"Friend, build your dreams and make them great! I have every confidence that—with this book—you are about to turn a corner in your ministry, a turning with lasting lifetime results.

"It is a turning that will take you from discouragement and near defeat to optimism and unexpected victories, from one level of success to another—to ever higher levels of accomplishment than you ever dreamed of before you started real possibility thinking!

"Why am I so sure? Because the principles of success are all here. Read them. Believe them. And then apply them!

"They will work, if you work them."

—R.H.S.

The Tower of Hope and the Crystal Cathedral rise majestically above the Garden Grove Campus.

ROBERT H· SCHULLER

YOUR CHURCH HAS A *Fantastic* FUTURE!

A Possibility Thinker's Guide To A Successful Church

Regal Books

A Division of GL Publications
Ventura, California, U.S.A.

Rights for publishing this book in other languages are contracted by Gospel Literature International (GLINT) foundation. GLINT also provides technical help for the adaptation, translation and publishing of Bible study resources and books in scores of languages worldwide. For further information, contact GLINT, Post Office Box 6688, Ventura, California 93006, U.S.A. or the publisher.

Certain portions of this book were previously published under the title:
Your Church Has Real Possibilities!

Published by Regal Books
A Division of GL Publications
Ventura, California 93006
Printed in U.S.A.

Library of Congress Cataloging in Publication Data

Schuller, Robert Harold.
    Your church has a fantastic future!

    Includes bibliographical references.
    1. Church growth. I. Title.
BV652.25.S38 1986   254'.5   86-11906
ISBN 0-8307-1126-0

1 2 3 4 5 6 7 8 9 10 / 91 90 89 88 87 86

The Secret of Success

Find a need and fill it.

Find a hurt and heal it.

Find a problem and solve it.

Find a chasm and bridge it.

Find somebody who's sick and
lead him to healing love.

Find somebody who's suffering from sin
and show him how he can be saved.

R.H.S.

Arvella and Robert H. Schuller

DEDICATION

To my wife, Arvella, the one person who, more than anyone else, was and is my God-ordained adviser, consultant,
critic and motivator on "how to build a positive church."

CONTENTS

8

What Makes a Truly Great Church?

"We don't have members—they're all ministers."

143

9

Are You Growing into Your Mission?

"The church must either grow or perish."

155

They Made Their Dreams Happen

10

Seven Principles of Success

"The parish church is in the business of 'retailing' religion."

245

FOREWORD

Robert Schuller is a breed apart from most superchurch pastors. Like the others, he is a person of extraordinary vision and leadership. Like the others, he has sensitivity to the needs of people and persistently gears his programs to meet those needs. Like the others, he knows how to manage well, how to make the big decisions, and how to rally the people for accomplishing goals. Like the others, he understands the function of religion and focuses the gospel of Jesus Christ on the hurts and hopes of people in such a way that they are drawn to the Saviour.

But beyond all this, Robert Schuller is gifted with the kind of mind which can analyze and communicate what is going on behind the scenes. Not only does he operate on the sound intuitions which eventuate in dramatic church growth, but he has an unusual ability to help others do the same.

That quality is what makes this book a church growth classic. Many pastors blessed with great church growth write books. Most of them are "here is how we do it" books, which in themselves are extremely useful and I highly recommend them. But *Your Church Has a Fantastic Future!* not only tells *what* Robert Schuller did to develop the Crystal Cathedral but also *why* he did it that way.

For more than ten years I have assigned the earlier edition of this book entitled, *Your Church Has Real Possibilities,* to every one of my Doctor of Ministry students at Fuller Seminary and have asked them to write reports on it. Many hundreds of pastors and denominational executives have written reports, and all have been positive. Few books have been so helpful in enabling pastors and other church leaders to understand the reasons for growth or nongrowth and to make the necessary adjustments to lead their churches into a better future.

As a professor of church growth, I am personally indebted to Robert Schuller for much of what I know and teach. I visit the Crystal Cathedral often. Back when it was called the Garden Grove Community Church, I had the privilege of attending a Robert H. Schuller Institute for Successful Church Leadership. It was a life-changing experience. Not only did I learn new principles of church growth, but I also received a fresh measure of inspiration and motivation which I had not previously known. This helped move me to what I now call in my own writings and classes the "third level of faith" or "possibility thinking faith."

A major contribution of possibility thinking to church growth has been to surface this unique dynamic of intelligent goal setting for doing God's work. Goal setting, as Robert Schuller persistently reminds us, is a form of biblical faith. "Now faith is the substance of things hoped for, the evidence of things not seen" (Heb. 11:1, *KJV*). If you have not released the power of this kind of faith in your own ministry, *Your Church Has a Fantastic Future!* is what you need. It will help move you to levels of effectiveness and satisfaction that may well transform your ministry.

For me 1955 was a banner year. Robert and Arvella Schuller set out for Southern California with $500 to begin what was then called "the Garden Grove Experiment." Donald McGavran wrote *The Bridges of God* and thereby launched the Church Growth Movement. And I was ordained to the Christian ministry, preparing to leave as a missionary to Bolivia. Little could I have realized how these streams would eventually converge and how indebted I myself would be to both McGavran and Schuller.

It is because of this sense of debt that I hasten to commend this book to you. Now, ever so much more valuable in its revised and updated form, it will help you as a church leader to understand your own church better than you ever have before and it will open up new horizons for growth both in quality and quantity. Read it and you will see how powerful faith, operating through a born-again Spirit-filled servant of God, has made an indelible impact on the lives of thousands of hurting men and women; how they have gathered together and formed one of America's great local churches; and how you can apply this dynamic to your own situation.

C. Peter Wagner
Professor of Church Growth
Fuller Theological Seminary
Pasadena, California

Dr. Robert H. Schuller

PREFACE

In everything you do, put God first, and he will direct you and crown your efforts with success (Prov. 3:6, *TLB*).

In the strong self-confidence that God has revealed certain techniques for success in our ministry, and in a stewardship of responsibility to share what I have learned with others, I submit my thoughts to you in this book even as I have been offering them in the Institute for Successful Church Leadership.

Hundreds upon hundreds of ministers of all denominations have attended the Institute which we conduct on the campus of our church in Garden Grove, California and in selected sites across the country. In preparation for their attendance at these Institutes, these ministers prepared Self-study Guides in which they took a long, hard look at themselves, their ministries and their churches. We then analyzed these guides and provided written evaluations of each one.

As I read the Self-study Guides of these pastors, representing churches of all sizes and all denominations from all parts of America, I became acutely aware of enormous misconceptions that block men and women from succeeding in the work of pastoral ministry today. At the same time, I feel certain that we have discovered solutions to many of these problems.

There is hardly a church problem a pastor faces that I have not faced during the years I have pastored in Garden Grove. I know what it is like to have a dream—only to see it obstructed by negative people. I know what it is like to have a great idea, only to see it crushed by insensitive people around me. I know what it is like to feel an all-consuming ambition to do something great for Jesus Christ, only to find myself hemmed in by small-thinking people; handicapped by no money, no trained lay leaders, no property, no members; and obstructed by an "impossible" city-planning department and unbelievable building restrictions.

The years have gone so fast that I can still remember the very dark times of my ministry, when I was still in the drive-in theater and had this magnificent dream of a great glass walk-in, drive-in cathedral. I found myself blocked by obstructions.

For two years I held on through black despair. For almost 24 months I went to my office and secretly hoped for a fatal heart attack! My enormous personal pride would never have allowed me to even contemplate suicide. But if God would have removed me with a heart attack, I would have been relieved of command with honor!

I could see no other way out. I held on, clinging to the words of Jesus who said, "No man, having put his hand to the plough, and looking back, is fit for the kingdom of God" (Luke 9:62). Then I gave Jesus Christ complete command in the leadership of the church and my life. Obstacles disappeared. The pathway opened brightly. Success was given to me by God. And I know God wants you and your church to enjoy success!

I know that some leaders who read these pages are today in a despairing time of life. I say to you, "Think with me—from chapter to chapter—and I believe God is going to give you marvelous success, too! I absolutely guarantee that if you will follow the prescriptions laid down in this book, your church will grow. And as your church grows, enthusiasm will mount. Dynamic energy will throb through the congregation. An authentic spirit of renewal will be felt, for such enthusiasm will attract new people.

Try it. And you will soon find that the same dynamic success cycle described herein will be operating for you there in your own home church, just as it does for us here at the Crystal Cathedral.

Garden Grove, California
1986

INTRODUCTION

There are two universal languages in our time, the language of ethics and the language of psychology. Unfortunately, the language of the Bible and its theology is no longer universally understood. Yet both ethics and psychology are deeply imbedded in the Bible and its message. Issues of love and justice leap out of the Old Testament and the New. And the healing of broken relationships is the very heart of the good news of Jesus Christ.

Robert Schuller majored in college in the field of psychology. Inspired by such preachers as E. Stanley Jones and Norman Vincent Peale, but adding his own special thrust, he has expressed the gospel themes of salvation and hope and healing and the individual's worth in terms which millions can recognize and respond to. It is said of our Lord that "the common people heard him gladly." The same words can be said of Dr. Schuller—"gladly"because common people understand him, and "gladly" because he makes them feel glad when they open their hearts to God's love.

The publication in 1974 of *Your Church Has Real Possibilities* was itself good news. Many pastors took its message seriously and found new joy in their work. Some of their stories are included in this new and expanded edition, *Your Church Has a Fantastic Future*. Then, too, the Crystal Cathedral was only a dream back in 1974 when the book first appeared. So much has happened since. The Garden Grove story has been brought up-to-date, and Dr. Schuller's "home congregation" continues to exemplify the promise of the original title.

Fifty ministries, more or less, can be identified as going on at the home campus. And the end is not yet in sight. What the impact on North America and the world could be if even 10 percent of Christian congregations unblocked the Spirit of God and dared to do possibility thinking, praying and acting simply boggles the mind!

This new edition of a treasured book now goes out to bless those who read it and translate its story into their own locale. To small churches and large, ethnic and white, denominational, Roman Catholic, "free" or "other," American and those in other lands, Dr. Schuller and those of us who work with him send his characteristic greeting: "God loves you, and so do I."

Harold N. Englund
Executive Director,
Church Relations

Dr. Schuller in 1955 preaching at the drive-in theater.

Chapter 1

THE GARDEN GROVE STORY

Nineteen-hundred-fifty-five. A dream is born!

In January, my wife, Arvella, and I arrive in Orange County, California to begin our ministry here. On Sunday, March 27, we hold the first service of the new Garden Grove Community Church in the Orange Drive-In Theatre. About 50 people are present.

A small beginning, yes. But today, 30 years later, our church has become one of the world's truly life-changing centers with more than 10,000 members. Has size alone made the difference? Obviously not, for we began small, as every church must, as your own church has. Rather, our present size is the result of our being faithful—from our simple origins to our present role as a great twenty-first century church—to one basic philosophy that any pastor and church can adopt: *a church should provide for the needs of the persons in its community*. We began that way, and now, three decades later, we can still say that our church is meeting the ever-changing needs of the persons in our community. To everyone under our ministry, we can honestly say:

Whoever you are, there is room for you.
Whatever your needs, we have the answer.
Whatever your interest, you can find your joy
here.

Of course, seeing a dream realized is no accident. We must work to see our dreams fulfilled. And we worked hard. But first, let me tell you how this dream began.

I was inspired in seminary by the example of the late Dr. George Truett. He spent 40 years in one church—the First Baptist Church of Dallas, Texas—and built what was in his lifetime the largest and, by most standards, the best Baptist Church in the world. I thought, *That's fabulous. I'd like to do that. I'd like to find one place and spend 40 years, devoting my life to one church.*

So I prayed, "Lord, just send me to some place where there are enough unsaved people that I can work my whole life and not run out of lost souls to work with." It was that simple. When the call came in 1955 to start a new church in California, I had no doubt this was what I had prayed for, as there were enough lost souls in the state of California to keep me busy a whole lifetime. In response, all I could say was "Hallelujah, here we come."

Getting Started

When the little church I had served for five years in Chicago heard that I was leaving to begin a new church in California, they gave my wife and me a farewell gift. It was a check for approximately $300, enough to make the down payment on a two-manual electronic organ.

I was delighted with this gift because, now that I was going out to start another church from scratch, I had determined to do two things: begin *with* an organ and begin *without* mimeographed Sunday morning bulletins. So en route from Chicago to California by car, we stopped at a music store in Iowa run by an old friend of mine, Howard Duven. He agreed to take the check from the Chicago church as the down payment on an organ, with the balance to be paid off in 36 monthly installments of $38 a month. With a salary of $4,000, I calculated that my tithe would make the monthly payment.

Possibility Thinking

I wrote a friend and said, "I'm out to start a new church. Would you find an empty hall and rent it for me?"

He wrote back and, in that letter, he used a word that would change my life. He said, "Bob, it is impossible to find a place to start a church in California."

Impossible?! I honestly thought that was a strange thing to say. As far as I knew, there was a whole desert in California with lots of space. So how could it be impossible to start a church there? Impossible is such an irresponsible word!

Since I don't believe in impossibilities, I practiced some possibility thinking on my way to California and made a list of nine possible places to conduct services: (1) a school building, (2) an Elks Hall, (3) a mortuary chapel, (4) a Masonic Temple, (5) an empty warehouse, (6) a Seventh-day Adventist Church, (7) a synagogue, (8) a drive-in theater or (9) an acre of ground and pitch a tent.

We arrived in Garden Grove, California and were given a check for $500 by our sponsors, the Reformed Church in America. I brought the check to a local bank and opened an account there under the name "Garden Grove Community Church" because I didn't think the name "Reformed" would bring the unchurched rushing in. Then I began working my way through the list of possible sites for holding church services.

Personal Contact

Within a week after arriving in California, I had already exhausted eight of the possibilities I had considered for holding services. State law would not allow churches to rent school buildings. There was no Masonic Temple or Elks Hall. The Baptists were already in the mortuary. The Presbyterians occupied the Seventh-day Adventist Church on Sundays. And there was no Jewish synagogue.

I finally came down to the one that read "rent a drive-in theater." So six days after our arrival, I went to the Orange Drive-In Theatre and asked the manager if I could use his place for Sunday morning church services.

He obliged, and I asked him what it would cost. "Oh," he said, "let's say $10 a Sunday which is what I have to pay the sound man to come out here and throw the sound control switch on and off."

Enthusiastic Publicity

I now began to spend the $500 that was in the church checking account. For $25, I had a four-by-eight foot sign painted, posted on a triangle and set under a palm tree in front of the drive-in theater. The sign announced that services would be held in this place every Sunday morning at 11 A.M., starting Sunday, March 27, 1955.

Next I spent $75 for a microphone which I could jack into an outlet of the sound system on the sticky tar paper roof of the snack bar of the theater. The plan was that I would stand up there, speak into the microphone and address the people who would be listening through the private speakers placed inside their automobiles.

Hard Work

I proceeded to spend another $110 for rough lumber which was delivered to our small house. There in our one-car garage, we stored our mahogany organ while awaiting the grand opening! And here, with only a hammer and saw, I began to build our first altar and a 15-foot cross.

My next item of expense was $25 for a used trailer upon which I placed the organ, pulling it behind my car every Sunday from the garage to the drive-in theater. I didn't realize then that I would do this for more than five years!

Then I proceeded to spend about $50 for brochures. Hoping to impress unchurched people, I wrote to Dr. Norman Vincent Peale, who wrote back a marvelous statement with his permission to quote extensively. So I grabbed hold of his coattails. Then we proceeded to buy advertisements in the papers, saying, "Come as you are in the family car."

By the time the first Sunday arrived, we'd spent almost the entire $500! But is was the beginning of something great! To our delight, we received $86.78 in that first offering.

Exciting Programming

From the very beginning, I was able to promise the people that they were "most fortunate to be a part of an exciting program that God was moving and planning in Orange County!" I believed it. I felt it. I knew it. And this conviction spread through the lives of those who listened.

About this time, Dr. Peale's book, *The Power of Positive Thinking,* was on the best-seller list. So I wrote to Dr. Peale and asked him to preach for me. I said, "I have the largest church in the state of California. It's 17 acres, almost all parking lot." I was positive, believe me! And I said, "It's an unusual arrangement. Everybody has a soft seat by an open window. And you can look up and see the sky. It's beautiful."

He said, "I'll come." And he did, in June 1957.

The Sunday that Dr. Peale preached at our church fell in the same week the drive-in theater was showing a movie on the life of Audie Murphy, the World War II hero. The movie would still be running that Sunday night, so when we arrived in the morning, the theater marquee read: "To Hell and Back. In Person—Dr. Norman Vincent Peale."

I don't know who was shaken up the most, Norman or I, but the place was packed with about 2,000 cars. When it came time for the sermon, I had to introduce him and I wasn't sure what to say. We really weren't an organized church, yet, so as far as I knew, these were people to be evangelized, not a body of believers. And there is a difference, you know.

I shot up a quick prayer and heard myself say, "Ladies and gentlemen, we have with us in person the greatest positive thinker alive in the world today. His name is a household word. Many of you have read His inspiring writings and, if you have, your life has been changed. I have gotten to know Him personally on a one-to-one basis, and if you get to know Him that way, you will be born again. How proud I am that He's with us today. His name is Jesus Christ. And here to tell us all about Him is Norman Vincent Peale."

I'll never forget how Dr. Peale started his sermon.

First of all, he blushed all the way, because he was enjoying the introduction immensely. As he mounted the podium, he said, "Pray for me." I did. He confessed later that he never planned his opening statement; it was a reaction to the introduction.

"If Jesus Christ could stand here today and talk to you, what would He tell you?" I've never forgotten that question or the message that followed. There's a great possibility that God was in it and not just Norman Vincent Peale.

Bold Planning

Now, with the financial support of the denomination, two acres of land were purchased at a cost of $4,000. And the church extension committee announced that one of the local ranchers "who puts up buildings on the side" had agreed to "design plans for your church for nothing." I gasped! I was a student of architecture, and to me this was intolerable!

I asked the extension committee to loan me the money to hire an architect. They refused. "We've never spent money for an architect yet and we're not about to begin now," was the verdict. To which the spokesman for the group added: "We just can't afford to hire fancy architects."

On my own initiative, I proceeded to contact a young architect in Long Beach. "My name is Robert Schuller," I wrote. "You don't know me, but I'm an honest man. I'm 28 years old, and I'm starting a new church. Its building must be designed by a good architect. I know what we want to build. Will you draw the plans for me? I promise you that you will be paid in full. I'm not sure how much I can pay or when you will get paid, but I guarantee that you will be paid completely in my lifetime."

Richard Shelley took a chance. He drew magnificent plans and submitted his first bill. It amounted to $1,000. I announced to what was already a growing congregation in the drive-in church that we would need to raise $1,000 for the first payment to the architect who was designing our new church. We took a special offering and the $1,000 was given!

When the last of the total fee of $4,000 was due, he submitted another bill. I challenged the people and they responded. He was paid in full and on time!

Much Prayer

Obviously, there was a great deal of prayer involved in all of this. And obviously we moved ahead with possibility thinking, believing that it would be possible to accomplish our objectives. We proceeded to build our first $70,000 unit on the two-acre parcel of ground. We were about to increase our corporate debt from the $1,600 still owed on the organ to nearly $70,000. But this was not done until I received pledges from the congregation assuring us of an increased weekly cash flow to cover at least the *interest* on the increased debt!

Meeting Needs

It was about this time that I was called to a nearby rancher's home and Warren Gray introduced me to his wife, Rosie. "She's been sitting in your drive-in church every Sunday since the beginning," he told me. "She can't walk and she can't talk. She can only grunt and drop a tear. You see," her husband explained with moist eyes, "my wife Rosie had a stroke a few years ago. And the drive-in church was just the answer for our needs."

When I left the Gray ranch, it was with the understanding that they were to join the church the following Sunday and would be baptized. This was exactly at the time when the pews were being installed in our pretty little chapel in the lovely suburb of Garden Grove. The question naturally arose: "Now that we have Rosie Gray, a handicapped old lady as a member, what are we going to do about the drive-in church when we finish and open our new chapel in a month?"

The board quickly made the decision with my enthusiastic approval: it was decided that I would conduct a service at 9:30 A.M. in the new chapel and then go to the drive-in theater to hold an eleven o'clock service for Rosie Gray. Soon she would die, they reasoned, and we could discontinue the work. Deep in my heart, though, I wondered if I would ever be able to give up what the drive-in theater offered: fantastic accessibility—and a parking lot big enough to invite Norman Vincent Peale to appear in!

Thinking Big

As it turned out, Rosie Gray kept living—year after year—and both churches grew in both places. The dream unfolded in our imaginations of a sanctuary where people could sit in a traditional pew arrangement, while others would sit in their cars parked in a landscaped drive-in church. It was an intriguing plan.

Finally, by a narrow and very noisy congregational vote, it was decided to establish the future direction of our church. We received the go-ahead to merge the drive-in and the chapel congregations into one church on a new relocation development. This was indeed a most dramatic undertaking.

Meeting Opposition

I was destined to have the unforgettable experience of being the pastor of a church during a major relocation experience. More than that, I was destined to be the pastor of a church that was split down the middle. Those who opposed the merger and relocation were vehement. Secret meetings were held through the week. This went on for over two years.

For these two years, I went to my study under the enormous weight of an awareness that nearly half of my people were violently opposed to the direction in which I was leading the church. For a period of a year and a half, I would have relished nothing more than a fatal heart attack. In that way, I would have been removed with honor from the unhappy scene! Nevertheless, we had to move ahead.

At this time, we had a net worth of approximately $10,000 and a debt of $70,000—against total assets of $80,000. It was about then that we were given the opportunity to purchase 10 acres of land a half-mile from the freeway, just west of the drive-in theater, at a price of $6,600 an acre, or $66,000.

"I believe the owner will sell it to you for $18,000 down, and he'll take $400 a month to cover interest and principal until the entire property is paid for," a realtor informed us, adding: "If you're interested, we can open a 120-day escrow tomorrow with only $1,000."

This proposal was first submitted to the church board and then, according to the practice we followed at that time, to the congregation. The congregation was consequently drawn into the entire nitty-gritty of discussing endless details in the process of arriving at a decision. In this way, we created a magnificent public platform for every negative thinker in the congregation to sound off and spread his negativism. Nevertheless, a motion was made and it barely passed, moving "that we purchase the 10 acres of ground at the above price, open an escrow tomorrow for $1,000, and instruct our pastor to close the escrow on or before the end of the 120-day period, providing he can raise the $18,000 down payment within the time allowed."

Raising Funds

That action kicked off a fund-raising project—the most intensive in my whole life, with the exception of raising the money for the first organ in my first church. I began by cashing in my life insurance policy and giving the proceeds to the church. I called my brother and talked him into loaning the money he had in his savings account to the church. I borrowed from my father, from my uncle, from my sister and from another uncle. I left no stone unturned.

Regrettably, nearly half the membership of the church was violently opposed to the entire project. Only about 60 people in all were actively behind the project at this stage. The others were doing all they could to kill it.

Suddenly, during this fund-raising period in 1958, property directly across the street from the piece of ground we were attempting to purchase was sold for $12,000 an acre—exactly double what we were asked to pay for ours! Clearly, we were on the right track.

I went now to Warren Gray, husband of Rosie, and he came through with a $2,000 gift. Going into the final week of the 120-day period, I was only $3,000 short of the full $18,000 that was needed.

Day 120 was scheduled to fall on a Friday. But there were still three people who had promised $1,000 each. So I knew we had it made.

I went to the first man and he shocked me by reneging on his offer. I went to the second. "Come back in a month, but right now, I'm flat broke." I was stunned.

Then I called on the third man, and he floored me by saying, "You know, Reverend, we just had my daughter's wedding. Do you know what that cost me? And my wife hasn't even balanced the checking account!" His voice trailed off in a ridiculous display of the kind of verbosity that flows out of a highly defensive mentality. I was sick!

Robert Moore, a faithful member of the church board, risked losing his job at Disneyland by spending the morning literally begging loans from his fellow employees. He called in to report that he's collected only $200. With that, every stone had been turned over and we had found nothing.

It was now Friday noon, and it looked like we were defeated! The escrow company's office was to close in only four more hours, and we were still $3,000 short. The sellers would rejoice, of course, if we were unable to close this deal, for the selling of the property across the street now proved that they could easily get $120,000 for their land instead of the $66,000 we were offering. A great bargain was about to slip through our hands!

I went to a pay phone in Santa Ana, listened to the dime clink to the bottom, dialed my home phone and talked with my wife at the other end. With trembling lips, I reported failure.

"But you mustn't give up, honey," she insisted, adding, "have you called Warren Gray?"

"I can't, dear," I insisted. "I can't ask a person to give twice!"

"Why not?" came her reply. "Besides, you'll have to tell him that you can give him his $2,000 back!"

"But, honey, I can't call him today. He's only been

home from the hospital a few days. You know they sewed him up full of cancer."

Again she insisted that I call his house. I did. The nurse gave him his telephone at his bedside. I explained to him that we failed to secure the down payment to close the escrow. "But we can keep the services going in the drive-in theater," I assured him.

"But, Reverend, you'll never get land near the freeway at that price again! You can't let the deal slide by. Give me a couple of hours and I'll meet you at the Bank of America at Eighth and Main," he said.

I objected, reminding him of his serious condition.

"But, Reverend, Rosie needs that land. And I've got the money for you if you can meet me at the bank." With that, he hung up.

Two hours later, I was pacing the floor of the Bank of America's lobby when I saw Warren come in, ashen-faced and hollow-eyed, his old rancher's hat topping his head of uncombed hair. He nodded to me, walked to a cashier's window, passed some papers to the girl behind the grill and a few moments later confronted me in the center of the bank lobby with the sweat running off his face. "Here you are, Reverend, here's $3,000," he said.

I shook his hand—hard. Then I went to the escrow company. *Sixty minutes before the deadline, God took title to His 10 acres of land!*

The immediate crisis had been met. However, the opposition in the church was convinced that we would be going bankrupt. They had now cut off their financial support and we were barely able to make the payments on our little chapel. And now we would also have to start making payments of $400 a month on our newly-acquired land. A battle had been won, but the war continued.

Then, on the Sunday after the land cleared escrow, a

deacon approached me, excitedly waving a check from an unknown family. "Reverend, look at this! A check for $100 from a stranger! If we got one of these every week, they would make our land payments!" The following week, another check for $100 came from the same party. And it continued week after week!

What happened? Obviously, God wanted this church built. And He directed a family to our church whose tithe amounted to precisely the same amount as the land payment on the new property!

And why was the family attracted to our church? Because they heard that "The Garden Grove Community Church was announcing plans to build the world's first walk-in, drive-in church on 10 acres of land on the east side of Garden Grove alongside the Santa Ana Freeway." That idea was big enough to excite these big-thinking people! And so they started coming at this precise moment in history!

Growing Pains

Now we placed our lovely, three-year-old, stained glass chapel in the lovely suburb up for sale! We sold it for approximately $40,000 more than we had invested in it. Why? Because it was the most beautiful church building in the village! Good architecture is always a great investment.

Then we hired Richard Neutra, considered the foremost living architect in the world at that time. Plans were drawn up for the walk-in, drive-in church. Finally, groundbreaking ceremonies were conducted in September 1959.

The next morning, the Monday newspapers blared out the news: "Ground was broken yesterday for the world's

The first Garden Grove Chapel soon grew too small.

first walk-in, drive-in church to be erected in Garden Grove, California. It will be the first church designed for people to sit outside and worship in their cars while others sit inside and worship in the traditional pew arrangement."

I was a happy man, except for the funeral that I had to conduct on that same afternoon. It was the funeral of Rosie Gray! God kept her alive through all of those years until we were publicly committed to building the church that God wanted us to build.

Obviously, if God is in on the planning, money problems have a way of solving themselves! Probably that's the reason we dared to begin to plunge further into what some people would have called "debt." We calculated that we would have to borrow approximately $700,000 to build the first unit, complete with fountains, pools, landscaping and gardens. This would give us a sanctuary seating 1,000 people, expandable to 1,700 in the future. It would also give us a three-manual pipe organ.

Boosting Income

We calculated that we could borrow the money at 6 percent interest. We assumed if we could boost our annual income to cover the interest on the $700,000 debt, even before we built the building, that the increased income generated by the new structure should help liquidate the principal indebtedness. But no commercial lending institution would lend us money.

We used professional fund-raisers instead. We conducted a campaign. We boosted our income well over $40,000 a year—enough to make the interest payments.

With that base established, we proceeded to borrow $700,000, offering only promissory notes as security. We approached members of our denominational family through our national periodical. It took us 24 months, but we succeeded!

Then on November 5, 1961, Dr. Norman Vincent Peale flew from New York City to dedicate the new Garden Grove Community Church, located just a half-mile west of the Orange Drive-In Theatre where he spoke for us five years before! We spent a few thousand dollars publicizing his presence in our church's services that day. Naturally, we had turn-away crowds. All of us were convinced this was a success!

Approximately four years later in November 1964, I preached a sermon on "How to Make Your Dreams Come True" and launched my dream of someday building the main tower structure in the total church building plan. I announced that the architect and I envisioned a 14- or 15-story tower with high-speed glass elevators, a chapel at the top, a 24-hour telephone counseling center manned by live human beings every hour of every day, offices for a

growing church staff and a professional psychological counseling center, and the balance of the floors to be used for
educational purposes.

I promised that the "little chapel in the sky at the top of
the tower would be a twinkling diamond of hope in the
black night sky at the freeway hub of this great county."
This tower would become a tower of hope representing
and saying to the public that "there is an eye that never
closes, there is an ear that is never shut, there is a heart
that never grows cold."

The idea caught fire!

An "anonymous" donor started things off with $25. I
announced to the congregation that a $25 contribution had
been made and that the Tower of Hope fund had been
opened! Someone else responded with a $50 gift! Twelve
months later, the fund had grown to almost $6,000.

About this time, someone said to me: "Reverend, at
this rate you'll never get a million dollars." That challenged
my imagination. I knew we were earning 6 percent interest on this $6,000. Rising early one Sunday morning with
pencil and paper, I scribbled out a rough calculation as to
how long it would take $6,000 earning 6 percent interest,
compounded annually, to grow into a million dollars. I calculated it would take just a little over 100 years!

That Sunday I announced to the congregation: "I have
good news for you! Sometime the Tower of Hope will
stand here in the heart of Orange County! It will be a powerful positive statement of the light and love of Christ! We
really have a million dollars right now. The only drawback
is that we can't cash it in for 100 years!"

At this point, everyone knew that someday we would
have a million dollars! The project became believable.
Then the idea began to catch on and many people said they
wanted to see it "in their lifetime."

Worship services at the first walk-in, drive-in church.

"Is there any *possible* way we can raise a million dollars faster?" That was the question people began asking. Well, perhaps if we broke it down in 10 years, $100,000 a year would do it. And so we conducted a fund-raising campaign to boost our annual income by $100,000 a year, with pledges extended over a 10-year period to raise "a million dollars for the Tower of Hope."

The project was a success! True, the people could not, and would not, wait for 10 years. The pressures grew to "borrow the money and build it today."

So we did!

By 1968, 13 years after we organized and began services at the drive-in theater, Orange County's tallest structure stood completed! The 90-foot cross atop the tower, visible for miles around, stood as a beacon of promise to all who passed by, its outstretched arms an invitation of welcome to all who come in. Telephones in the 24-hour counseling room at the top began ringing. An unbroken lifeline counseling program was started. The number was easy to remember. Dial: N-e-w H-o-p-e! So, Garden Grove Community Church became the first church in America to man a 24-hour live telephone counseling center.

By now, we had invested nearly $2 million in property, the original sanctuary, classrooms and the Tower of Hope. None of us suspected that a year and a half later we would plunge into another million-dollar project to purchase 10 acres of additional land to provide desperately-needed parking space.

Setting Goals

Set goals beyond goals!
By 1970 the dream had branched out into television.

We started with one station in Los Angeles, and today our TV ministry reaches nearly 3 million viewers every week in the United States, Canada and Australia. I tell the story of how God led us into this wonderful ministry and provided for it in *Possibility Thinking Makes Miracles Happen*. But it all grew out of our desire to find a need and fill it.

Surely no one would ever have dreamed that before we reached our 20th birthday, we would be launching a 36-month capital funds campaign to raise another $1.5 million preparing the financial base to build a larger 3,000 seat auditorium. Yet after two decades of phenomenal growth, our church faced a critical situation, for we were literally bursting at the seams. Every Sunday each seat was filled, and hundreds of persons were standing in the aisles and sitting on the grass outside the sanctuary. And we were turning people away.

It became evident to everyone that the church needed a new sanctuary. To describe the situation we were in and the need we faced, I coined this phrase: "The shoe must not tell the foot how large to grow." It was another way of saying that we were refusing to surrender leadership to our buildings. Rather we determined to live by our own principle of grow or perish.

Reaching Out

Let the unchurched population set your goals!

Had we not elected to build a larger sanctuary, we would have ignored the fact that an estimated 500,000 unchurched peopled lived within a 15-minute driving radius of our church.

In raising money for the enlarged facilities and focusing on the problem of the unchurched in the shadow of our cross, we were making a promise that, in our second 20 years, thousands of desperate and despairing people would be able to come here and find Christ—all because so many cared enough to make room for others. It was at this point that the concept of the Crystal Cathedral was born.

In November 1975 at the 20th anniversary celebration of our church—held in the Anaheim Convention Center and attended by some 7,000 guests—I held up a tiny model six inches high of a proposed new sanctuary. The revolutionary design by Philip Johnson, a New York architect, was shaped like a star and was to be constructed of concrete, steel and glass—a whole new approach in the field of church architecture.

From the beginning, I had felt that our dream church should have two qualities: it should be unique and it should be a work of art in its own right. Beyond that, I wanted a structure where no chunk of plaster or two-by-four would block our view of the sky, the clouds and the birds as we worshiped together. In designing our future church as a star of concrete and steel with mirror walls of glass, Philip Johnson proved he could dream our dream with us.

The design and the name "Crystal Cathedral" caught the imagination of people across the nation and around the world. By the spring of 1976, thousands of persons had pledged their support; they donated the 10,000 mirrored windows of the Cathedral as memorials in honor of loved ones and friends. In this manner, nearly $5 million was raised for the Cathedral's construction.

It was my dream—and my goal—to build the Cathedral debt-free, and it was validated by an extraordinary gift of $1 million from John and Donna Crean. Along with their gift came the challenge to "dig a hole," even though the balance of the construction money was yet to be raised. "Make a decision and then solve the problems" is another

Great concrete balconies—like giant wings unfolded.

The skeleton of the Cathedral—a lacy web of white steel.

of our guiding principles, so we made the decision to begin. In December 1977 construction started.

1977 was an excited year of growth as one fantastic event followed another:

January   The Hour of Power headquarters building opens.

March   The Chapman Avenue pedestrian bridge opens, linking the Hour of Power headquarters on the Orange city side of the street with the church campus on the Garden Grove city side.

December   Crystal Cathedral groundbreaking takes place.

From a huge hole in the ground at the beginning of 1978 to the completed balconies and main floor at the end of the year, construction progressed on the Cathedral. A crisis arose at midyear when a $1 million payment became due and the money was nowhere in sight. The builders threatened to halt work unless the payment was made in full. Rather than see construction stopped for lack of funding, I appealed to our members and friends at a special service on Father's Day, June 18, to give the total amount in one offering, placing their gifts in wheelbarrows and cement buckets. When the offering was counted that day, contributions from the local congregation totaled $1.5 million. The dream had been tested! Now the dream could continue to expand!

By May 1979, the lacelike steel network comprising the "space frame" of the Cathedral was ready to be erected. The wall and roof sections of this frame, the largest ever attempted in America, are made up of more than 16,000 individual pieces of steel that together form a canopy of white filigree, spanning the entire structure. Individuals giving to this stage of construction gave gifts that were designated "Pillars of Steel," securing another $1.5 million toward completion of this project.

Even though a year's work remained to be done on the building, nearly 6,000 people met on two November 1979 Sunday afternoons to witness the opening of the great 90-foot doors behind the pulpit and to view the graceful leaping of the fountains. In thanksgiving to God, they subscribed the largest budget in the history of our church—$2.7 million! The dream is blessed by God!

Another $3.5 million toward construction costs was raised through an additional program of memorials—a glittering ceiling of 10,000 gleaming mylar stars suspended high above the choir and reflecting sunlight by day and Cathedral lights by night throughout the sanctuary. Subscribed for at $500 each, the glistening memorial stars formed a giant mobile of luminous jewels, adding their own radiant beauty to the majesty of the Cathedral itself.

The stars collectively, as a ceiling, performed their function admirably until one Sunday, soon after their installation, when a few of the stars decided to stage an encore performance of their own during a morning service. Even though we were in the season when the hot, Santa Ana desert winds were gusting strongly through the countryside, the great pulpit doors were wide open for the service. At one point in midworship, a great burst of wind blew in through the doors and dislodged several of the new stars from the ceiling. Fortunately, they are made of very light material, so they slowly wafted down from their moorings 128 feet above the floor like autumn leaves from a tree. But instead of staying over the choir, they drifted out into the congregation and settled gently into the laps of some very astonished worshipers. Ushers quickly and quietly gathered up the errant stars, so they could be restored later to their rightful places. After that, we made sure all the stars were properly secured.

Despite all our efforts, by January 1, 1980, we were still $4.5 million short of the $18.5 million we now needed to cover the rapidly rising construction costs. And the amount we had already raised included five gifts of $1 million each—two such gifts from one couple. At this time, Beverly Sills, the most prominent soprano of the New York Opera Company, had announced her retirement and was touring the nation, giving a series of farewell concerts in major music centers. She consented to give a benefit performance in the Crystal Cathedral to help us raise the final amount we needed to open the sanctuary debt-free.

The Beverly Sills Concert was scheduled for May 13, 1980. Since the Cathedral would not be completed before fall, this meant we had to step-up work on the interior of the sanctuary, so it would be ready for its first official public function a half-year ahead of schedule. In anticipation of this glorious night of song, 3,000 friends of the ministry gave $1,500 per seat to fill the nearly completed Cathedral. Preconcert concerts on Mother's Day, featuring famed pianist Roger Williams, the Hour of Power choir and other musicians provided a splendid musical experience for our many members, staffers and friends who would not be able to attend the Sills recital. And it also gave us an opportunity to test our sound facilities in a full house before the big night.

The Beverly Sills concert proved to be a truly historic occasion. The construction site on campus had been "landscaped" with artificial grass and container plants of all kinds and never looked more beautiful. The lighted cathedral glowed like an enormous gem in the California night. And fingers of light from enormous spotlights sweeping

The congregation at worship in the Crystal Cathedral.

across the darkened sky announced to the world that a very special event was taking place.

Miss Sills was superb, and the audience, resplendent in formal attire, loved her. The entire occasion was a critical success, with both artist and auditorium surpassing all expectations. The public life of our new sanctuary had been auspiciously launched. And we now had the funds to complete work on the building.

Six months later, on Sunday, September 14, a monument to God's glory became an instrument in His service, as the Cathedral was dedicated debt-free just as had been promised! The dream had become a reality at last! The Cathedral, in all its magnificence, stands 128 feet high, 207 feet deep and 415 feet wide and seats 2,890 persons in opera-style seats. And yes, it is "quake proof," having been designed to withstand an earthquake of 8.0 on the Richter scale and winds of close to 200 miles an hour.

In thanksgiving to God for demonstrating through this beautiful building that He did indeed have a better idea and in gratitude to Him for providing us with this sanctuary free of any indebtedness, we applied the entire offering on Dedication Day to the building of an emergency medical relief center in Chiapas, Mexico, a new work for God to serve 500,000 non-Spanish-speaking Indians in both Mexico and Guatemala.

Healing Hurts

Our sanctuary is both a witness to God and a beacon to mankind. And now that this great dream is realized, some may wonder if we are through dreaming dreams. Not at all. Having this great edifice to worship in gives us even more reason for dreaming our greatest dream yet—to extend our arms of healing, light, hope and love to the hurting around the world. Because the Crystal Cathedral was dedicated debt-free, our ministry does not labor under the restricting confines of an interest-laden mortgage. So with many hurts still to heal and so many needs yet to meet, more dreams are waiting to be dreamed. Making these dreams come true ensures that this great monument to God—the Crystal Cathedral—will truly be an instrument of ministry and service.

In fact, some of our various ministries have already been underway for some time. In 1971, we established our Lay Ministers Training Center. In 1972, our involvement in Keochang High School in Korea began. In 1974 a Performing Arts Center was opened. And, in the same year, the Garden Grove Community Church financed the

The Last Supper from the "Glory of Easter" pageant.

printing of the Bible into the new Maoscript for the benefit of China's millions.

In 1977, our church provided the Missionary Aviation Fellowship with the Good Samaritan Helicopter for service in New Guinea. That was the same year our church opened the Crystal Cathedral Academy with its first 51 students and established a "daughter" church in Zellwood, Florida.

A unique ministry of the Crystal Cathedral since 1981 is the annual living nativity pageant, "The Glory of Christmas," a spectacular production presented by the congregation and the musical organizations of the church. "The Glory of Easter" was added in 1983, and together these two glorious presentations fulfill a dream of reaching—with the message of faith, peace and hope—people who otherwise might never come to a church for any other reason.

January 1985 saw the grand opening of Rancho Capistrano Renewal Center, a conference center situated in a beautiful 93-acre garden with a lake and accommodations for 30 guests at a time. Seminars are held year-round at the center located in the heart of Orange County to meet human needs and hurts of the heart.

Also under consideration by the city council is our proposed Leadership Training Facility and memorial gardens. When erected, this desperately needed building will house the burgeoning Christian education activities of the church.

Plans are also underway to create a prayer chapel on the northeastern corner of our campus. Formed of white limestone from the Holy Land, it will have a glass roof and a glass floor and will appear to float on a beautiful reflection pool. Isolated from the busy activities in the heart of the campus the prayer chapel will serve as a peaceful prayer and meditation spot.

So you see, because we foresee a fantastic future for our church, we never stop dreaming great dreams. Nor do we ever stop working to see them realized. But the Crystal Cathedral congregation has no monopoly on dreams. Just make a decision to become a possibility thinker and you, too, can dream great dreams for your great God. Your church can also have a fantastic future!

Chapter 2

YOUR CHURCH HAS A FANTASTIC FUTURE!

I predict a fantastic future for the Church in the United States of America! And in doing so, I realize that my prediction is contrary to much that is being written and offered as opinion by many ecclesiastical theorists.

If I am still alive in the year 2000—and I hope I am—I will be 74 years old. At that time, I expect to be addressing a group of young ministers and saying to them:

"It's a thrilling thing to feel the power and the impact of the enormously strong Church in America today. Some of you would never believe that in the 1960s and in the early 1970s, leaders of the Church were predicting its demise.

"They were gloomily prophesying, 'The Church in the future will be away from ground and buildings and into small homes and private cells in communal groups.'

"How wrong they were!"

It will be a thrill to look across America in the year 2000 and see tremendous institutions in every significant city carrying out fantastic programs to heal human hearts, to fill human needs; enormous centers of human inspiration where people rally by the thousands and tens of thousands on Sundays and gather seven days a week for spiritual and personal growth. These tremendous spiritual-growth centers, these dynamic inspiration-generating centers, these great family-development centers will be proof positive of a renewed, revitalized and resurrected Church.

Begin Now

Any church that really wants to be a part of this vigorous and vital church of the twenty-first century can be. But it won't just happen—that church will have to work at it—and will have to *begin* working at it *now*. How? Through the application of certain universal principles.

Apply Anywhere

These principles will work anywhere we work at applying them—they really will. Let us take a case in point of a certain church located in the South Bronx, New York—certainly one of the worst inner-city sections anywhere in this country. If you drew a circle with a half-mile radius around the site of this church, you would enclose eight solid square blocks of deserted buildings, many of them four, six, eight stories high. The windows are knocked out. They are inhabited by gangs concocting Molotov cocktails.

These eight blocks were purchased by the Federal Government some years ago for demolition. The government planned for a brand new model city to rise from the former slum. But what happened? After the government bought the eight square blocks and evicted all the tenants, Congress failed to appropriate the money for the new model city. So the government property simply sits there, eight square blocks of empty buildings that have become a brick-and-concrete jungle.

Would you like to have that territory for your parish?

I have been to the South Bronx and to that church. During my visit there, the pastor asked me, "Have you ever seen a 'shooting gallery?'"

"No," I answered.

He took me across the street and to the roof of one of those abandoned buildings. And there I saw cans with blood in the bottoms and perhaps 150 to 200 little white postage-stamp size squares—empty heroin bags—lying around.

"Are there still people here?" I asked.

"Are there people here? This place is full of junkies!" he replied. "They're hurting, and they're scared. They've got problems, but I believe Jesus Christ can save each one of them."

That pastor came to one of our Institutes, and when I saw him, I asked myself, "Why did he come? What we have here won't work for him."

But he got so turned on—so excited—he went out of here believing he had a greater opportunity to serve Christ there in the South Bronx than anywhere else in the United States. He looked at his parish and developed the "inventory" of his community. What kinds of needs did these people have? These needs determined and established the architecture for the building program of his church. He envisaged a building *for people,* not just for an artist. He operated on the principle of biological realism.

Imagine having to seek bank financing in that community! But he did it, and he and his church built a new $700,000 building. No, it isn't the traditional house of worship with stained-glass windows. It's a multipurpose facility where basketball backboards hang down during the week. For Sunday worship, the backboards are folded up, and during the services only the reverse sides with the religious symbols on them are seen.

That church has been growing ever since its new building went up. But the biggest thing in their entire program is the day-care nursery. The church runs it all week long, because there are mothers there with illegitimate children, and other mothers—if they are lucky—who are working. So somebody else has to take care of the babies, and this is where the church has stepped in. Actually, the day-care nursery helps pay the mortgage, because the city of New York subsidizes much of this sort of activity.

Of course, no two communities are alike, and you have to find out where people are hurting in your community. The theme of this book could be: The secret of a growing church is so simple—find the hurt and heal it!

We have another graduate of our Institute who is the Chinese pastor of a church in the slum section of Calcutta. Now, downtown Calcutta is worse than any city ghetto in America, including the South Bronx! As that pastor sat here in our Institute, I again thought, "Can these principles work for him? He'll go back to Calcutta and then say, 'Yeah, Schuller, it works for you in Garden Grove. But look at all the rich, white, upper-middle class, affluent Americans you've got to get it all together for you.'"

The pastor is neither white nor rich. But he has such a positive attitude. He listened to what we were saying, and then he went back to Calcutta—and went back to work. I visited him there recently and discovered that this pastor now has three churches.

He has one church of about 200 members that worships on Saturday night. I preached there one night, and the place, as usual, was jammed. The next morning we had a second service in a second church. About 300 people attended. Then in the afternoon at his third church, there were about 400 more people in attendance. Three different congregations, three different buildings, three different locations!

Outside one of the churches, I saw pigs roaming the streets, and in those same streets, people slept wherever they could find sufficient place to lie down. There were no sidewalks. Across the street from the church was a large piece of property that had sunk some 20 feet below street level. Its vast crater was filled with foul-smelling water.

The pastor saw me gazing at the eyesore across the street, and he said, "Dr. Schuller, I use possibility thinking. That's a great big sewage hole now. But one day there'll be a hospital there!"

"But," I pointed out, "you've got a drainage problem there."

"*That,*" he answered, "is an understatement. But what we are going to do is build a moat and then turn that big sewage hole into a little lake with a bridge coming over it—right to the church."

Now that's a bright idea. And the pastor is already collecting funds for this project. He'll build it. It *will* be built. It's as good as built now, because he already sees it in his mind by faith.

Believe God

Many of you have heard the statement, "I've got to see it before I believe it." That's a negative-thinking statement if there ever was one, and it's as wrong as can be!

Learn to say it right. Turn it backwards and say, "I've got to believe it before I see it." That's truth! So don't ever say, "I've got to see it before I believe it," because you've got to believe it before you'll see it! You see, it is God at work in us, giving us the will and the power to achieve His purpose. (See Phil. 2:13).

God doesn't go to work in you to achieve these big, thrilling break-through ideas until you've demonstrated faith. That's how God works, for "without *faith* it is impossible to please him; for he that cometh to God must believe that he is, and that *he is* a *rewarder* of them that diligently seek him" (Heb. 11:6).

"If you have faith as a grain of mustard seed, you will say to this mountain, 'Move . . . ,' and it will move; and nothing will be impossible to you" (Matt. 17:20, *RSV*). But nothing is more important than faith, and faith is believing it before you see it.

You've got to believe it before you see it! So believe you can build a twenty-first century church now! You can be the founder and the leader of such a great new inspirational center. You can make your church a great church for Jesus Christ.

Consider how many years are left between now and the year 2000. Then ask yourself, "What kind of a job can I do for God between now and the beginning of the next century?"

If you believe it, you'll see it. It will amaze you what dreams He will unfold into your imagination, and it will amaze you even more when He causes those very same dreams to come to pass.

Chapter 3

SET YOUR GOALS
FOR SUCCESS

The first step toward making your dreams come true is to set some goals. Set successful goals and you will succeed. Fail to set successful goals and you can be assured of failure.

Success or failure starts at this point, for goal setting is nothing more than planning ahead. And when you fail to plan, you plan to fail. Putting it another way, *when you set no goals for growth, you set your goals for no growth!*

Lack of Goal Setting

The terrible truth is that tens of thousands of churches around the world today are experiencing no growth simply because nobody established any growth goal. I have talked to pastors of churches in Hong Kong, Japan, India, Korea, Greece, Europe, the Middle East and America. I have read hundreds of Self-Study Guides of ministers and church leaders who enter our Institute for Successful Leadership. And I can report that few pastors and few churches have set any firm, clear-cut goals for growth.

Now this is an unforgivable sin for a person who is supposedly a leader in the movement which is commissioned to go "into the world, and preach the gospel to every creature" (Mark 16:15).

What are the reasons for this lack of goal setting?

Transiency of pastors

Perhaps the biggest single reason is that the typical pastor comes to the church *without the determination to stay there long enough to make it a great church.* I have done enough private counseling with ministers of all denominations to report that the majority of ministers accept the call or assignment to a church with the expectation of staying on only until something better comes along.

Others look upon the church that is financially self-supporting as a "success." They see their goal as nothing more than "greasing the machinery" and keeping the machine going. Obviously, such an attitude is not going to produce a dynamic evangelistic spirit which will produce the new blood which keeps the church lively and exciting.

I am certain the Crystal Cathedral would not be the church it is today if I had not been deeply impressed earlier in my life by two persons. One of these was Dr. Raymond Lindquist, then pastor of First Presbyterian Church, Hollywood, California, who challenged us never to take a church "unless you can envision spending your life there."

At this same time in seminary I was asked to write a term paper on George Truett. When the assignment was given to me, I hadn't the faintest idea who he was. But I soon found out, and I've never forgotten it.

George Truett, as I previously mentioned, accepted a call to a small Baptist church in Dallas, Texas. He took the long look and envisioned spending his life there. And he did! He devoted more than forty years of his life to this congregation where he was able to think long thoughts, plan great dreams and set enormous goals. The real proof of the success of his ministry lies in the fact that now, many years after he has gone, the church continues to grow in a vital and dynamic way.

So it was, through the comment by Dr. Lindquist and the inspiration of Dr. Truett, God gave me the desire to find a church where I could devote my entire lifetime.

Fear of failure

Another major reason for lack of goal setting by church leaders is *the fear of failure*. When I had established a clear mental picture of the walk-in, drive-in church that I hoped to build, complete with fountains, landscaping and tower, I was a very excited young man. Remember, goal setting is a major source of enthusiasm—and enthusiasm is all-important for success.

I did not dare at first to reveal my dream publicly. I had a dream, you see, but it was not yet a goal. Why not? Because I kept it a secret, and only dreams that are publicly announced become goals.

I was afraid that if I announced my dream and accepted it as a goal to be sought, I would run the risk of failure. And the fear of failure, perhaps more than any other single factor, is the reason why the average human being does not establish challenging goals for himself.

What cured me of my fear of failure? I once saw a calendar with this slogan written across the top: "I'd rather attempt to do something great and fail than attempt to do nothing and succeed." That did it! I realized that "not failure but low aim is crime." Since then, I have never been afraid of publicly establishing and announcing great goals.

Overcome your fear of failure. As one of my books states, there are seven ways you can do so.[1] I do not believe that God will ever scold you for having attempted to dare something for Him. But I do believe that some of us will stand before God someday and be accused of having had too little faith.

Lack of self-confidence

Still another reason why people resist setting goals is *their own lack of self-confidence.* At this point I urge you to read most carefully another of my books, *Move Ahead with Possibility Thinking.* [2] You can accomplish anything you can imagine, providing your goals meet certain principles. You can, in fact, test the success potential of your goals before you actually launch them. If your goals meet the following criteria, they will succeed—if you only have enough nerve to announce them, begin them and never give up.

Test Your Goals

Test your goals in this way: ask these three questions to determine whether your goals are wise and attainable.

Is this a problem-solving goal?

Does this goal—this dream—solve human problems? This is the test of practicality.

The terrible thing is that most people begin by asking the question: "Can I afford it? Do we have the money?" This is the last question to be asked.

The first questions must always be: "Would this be a great thing for God? Would it be a great thing for Jesus Christ? Would it be a great thing for our community? Would it help a lot of human beings? Would it solve a lot of human problems? Is anybody else doing the job right?"

If your goal would help to solve human problems, move ahead to the next question.

Can this dream, my glorified goal, be pacesetting?

Obviously, if another church or several churches in your community are already succeeding in doing what you hope to do, then you can expect some rough competition. I was enormously encouraged to build our walk-in, drive-in church and was confident of success because this was the only walk-in, drive-in church in all of Orange County. We have succeeded, not because we are so smart, but because the competition just didn't exist!

If your glorified goal, your exciting dream, is pacesetting, you can be assured of enormous publicity. As a result, the people who stand to benefit by your services will know you're in business! And this is all important—for people must get behind any goal to make it succeed. Even the artist who works completely alone on a canvas needs customers to buy his paintings or he will starve.

If your goal passes the first and second questions, then move on to the third question.

Can this goal be exciting—really exciting—to people?

Obviously, if it fails to excite people, they will not get behind the project. And people will get excited about goals if they see that these goals are really practical—and if they will help human beings who are hurting. People will get excited about goals if they see that these goals can be creative and can lead to something beautiful.

I tell the members of my staff that I will listen to any suggestion if it has a superlative in it. If it is the "first" or the "longest" or the "shortest" or "newest" or "oldest." If it excels, it will attract attention because it is an award winner, then I know that it has excitement-generating potential and will become relatively easy to sell.

The goal of a walk-in, drive-in church was established firmly in my mind as a guaranteed successful idea because it passed the above three questions. People who are physically handicapped or have mentally retarded children or want to avoid crowds or are mourning and given to crying in a sanctuary or wish to maintain their privacy—these are some of the people with problems who are benefited by a drive-in church. Obviously, a walk-in, drive-in church could solve human problems.

Furthermore, there was nothing like it in the United States or, for that matter, in the entire world, so it was pacesetting. I could be assured that I would get the attention of many people. And I would need the attention of many people in order to attract the support that would make success possible.

Beauty as a Goal

Beauty is practical as well as desirable! That's why I could envision the walk-in, drive-in church being designed so attractively, so beautifully, that people would be magnetically drawn to it. People run away from ugliness, people run to beauty. Beauty excites. Beauty generates enthusiasm. Beauty marshals enormous support. I envisioned reflecting pools, fountains, green grass with splashes of flower gardens. I envisioned award-winning, futuristic architecture.

Set Membership Goals

So test your dreams by the above questions and begin now to set growth goals for your church. But how do you begin? First, *determine what the unchurched population of your community is today, what it will be 10 years from today, 20 years from today and 50 years from today.* Your local chamber of commerce will have studies that will give you the answers.

Then ask yourself this question: "What percentage of

the unchurched population from our community could we win into our membership if we had a tremendous staff, marvelous facilities including surplus parking, and a program for all ages?" In arriving at your answers, you can assume that people will drive as far as 20 miles one way if you are near a major freeway. Or most people will be willing to drive 20 minutes to a church that has the goods!

For myself, I find that 20 minutes or 20 miles, or 10 stoplights is the limit of my tolerance. And I believe that this applies to many people in our modern society. In arriving at the population of your potential parish zone, draw a radius of 20 minutes' driving distance, or 10 miles if there are several stop signs or stoplights.

Perhaps you should establish a goal of canvassing door-to-door, all of the homes in your community. Then actually *draw up a mailing list of all the unchurched people in your territory*. When you have done this, you will know more realistically what the prospects for your church membership growth will be. Do not assume that thousands of homes are too many to canvass.

In the early days of our church, when we had less than 200 members, we canvassed 14,000 homes in only two weeks. It can be done very simply. All we did was have one person ride down every street while his wife drove the car. He wrote down the name of the street and the number of every house. Forty addresses appeared on a sheet of paper from the top to the bottom. And so a total of 350 sheets with 40 addresses on a sheet amounted to 14,000 addresses.

We recruited 35 teams of persons and gave to each team 10 sheets with 40 addresses—or 400 calls to make. They did this in two Saturdays. They simply went from house to house and asked one brief question: "Are you an active member of a local church?" If the answer was no they made a simple check mark on the sheet, left an invitational brochure and moved on. The names and addresses of all the unchurched people were placed on a stenciled mailing list and we had the beginnings of a tremendous field that we could work!

No matter how small your church is, you must begin by setting membership growth goals. If you have a very small church, you can begin by keeping on your desk a list of all the prospective members of your church. I did this for years. If you don't have a prospect list on your desk, then go out and call from door to door to build a prospect list! *And begin by working the prospect list.*

Then establish quarterly goals to win people to Jesus Christ. Really, the secret of winning people to Christ and into a growing membership of the church is so very simple! Success starts when you start to set goals!

How large should a church ultimately be? *The answer to that question must be based on the unchurched population of your community.* Calculate what percentage of the unchurched you can reasonably expect to win in the next 20 or 30 years, and let this determine your ultimate membership goal. The ultimate potential membership of your church, based upon prayerful expectations of the maximum number of unchurched people you can win to Christ out of your large community in the next 30 years, should be the *only* basis upon which your membership goals are established.

I cannot urge too strongly that word, ONLY! No other criterion should determine your membership goals. Not the theories of some writer. Nor the ideas of some "management consultant." Nor the seating capacity of your sanctuary. Nor the size of your parking lot! One factor and one factor only sets the membership growth goals. And that is *the number of unchurched people in your community!*

Set Attendance Goals

Now that you've set membership goals, establish church attendance goals. Up that goal! If your sanctuary is almost filled, plan two services. Let your goal be to fill the church twice. When you force yourself to establish these church attendance goals, you will be forced to think of possible ways to raise the attendance. This will force you to think in terms of better programming, better public relations, better advertising and more aggressive door-to-door calling. Up that church attendance goal right now!

Set Program Goals

Now begin to work on program goals! And how do you establish goals for programs? You might find yourself stimulated by reading material that comes from your denominational headquarters.

But let me give you a very practical assignment that is the best advice anyone will ever give to you on establishing program goals for a successful, growing church in your community.

Have your secretary (if you don't have a secretary, you'd better get out and make your church grow large enough so you can afford one!) block off two weeks in your calendar when you will attend no committee meetings, accept no public assignments, and perhaps have your board bring in two guest ministers for two Sundays.

Allocate these two weeks *full time* toward the following project: begin by calling door-to-door in the immediate vicinity of your church. You have called on some of these homes before, but you are going to call now with a different purpose, a different motive and a different question.

You are going to ask: "Do you attend our church regularly? Have you ever attended it? Do you attend any other church?"

If they give you a negative answer, you will reply by saying: "I'm delighted to hear this because I'm anxious to find out how I can improve this church and make it such an exciting church that intelligent and wonderful people like you will want to come. You are obviously an intelligent person, so you undoubtedly have good reasons why you don't attend the church. Would you please tell me what they are? And could you tell me what our church could possibly do to help in any area of your life? Is there any program that you would be interested in?"

Generally, after you have asked the first one or two questions, the answers will be forthcoming. I did this years ago and it was an eye-opening experience! I heard criticisms of "typical sermons." And I heard criticisms about other gaps in the church program. The criticisms of unchurched persons in my community became a major learning experience!

If you will spend two weeks calling door-to-door in an ever-widening circle, beginning from your church property, and will listen with an open mind, then indeed you will have the education of a lifetime! Listen to the individuals you talk with—listen to them carefully.

Do not be defensive! In spite of all that you have ever been taught, assume—for one humble time in your life—that you may have been wrong about a lot of things! So, listen to what the unchurched are saying and you will find out where they are hurting, where they are frightened, where they are worried. Take careful notes. Keep a daily diary detailing your calls.

After two weeks you will know what kind of a church program you have to design to meet the needs of these people in your community. You will know what kind of messages to give in order to bring them into the church. Not only will you be enlightened, but you will be mentally and socially prepared to establish program and sermon goals. You will even discover what kind of staff members should be added to your church.

Set New Goals

Never allow anything to keep you from setting new goals once the old goals have been attained. Where there are no goals—then and there the seeds of death are sown. The dullest, deadest and most unpleasant time in my life came when, after 14 years in the Garden Grove Community Church, I found my 40 years' goals accomplished!

Victor Frankl said in a lecture once: "The *is* must never catch up with the *ought*." When the Israelites traveled across the wilderness, they never caught up with the cloud by day or with the fire by night. There must always be the tension between the unreached goal and the present state of affairs. When there are no challenging goals, then death has already set in.

If anything blocks the way to establishing larger and more challenging goals, then by all means remove these obstacles to growth goals! Growth-restricting barriers must be removed at any cost or the seed of death is planted. Our original church property was 10 acres in size. This allowed for 700 parking spaces off the street. When the parking lot was filled twice on Sunday morning, I could see cars drive in and out and storm away because they could find no parking space.

We had a growth-restricting problem. Either we would create more parking or growth goals would be unattainable. At a price of $1 million, we removed the problem of inadequate parking. We bought 10 acres of land next door. It was one of the smartest things we ever did in the history of our church!

When our sanctuary was enlarged to its maximum seating capacity of 1,700, and when it was filled to overflowing in two morning church services, we had another growth-restricting problem which threatened the realization of our goals in increased membership. As a result, we determined to solve this growth-restricting, goal-frustrating problem at any cost. We were prepared, if necessary, to destroy the entire sanctuary to build a larger one if need be.

It would be a sin, we felt, to allow a building made out of glass and steel and aluminum to frustrate the winning of more people to Jesus Christ! We would not surrender leadership to a chunk of real estate. So we solved the problem by announcing three morning church services and I began preaching at 8:30, again at 10:00 and again at 11:15 A.M.

Again, because unmet needs outgrew our capacity to meet them, we built a larger sanctuary, the Crystal Cathedral, with its 3,000-seat capacity. This larger facility and others already on the drawing board affirm that we will never allow the shoe to determine how large the foot can grow. Why? Because within a 15-minute radius of our church are still hundreds of thousands of unchurched people. We have an idea how many unchurched people we can win in our community. With this knowledge, we plan the facilities we must have to meet the needs of each one.

Other than our commission from Christ, *the challenge of the unchurched people—more than anything else—sets the goals in our church.* And if that should ever change you will see the Crystal Cathedral begin to die.

Set Goals Beyond Goals

By all means, set goals *beyond* your goals. And if there are any obstacles in the way that would keep you from establishing larger goals, realize that these obstacles must be removed at any cost—or accept the fact that the seed of death and decay is already planted. If you can't afford to pay the price of removing your growth-stifling obstacles, then be prepared to pay the price of "not being able to afford it"—and that price tag is *death!*

What this means is that you must become a possibility thinker to succeed! In setting your goals, believe that anything is possible if it can solve human problems and if it can be a great thing for God.

Use possibility thinking to set your goals. And then use possibility thinking to dream up all of the possible ways to reach what may seem now to be an impossible goal!

Notes

1. Robert H. Schuller, *Self-Love: The Dynamic Force of Success* (New York: Hawthorn Books, Inc., 1969).
2. Robert H. Schuller, *Move Ahead with Possibility Thinking* (New York: Doubleday & Company, 1967).

"An eye that never shuts. An ear that never closes."

Chapter 4

POSSIBILITY THINKING MAKES MIRACLES HAPPEN

The greatest power in the world is the power of possibility thinking. If your dream has come from God then you need only to exercise this miracle-working power, and you can reach the seemingly unattainable goal! Believe me, I know!

All right, your goals are already firmly established in your mind. And they have successfully passed the three-way question test. So far, so good. But now at this point, your biggest problem is you. Yes, you! The hardest job before you now is to make yourself believe that the apparently enormous goal is somehow, some way, somewhere, some time attainable.

Impossibility Thinking

But you can do it, unless you are a victim of impossibility thinking. Yes, only you can make the possible goal impossible. How?

You make a possible goal impossible when you do nothing about it. You make a possible goal impossible when you quit somewhere along the way. You make a possible goal impossible when you accept failure as final.

Possibility Thinking

So what then is possibility thinking?

Possibility thinking is maximum utilization of the God-given powers of imagination exercised in dreaming up possible ways by which a desired objective can be attained. Possibility thinking is also called faith, the kind of faith Jesus Christ was talking about when He said, "If you have faith as a grain of mustard seed, you will say to this mountain, 'Move . . . ,' and it will move; and nothing will be impossible to you" (Matt. 17:20, *RSV*).

The principles of possibility thinking are these:

Possibility thinking assumes that there must be a way to achieve a desired objective.

This is so when it is established that that same objective would be a great thing for God, a tremendous thing for Jesus Christ and a problem-solving means for helping many hurting human beings.

Possibility thinking makes great pronouncements.

In this way you reveal to the public your sincere intention to accomplish this exciting and most necessary objective.

Possibility thinking results in brainstorming.

Motivated by the assumption of achievement and committed by public pronouncement, possibility thinkers begin to brainstorm. And in brainstorming, an amazing assortment of creative ideas will be forthcoming—ideas which will unlock possible ways to success that you would never have thought of at all, if you had not exercised possibility thinking in the first place!

Possibility thinking brings in support from unexpected sources.

The positive idea let loose will be grabbed hold of by people who will become the followers of the idea and will not let it die. At this point, the goal is already halfway attained!

Never Say No!

I have adopted a policy never to make a no decision on a potentially good idea. If any idea is ever suggested to my mind by God or by a fellow mortal, I—by an act of sheer willpower—refuse to make a negative response. I intuitively test proposals by the three success-spotting questions and, if I get the right answers, I move ahead and *assume* that the objective can be accomplished. If it is not God's will for success to be forthcoming, I will let Him make the no decision! There are a million ways in which God can stop us!

God Is Unlimited

God has unlimited financial resources and unlimited intelligence to achieve His goals. *Possibility thinking is simply opening your mind for God to unfold the ways in which His will can be accomplished.* Thus God performs miracles in those people who, unafraid of failure and public embarrassment, move boldly and bravely forward, attempting big things for God and expecting great things from God.

Nothing Is Impossible

At this point, let me share three never-to-be-forgotten

experiences that I have gone through since I published the book on possibility thinking some years ago.

Our original walk-in, drive-in sanctuary was built on 10 acres of land which we purchased at a total cost of $66,000, or $6,600 per acre. At that time, we tried to buy an additional 10 acres of adjoining land, anticipating a future need. We offered the owner $12,000 an acre, an unheard of amount! The offer was refused. Later, we offered him $25,000 an acre—a quarter of a million dollars! Again the offer was turned down.

Many years later, we offered him $50,000 an acre, or a half-million dollars! Believe me, it took an enormous amount of possibility thinking to offer $500,000 for the same amount of ground we had bought only a few years earlier for $66,000! Once again our offer was refused.

A few months after this last offer was rejected, a huge development combine came in, purchased 200 acres directly across the street from our church, and took out a lease-option on the adjoining 10 acres that we had bid for unsuccessfully. The lease they secured on the land was for five years, with an option to buy the acreage at the end of that period for $500,000. When I discovered that we had lost out, I accepted defeat. "We'll never get it now," I thought to myself.

In spite of the apparent setback, we proceeded to enlarge our sanctuary from its original seating capacity of 1,000 to its master-plan size designed to accommodate 1,700 persons. We proceeded to erect the Tower of Hope, a 14-story structure housing the 24-hour telephone counseling services in the chapel at the top, offices for the growing staff, counseling clinic and classrooms. By now the added stimulus of the additional building projects created so much publicity and attention in the community that attendance soared.

Twelve months after we enlarged our sanctuary, we found ourselves with a parking problem. I had now moved into my office on the twelfth floor of the Tower. From this vantage point I could see what was going on in the parking lot and in the adjoining streets.

I realize now that, if we had not built the Tower, and if my office had remained in its former cloistered, paneled seclusion of the garden setting, our church would not have grown as it has today, for I would not have been aware of the parking and traffic problem. But when I was elevated high in the sky and looked down on the congestion on the streets and the futility of cars driving in and out looking for a place to park, I became deeply aware of the fact that our success was about to strangle us.

Addressing the church board, I made the following comment, "Growth will lift you or it will level you. It can propel you forward or it can knock you down and grind you into the ground. Look at the old downtown sections of cities in this country.

"The original merchants were so swamped with new customers when the first suburbs were built that they were confident of continued success. They were not, however, sustained by growth for long. Soon they found that they were incapable of handling the crowds. Parking became impossible.

"So, enterprising merchants began building great new shopping centers on the outskirts of the old towns. The result? With the new shopping centers in business, the old downtown merchants died—strangled by growth."

It became clear to us that we would have to obtain additional parking. There were only two possible ways in which this desired goal could be accomplished: either buy more land or build a high-rise parking garage on our present land.

First, we investigated the possibilities of the high-rise garage with its racks or elevators lifting cars to the second, third and fourth stories. Our findings indicated that it would cost approximately $5 a square foot. At the same time, it would necessarily be a huge structure creating an undesirable visual intrusion into the spacious atmosphere of the 10-acre property.

Suddenly our thinking had been enormously stretched, and the biggest job in the world is to think bigger than you've ever thought before! So, we made a new approach to the syndicate that held the lease-option on the adjoining 10 acres. We were prepared to offer more than $50,000 an acre, which was their option.

Upon approaching them, however, we were informed that the property was not for sale at any price. We prayed. We practiced possibility thinking and believed that somehow it might be possible to acquire the land. About that time, I called our banker and he told me, "Did you hear the news? Edgar Kaiser has taken over control of the combine that owns the property around your place."

I prayed and suddenly I remembered reading, some 20 years before, a lead article in the *Reader's Digest* which was a condensation of the layman's sermon preached by Henry J. Kaiser, Edgar's father, at New York's Marble Collegiate Church where Dr. Norman Vincent Peale is the pastor. I immediately called my friend Norman Vincent Peale and asked him, "Do you know Edgar Kaiser?" He replied that he knew Mr. Kaiser very well. At my request Dr. Peale appealed to Mr. Kaiser to sell us their "option." Within 48 hours, I received a call from Charles Cobb, Kaiser's man in control, inviting me to come in and negotiate for the property!

It was then the middle of February 1969. The business administrator and I met with Mr. Cobb who told us that the property, on the advice of Mr. Kaiser, could be made available to us. The price would be $135,000 an acre or $1,350,000! Now, by all human rationale, that figure was out of our reach. We countered with an offer of $1,000,000.

Mr. Cobb subsequently agreed to sell the property to us for that sum, "Providing," he said, "that I can get $500,000 cash for our position by March 31"—just six weeks away. He explained that the payment was needed to get his firm's apartment project off the ground ahead of schedule. This, he said, would generate increased income by the apartment project, justifying the lower sale price.

I called a church board meeting and appraised them of the facts. "For the first time in our history—and for the only time—you have an opportunity to buy the adjoining 10 acres of ground. It is an opportunity that has never come before and will never come again if you turn it down today. We can buy the property for $1,000,000. That's about $2.50 a square foot—half the price the parking structure will cost and you get full frontage rights and all air rights! It's a bargain! The only thing is, we have to come up with $500,000 in cold, hard cash in the next forty-five days."

The board passed the following resolution: "To give God a chance to work a miracle, we would have Dr. Schuller announce on the coming Sunday our intention to raise this amount of money and buy the property." The resolution passed without a dissenting vote, and the next Sunday we made the announcement to the congregation.

Now you know, no conventional fund raiser is going to come in and attempt to conduct and wrap up a campaign from beginning to end in six short weeks. It just can't be done—or so they say. So I called in a friend of mine who operates a professional fund-raising organization and we hired him to recruit and train members of our church for an accelerated money-raising campaign.

And we did it! It was the most concentrated, most urgent appeal for financial help we've ever made in the history of our church.

As soon as we announced publicly our intention to buy the property, I received a phone call from the banker of our church who asked, "What are you doing?"

We told him. Without hesitation, he replied by saying, "I think it's a great idea! If we can help you out, we'd like to do so. In fact, if you people can actually collect $250,000 in cash in the next six weeks, we will loan you the other $250,000 for a period of 24 months."

This was great news! Now it meant that all we'd have to collect from the congregation during those 45 days was $250,000. Time passed with amazing swiftness as the campaign progressed—much too rapidly. Just three days before the payment deadline, we found we had only $160,000 on hand!

Suddenly the phone rang. It was the lawyer from the Kaiser group. "You know," he said, "we aren't going to be able to finish the legal work before March 31. There are some signatures we need from some of our people who are out of the area. Is it all right if we extend the agreement for another three weeks?"

"I will have to discuss it with my advisors," I replied. Then after a very short pause, I said, "Oh, that will be great! That will be just fine with us!"

By the third week of April 1969 we had the required $250,000 and had also borrowed $250,000 from the bank. The $500,000 was deposited and we took over the option to buy the 10 acres from the original owner for $500,000. After all the legal papers had been signed, our treasurer, Frank Boss, and I went back to our office jubilantly carrying the legal document, which was about three-quarters of an inch thick!

Then we began wrestling with the next problem. Where were we going to obtain the remaining $500,000 to complete the purchase in July? Imagine our happy surprise when we opened the document and read the fine print. In addition to verifying the fact that we had the right to purchase the land with a down payment of $500,000 in July, the document specified: "This price offer will hold firm for the next five years."

At that time, if we elected to exercise the option and actually purchase the property for $500,000, it would be sold to us on the following terms: $100,000 down, with 10 years to pay off the balance at 6 percent interest. And *so a million-dollar financial package fell together in less than two months time!*

Today that property is developed and our parking has been increased by 700 cars. A youth center stands in the corner of that additional property, and the Crystal Cathedral is sited in the middle of that land.

Without any doubt, the addition of that property kept our church from dying! And it opened up a fantastic future for us! We now have 20 acres at the freeway hub of Orange County. And it all became possible simply because we got out of God's way, assuming and believing that when we get out of His way, *God specializes in turning impossibilities into possibilities!*

Only five months after this enormously aggressive and successful fund-raising program, I made the acquaintance of Fred Dinert. Fred and I were chatting in my office about the prospects for a television ministry emanating from the Garden Grove Community Church. I could envision a most spectacular color telecast of our church services. We do have a phenomenal natural setting, with trees, flowers and fountains lending a spirit of beauty and serenity to the church grounds.

Fred and I discussed the possibility of an hour-long television color program and he agreed to give me an estimate as to the cost. He came back with this report: "It can be done, Bob, but it will cost around $400,000 a year."

I replied with this impossibility statement: "We can never do that. Certainly, we couldn't do it today. Perhaps in four years we could. But at this point in time it would be impossible to try to raise any extra money from our people who have just been hit for all the money we could get out of them."

Then, like a real impossibility thinker, I added, "Furthermore, in November—only a few weeks from now—we'll be asking them to underwrite next year's budget which is going to be increased over this year's by $100,000! So I suppose we'll simply have to forget the televising idea at this time."

Well, Fred Dinert called me a few weeks later. "Bob, I think you should let God decide whether it is possible. Why don't you and I give God a chance to make this decision. *If the decision is no, let God make it.* Next Sunday have your people come to church and lay the plan before them. Let them respond.

"You and I and your business administrator, Frank Boss, will make a quiet prayer covenant with God. We will tell God to show us $200,000 worth of support in two weeks time, if He wants this television ministry to begin. If we can receive pledges in that amount, we will go on the air in January and trust that the balance of the money will come in the next 12 or 24 months."

So Fred Dinert in Philadelphia, and Frank Boss and Bob Schuller in Garden Grove made this quiet prayer covenant with God.

On the following Sunday, the people came to church after being notified in advance that "Dr. Schuller was about to make one of the most important decisions of his life and that he would ask the members of the congregation to direct him." Persons in attendance that Sunday morning found pledge cards in the bulletin. That morning alone, 1,100 families pledged $186,000. And on the following Sunday, the pledges totaled $203,000!

God had taught me a big lesson. He taught me that I was a "too little" thinker!

We proceeded to form a corporation which we called The Robert Schuller Tele Vangelism Association, Incorporated. I selected the treasurer and business administrator of the church to be the treasurer of the new corporation, so that I would be personally immune from financial criticism in the handling, receiving and discharging of funds. I hired Stuart Ehrlich, a layman from the church to be my full-time administrative aide, handling the administrative details of this new project as well as the details connected with the Institute for Successful Church Leadership, another project I was about to launch!

By the first Sunday in January, the first pledge payments came in, totaling approximately $4,000. Since we were beginning from scratch, we wanted to postpone the beginning of the telecast as deep into the year as we could in order to build up a small financial base. So we announced to the congregation that we would videotape our first service on the third Sunday in January 1970, and would begin actual telecasting the first Sunday in February.

It was on a Wednesday morning in the middle of January that Frank Boss came into my office with bad news. "Bob, in order to live up to our word and begin videotaping on the third Sunday in January, we are going to have to have special lights installed *tomorrow!* And here's the bad news—the lights, plus a new transformer, will come to $20,000! And to make matters worse, they demand cash on the line—no credit. All the money we have available at this point is $10,000!"

Well, I had one day's time to find the solution to the problem. Deep within myself, I couldn't condone the idea of "borrowing" from the church corporation. I knew they simply didn't have the surplus cash.

Frankly, I didn't know what to do. Furthermore, I didn't have time to think about the problem during the course of the day because I had a heavy schedule of commitments. I decided to finish my work and then put my mind to confronting this latest crisis.

My last appointment for the day was a couple whom I had never met before. They walked into my office that Wednesday night with beaming faces. "What's your problem?" I asked. They informed me that they had no problem but that they wished to discuss another matter.

The husband explained: "When we became Christians, we decided to tithe. Our business has just been fantastic ever since! When you asked for pledges in November for the television ministry, we wanted to pledge something but didn't know how much we would be able to promise.

"But now we have a report from our accountant which indicates that the profits of our business in 1969 have been so good that we are in a position to give the Lord a substantial amount, enough to bring in our full tithe. So we have a check that we would like to present to you for your television program."

They handed me the check. I took it, looked at it, and tears flowed from my eyes. It was a check for $10,000!

It was God's way of saying, "Schuller, this is my project. Stay out of my way. Only be wiling to think big, believe big and pray big—and big things will happen!"

An inspiring "Hour of Power" telecast in the making.

Vice-President George Bush on the Jumbotron screen.

The next morning Frank Boss signed the contract with the lighting contractors. The lights were installed and the transformer was connected. And right on schedule, we videotaped our first program on the third Sunday in January! We began televising, exactly as we had promised, the first Sunday in February.

Impossibilities Become Possibilities

Why did these impossibilities prove, with God's leadership, to become possibilities? Both the acquisition of the extra 10 acres and the television project illustrate the three principles of spotting success before you launch your goal.

The television program solved many problems. It filled a vital human need. It was a great thing for God and continues to be a great thing for God. People need inspiration. And in our own area alone, 13 million people live within the range of the television station over which we televise.

The second principle is also in operation here: Our one-hour color television church service is pacesetting. Even today, ours is the only Protestant church in the nation that televises its services every Sunday. Nobody else is doing the job.

The third principle comes into play as well. Our program contains both beauty and creativity. We make full use of our magnificent setting of orange trees, fountains, walls that open to let in all the beauties of earth and sky, worshipers from all over the nation in the gardenlike sanctuary, on the verdant lawns and in their cars—all are captured by the television cameras to present an excitingly attractive program that generates great enthusiasm and consequently marshals enormous support.

If the goals you are establishing in your mind meet the three success-spotting principles—then *only you can make these goals impossible by doing nothing about them or by quitting too quickly.*

Play the Game

For the most productive and exciting time of your life, pick some fantastic goal, some tremendous goal that will pass the three success-spotting principles. I've got some great goal-setting suggestions for you later on in chapter 11, so be sure you're familiar with them. Then get together with one, two or perhaps three possibility thinkers and play the possibility-thinking game!

When you start playing the game, here's what happens. The wild and reckless ideas that you have allowed to be expressed in your slumbering subconscious get stirred up. So wild and reckless ideas bump into some snoozing, creative brain cells that, once jarred out of their slumber, perk up and listen to what's going on. They emerge from their hibernation to join the party and offer their own suggestions.

After awhile, more sleeping, creative brain cells are aroused by all the activity and great ideas come forth until the "list of possible ways" is lengthened and, generally speaking, a more probable solution is mentally generated.

What are your goals? What are your dreams? What great thing can you imagine for God? Play the possibility-thinking game.

"If you have faith as a grain of mustard seed, you will say to this mountain, 'Move . . . ,' and it will move; and nothing will be impossible to you" (Matt 17:20, *RSV*).

While we're being wildly creative and stepping out in faith into new areas of possibility, let's tackle something else equally important to the future of your church. And that is to put to rest once and for all a false dichotomy in the thinking of American Christians that has strangled, stifled and strait-jacketed the Church in this country for over 200 years. In our minds we have created an unbridgeable gap between the secular and the sacred.

Even though, in fact, no such estrangement exists between the two, many Christians think and act as though a state of war exists between the secular and the sacred, a war that gives no quarter and appears to offer no hope of resolution. The tragic result of this unfortunate mind-set in the Church is to retard growth, discourage creativity, destroy enthusiasm, limit effectiveness and cancel any hope of success.

So let's look now at this problem, and together we can eliminate from our midst this imagined conflict that has done more damage to the Church than most of the real ones put together.

Chapter 5

THE SACRED AND
THE SECULAR

I am always uncomfortable with statements of "we" versus "they." When we put positions or people in adversarial relationships, we run the risk of over-simplification. Such, it seems to me, is the assumed conflict between the sacred and the secular. This imagined opposition could lie at the root of most of the problems that face the Church today.[1]

If not, how do you account for Christians who lack the emotional and spiritual wholeness that a healthy Christian religion should produce? How do you explain or justify the destructive suspicions among the various parts of Christianity? How is it that theologians have failed to use and apply the insights into human behavior discovered by twentieth-century psychologists? Why the failure of so much of Protestant Christianity to come up with dynamic movements to correct social injustices after proclaiming the gospel?

Can there be a fundamental defect in our theology? And how do we resolve the perceived conflict between the so-called "theology of success" and the theology of discipleship under the Cross?

The questions go on: Is it possible to reconcile the tensions that exist between Christians who use some of the insights of Marx and those who see themselves as anti-Marxists? If the gospel of Jesus Christ is the truth that we proclaim it to be, why is the Church in Europe—established for centuries—declining? And why is the mainstream of Protestantism in America declining? Why is the world not rushing to embrace the good news? Can the human needs which seem to be met adequately by a growing secularism not be met more effectively by the gospel of Christ, if it is rightly interpreted and proclaimed?

It seems to me that all such questions can be spoken to in this one sentence: *The sacred must become secular, and the secular must become sacred.*

My thoughts here cluster around three great words: *Incarnation, Resurrection and Crucifixion.* And no, I don't have the Resurrection and the Crucifixion out of order. Wait, and you'll soon see why.

First, let's think together about the Incarnation.

Incarnation

"In the beginning was the Word, and the Word was with God, and the Word was God . . . And the Word was made flesh, and dwelt among us" (John 1:1,14).

For 30 years my ministry has been a mission to unbelievers. If I were a churchman talking to church leaders, I would have used a theocentric approach. However, I have seen my calling as communicating spiritual reality to secular people, people who aren't ready to believe in God. I have been trying to carry on a dialogue with persons who aren't ready to listen to God-talk. And as a missionary, I feel that a respectful contact with secular people must be based on a human-needs approach rather than a theology approach.

It is precisely at this point that I feel the Church must be reformed. For the Church to address the unchurched with a theocentric attitude is to invite failure in its mission. In the incarnation of Jesus Christ, the sacred became secular, the Word became flesh. Christianity is the result of God's foreign mission enterprise, and Jesus was God's first foreign missionary.

When the sacred became secular at Bethlehem, the secular was honored. The Christian faith honors the secular; it does not condemn it. To be secular is not a sin. To enjoy food and drink, clothes, sexual experience and material things such as a house and a car is not sinful. Paul tells Timothy that it is "God who richly furnishes us with everything to enjoy" (1 Tim. 6:17 *RSV*).

Much secularity is the result of God's creative enterprise. We have had enough negative reactionaries who say every Christmas, "It is all so secular—the Christmas trees, the spending of money on gifts; it's terrible!" The truth is that God can come to us in the tree, in the gifts, in the beauty. It can all be part of God's creativity.

When we built the Crystal Cathedral, we did not assume that it would be wrong to have secular activities there. Secular*ism* is what is sinful. Secular*ism* is a philosophy that seeks to sustain human life with only secular resources, with nothing that is sacred or divine. Now, of course, the secular that doesn't become sacred is dangerous, demonic, not because it's bad, but because it's good. It pretends to be adequate. Even as it is dangerous when the sacred fails to become secular, likewise it is dangerous when the secular fails to become sacred.

The Church can be and remain a Church, but unless it becomes secular it loses its mission posture, its mission role, its call, its commitment. If our music, for instance, must all be "religious," every selection used in morning worship needing to contain references to God or Jesus or the Holy Spirit, or to sin or salvation, we are going to reduce our effectiveness as a mission. Will we not dare to sing "The Impossible Dream" on a Sunday morning? Might it not be more suitable at a special moment than anything in the hymnbook?

When the sacred becomes secular, you've got a mission going. It's Jesus Christ coming to Bethlehem. It's Albert Schweitzer going to Africa. When our denomination sends a mission to Africa, the sacred becomes secular. What do we send? We send a veterinarian, chickens, Holstein cows, hogs, seeds. We send doctors, translators, evangelists. Again, the Word is made flesh and dwells among needy people, full of God's grace. Grace, God's love in action, is where sacred becomes secular, where the rubber touches the road.

On the other hand, when the sacred remains sacred, death is certain. Our problem is often that we do not dare to let the sacred part of our Christian life become secular for fear we may lose our life. Our spirituality—isn't that, after all, our life? And if we become secular, don't we lose our integrity? So what do we do?

We have done all kinds of things in the centuries of Christian history to protect our sacredness so we will not be infected with secularity. We have developed a holy language of words and gestures that is "Greek" to unbelievers. We have used standoffish architecture. We have developed a liturgy with put-down prayers and music and rituals that communicate little. We stand apart from the common life while two blocks from the church hookers are parading and pot is being sold. How does what happens in church relate to life as it is being lived two blocks away?

Many are saying, "Why, it doesn't connect at all!"

As a result, the Church in maintaining its sacredness, in shunning secularity, is dying. In trying to save its life, it is losing it. Why is the sacred so afraid of becoming secular? Don't we realize that it is our fear that is destroying the life of the Church? And fear is the opposite of love. Yet the fate that is feared is the key to life. When the sacred gives up its holy isolation and enters the common life, it is like a grain of wheat that falls in the ground and dies, only to sprout and bear fruit (see John 12:24).

Let me give you an illustration. I am a pastor in the Reformed Church in America. In Southern California when I was preaching in a drive-in theater to unchurched people, I was terribly criticized; criticized for preaching psychology and not the Word, for preaching shallow talks instead of profound theological sermons or glorious expositions of Scripture. During those days one of the Reformed churches in my classis tried desperately to have me stopped. It was a very Dutch church.

And in a consistory meeting, someone said, "Ve got to do something about Schuller! Ve can't have a dominie in a drive-in church. Ve can't have him do that!" Some time later, the dominie of the Dutch church left. I am still around.

The congregation called a pastor who had sung in a college quartet with me, Ken Leestma, who convinced the congregation to give up its sacred isolation and become secular. The miracle happened! They "died" as a church and were "re-born" as a mission. They bought property and built a new church with open windows permitting worshipers to participate both outside and inside the building. They called it the New Life Community Church. Today they are probably the second largest church in the classis! When the sacred dares to die there's hope!

The first walk-in; drive-in church—now the Arboretum.

Look at Christ's incarnate ministry. Look at His preaching ministry. Where did He preach? In the synagogues? Not usually. More often He preached and taught "by the sea," "on the way," "as He went." What was His subject matter? Scriptural exposition? Only rarely. Usually He told stories, wonderfully secular stories, and yet they were about the Kingdom of God. The common people heard Him gladly!

By contrast, sacred sermons that do not dare to become secular turn people off, or bore them, or at least fail to redeem them. Religion must become human. I am not nearly as concerned about secular humanism, though I see its danger, as I am about orthodox religion that fails to become human. This is for us the greater danger.

But when the Church decides to be a mission, to touch human life, all kinds of things begin to happen. One thing that is changed is church architecture. When the architect, Richard Neutra, designed our first church which today is our Arboretum, I saw all the proposed windows, and I said, "We can have a whole panorama of Scripture—creation, the prophets, the lot—in stained glass! We can portray events in the life of Christ, the dreams of the end of time, something about the modern church in mission."

I will never forget Mr. Neutra looking at me and saying, "Well, that's fine if it's just for your own religious people, but what will it do for all the non-religious people who come in here? I'm Jewish, but I don't practice the Jewish faith. And when I go into a place that surrounds me with stained-glass windows I feel threatened. I feel people are shouting sermons at me. Who is it you really want to impress?"

"Well," I thought, "I don't really want to impress believers; they've already accepted the message." So I had to transform a decision to be secular into an architectural statement. *We would be a mission first and a church second.* This meant giving up stained-glass windows all over the place, with their lambs and bunches of grapes and the whole colored array of holy symbols. To be a mission first meant a building that was comfortable for the uninitiated, understandable, yet beautiful too.

We also built the building so we could serve people who didn't come in but who stayed in their cars. Jesus met people outside the Temple, outside the synagogues; so did we. We did not say, "You come to me and meet me at my level; I'm not going to meet you at your level." We did not say, "You come to my turf; I won't go to your turf." Later we built the Crystal Cathedral—transparent, so that one could in a sense be out-of-doors even while he sat inside. Our idea was that the building, once built, would "go away."

Stewardship was in our minds too. We thought it would be a sin to create a crystal cathedral just for the purpose of being a sacred structure with its use limited to proclaiming the Word and administering the sacraments on Sunday mornings. It would be far better stewardship if we made it possible for the building to be used by the community during the week. If it could be a church, it could also be a concert hall. Psychologically, that would be good because we could meet people at secular events, and that would be pre-evangelism.

This thinking led on to other things. Some said, "Let's not have pews; let's have individual seats and number them."

I said, "Well, the sacred must become secular, but we must not forget that we're also sacred, because the possibility of forgetting that is the other danger. Let's keep an equilibrium, a balance. Let's have individual theater seats, but let's keep the pew backs and the pew ends." So that's how we did it.

Then we talked about the altar-table, the pulpit, and a cross. The minister of music said, "Let's make the altar-table so that we can move it to the back of the worship area."

And the comptroller said, "Let's place the cross so we can take it up, because when the community uses the building, there will be Jews and Buddhists and other non-Christians, and let's not offend them. Let's have the pulpit portable too, multipurpose."

But I repeated our need for balance, for equilibrium, and I said, "Wait a minute! The sacred must become secular, but the sacred must not forget where it's coming from and where it's got to get back to in the process. It is a process. That's the right word. So look, the cross will be bolted to the concrete altar. Because if you're thinking the way you are, and if I drop dead, someone who follows me may think the same way, and that would be a mistake.

"So we will not have a portable communion table, but we'll make it out of granite and it will be cemented to the concrete floor. The altar-table weighs three tons! And the pulpit will be made of granite and we'll fix it in wet cement and make it immovable. Then I'll screw a little brass plaque to the top of the pulpit with the words, 'Sir [that's me], we [that's the congregation] would see Jesus.'"[2]

In the process of allowing the sacred to become secular, I believe we have kept our balance and maintained our equilibrium and nothing has ever happened to our sanctuary fixtures. They have never been hidden or covered or removed.

Yes, the sacred must become secular, and the secular must become sacred. This double process not only affects church architecture, it also affects the social ministries of the church. So it was that the Church in years past led the antislavery movement, the reform of child labor laws and other great causes.

On the psychological level, if the sacred is willing to become secular, what then? Then we develop a theology that incarnates itself in psychology, and the two are not antithetical at all. If you don't have a theology that is really good psychology, then you haven't brought the sacred into the secular.[3]

On an ecclesiastical level, what happens? Early in my ministry I said that the Church of the future must not think of itself as just a worship center, but it must be "a shopping center" for Jesus Christ. It must think of itself as meeting all the needs of a community that are not being met by any other institution. Now I rue the day I used that term because it keeps popping up all over, as if my motivation were commercial. But a shopping center is a place where you can buy shoes or medicine or clothing in a one-stop location, and I think that's a hint of what the Church of the future is going to be. It will be specializing in meeting the many needs of a secular society and doing it in the name of Christ and for the glory of Christ.

If the sacred becomes secular, it affects faith, and faith becomes positive thinking, possibility thinking. What do I really mean by possibility thinking? It is God sending ideas into our heads, His Word becoming, in a sense, our flesh—again, the sacred becoming secular.

Resurrection

My second point is the other part of the process; the secular must become sacred. I call this "Resurrection." In the Incarnation, the sacred became secular. In the Resurrection, we have unfolding the possibility that the secular can become sacred. For Christ rises, He lives today through the Holy Spirit—actually, really, not just symbolically, penetrating human lives. Because Christ lives in me, these hands of mine can become the hands of Christ today, this voice can become the voice of Christ, this heart can become His heart.

Yes, the sacred can become secular and the secular can become sacred when "Christ lives in me" (Gal. 2:20, *TLB*), incarnated again in my life. That is what a Christian is—a mind through which Christ thinks, a heart through which Christ loves, a hand through which He helps, an eye through which He sees. And then what do we have? Through the Resurrection, I rise in Him and my whole secular life becomes sacred. As the stonemason in the Middle Ages remarked, "I'm not just working for a living. I'm building a cathedral for God!" You know the story well.

And money? Money is not something evil you preach

against. Making money is not a terrible thing. John Wesley had it right: "Make all you can; save all you can; give all you can." [4] I make all the money I can, and I give a lot too. I've given to the church nearly three-quarters of a million dollars, and the most I've ever been paid by the church is $44,000 a year. Since the church always needs money, I decided it could not pay me a salary which would let me put my kids through school. So I had better earn all I could to meet my family's needs. Paul had his tent-making ministry too.

In God's hands, money which is secular becomes sacred. When the cathedral was started, it was going to cost $7 million. Then costs rose and it became $15 million, then $20 million. At that point, I had a thought which I believe came from God: a lot of money is held by non-Christians. "But I can't go after that, Lord, because they're not your dedicated people; I can't take money from non-Christians."

Then I remembered the old joke about tainted money. The punch line is that the only reason it's tainted is because 'taint mine. Maybe, if I could get it, it could be redeemed. Save it, don't condemn it! Money can be born again too!

Labor, money, sex—what is a more secular subject than sex? Sex, if it is only secular, as it is in so much of our society, can be disappointing. But when sex becomes sacred through commitment, we have the most beautiful thing in the world. We have a family!

People sometimes say to me, "You have people on your telecast I don't think are born-again Christians." Well, I don't think they all are either. I didn't say they were. But here's what is important: they got into our church and sat through a whole sermon before they got out!

But they also had something to contribute. Do you say,

"We can't use their contribution unless they are Christians?" Would you say the same about a surgeon if you needed brain surgery? Suppose the best surgeon is Jewish? Or just non-religious? Do you really want to follow your principle consistently?

Why did I ask Milton Berle to be interviewed on the program? Well, he made people laugh. That was his contribution, and it was an important one. God gifts some rare individuals with the ability to make us laugh. God has a sense of humor, else where did we get ours? My role that Sunday was to preach the gospel; Milton Berle's role was to make us all laugh. It was a great Sunday!

Entertainment can be resurrected to become something wonderful. If it only distracts from reality, it is secular. But if it uplifts, inspires, amuses, lightens loads, helps us see ourselves and stimulates the positive emotions to produce healthier and more fulfilled persons, then entertainment becomes an ally and not an enemy of the Christian enterprise.

Critics have called Robert Schuller a secular humanist. They couldn't be more wrong. I feel sorry for them because they have missed the point. When the secular becomes sacred through resurrection, then the I-it people and even the I-I people become I-you people. I-I people, those who find their emotional nourishment through ego trips, are produced by secular humanism, as are I-it people who find emotional fulfillment through things. Bored? Get a motel room in Las Vegas and pick up a chick at the bar. Having trouble relating to your wife? Buy her flowers or candy or playthings. But when secularists are born again they become I-you people, and they find their fulfillment in relationships, in cherishing people, in giving themselves to people, and, in this new posture, they find both security and self-esteem.

Sometimes people say, "Dr. Schuller, your ministry changed my life!" Why? Because a real theology is at work. I make it so simple that most people think it isn't there. Yet it is. That's why people change. A lover, instead of packing his suitcase and taking off while she's still sleeping, becomes a husband. A sire becomes a father. A teacher becomes someone who sees possibilities in the dumbest student and believes he or she can become great. A pastor becomes the town psychologist, and his church becomes a mission station and a meeting hall. And the doctor becomes a healer of persons, not just a treater of symptoms. This is the sort of thing that happens when I-I people and I-it people become I-you people.

So, in the Incarnation, the sacred becomes secular. And in the Resurrection, Christ set it up so that the secular could become sacred.

Crucifixion

Now the third point: between the Incarnation and the Resurrection is the Crucifixion, the Cross. The Cross is not the final word in Christianity, but it is the central word. The secular cannot become sacred without a cross, even as the sacred cannot become secular without a cross.

God's great yearning to win us to Himself could not be fulfilled without the Cross. "Christ died for our sins" (1 Cor. 15:3). There it is in words of one syllable! The Cross is how far divine love was willing to go to save us. And if God could not go from Incarnation to Resurrection without the Crucifixion of His own dear Son, we cannot avoid experiencing our cross as we try to obey our mission to make His Son known.

I'm not sure what is most damaging to the cause of

church growth—a church that is so sacred that it cannot become secular, or a church that is so secular that it loses its sacred spirituality. Illustrations of both dangers abound. But one thing I am certain of, a cross is required in both instances.

People say, "Dr. Schuller, you don't preach the Cross." But wait! Possibility thinking is the positive proclamation of the Cross, because when God gives you His idea, the sacred again becomes secular, and when you make a commitment to do that new thing for God's sake, the secular can glow with a sacred purpose—providing you are prepared to be misunderstood, opposed, persecuted, crucified.

There is no success without a cross! Not for God. Not for us.

Notes

1. This is the same point I was trying to make in my book, *Self-Esteem: The New Reformation* (Waco, TX: Word Books, 1982).
2. John 12:21.
3. Others may do it better, but developing a theology that incarnates itself in psychology is another point I discussed in *Self-Esteem: The New Reformation*.
4. Quoted in Sherwood E. Wirt and Kersten Beckstrom, *Living Quotations for Christians* (New York: Harper & Row, Publishers, 1974), p. 159.

Chapter 6

SELF-ESTEEM: THE DEEPEST NEED OF THE HUMAN PERSON

All theology begins with some central premise. If you listen to or read many systematic theologies, you'll find a lot of them begin with the doctrine of God, theocentric theology.

Many years ago when I began to get into self-esteem theology,[1] I began from a different premise; not the doctrine of God, but the doctrine of the human person. In my opinion, you cannot possibly talk about the nature of the human being without being in the theological realm because the human creature is created in the image of God.

The Psychological Background of Self-Esteem Theology

A pivotal moment in my life took place at a school of theology in Claremont, California. I went to hear a visiting lecturer, Dr. Victor Frankl, head of the Psychiatry Department of the University of Vienna,[2] speak on logotherapy. After his lectures, we talked together at great length.

Frankl represents a progression of psychological thinking that begins with Sigmund Freud, evolves through Alfred Adler and culminates in himself. Freud, Adler and Frankl come out of a background of Judaism, for they are all Jewish. So is Jesus.

As Frankl explained, Freud believed that man's ultimate drive was pleasure. If you want to understand why some people do dumb things, Freud said, you have to realize they're frustrated because their pleasures are being blocked. Freud placed most pleasure drives in the realm of sexual behavior.

Then Adler came along and said that Freud was too shallow and had missed the point. Adler's position was that the drive for power is greater than the drive for pleasure. He said that human beings will deprive themselves of all kinds of pleasures to become number one. And you can see it, not only in the American culture, but in cultures all over the world. People in a desire to be at the top of the power pyramid will sacrifice family, friendships, ethics and morality. So, said Adler, the will to power is more important than the will to pleasure.

Now Frankl comes on the scene and says the deepest desire of the human person is not for pleasure, nor for power, but for meaning. His being Jewish led to this conclusion. His first wife, his children and his parents were all exterminated by the Nazis in the Holocaust of World War II. He alone survived. When he was brought before the Gestapo, they stripped him naked to see if he was circumcised. If he was, they would know he was Jewish. And that was all the evidence they would have needed.

So he stood naked before the Gestapo. And, noticing that he wore a slim, gold wedding band, they ordered him to take it off. As the ring was being removed, this thought came into his head: there is one thing no person can take from me, and that is my freedom to choose how I will react to what you do to me.

An incredible revelation. Frankl believes it came from God. So do I. It helped him survive unspeakable indignities in the concentration camps. Later, he built his whole system of logotherapy on this concept that every situation can have value and meaning. You can see the New Testament in that thought—that in all things God is at work for those who love Him and keep His commandments (see Rom. 8:28). That's the Scripture.

So Victor Frankl said, "The deepest will of the human person is not pleasure, it's not power; it's meaning." I thought about that concept, prayed about it, read about it and studied it. After two years, I said to Dr. Frankl, "But I think there's something deeper than meaning."

And he said, "What could it be?"

I said, "It is human dignity. What gave value to meaning was the fact that it fed your dignity, your worth, your respect, your value. You had value as a person so long as there was meaning in the horrific tragedy you were going through. Even meaning is meaningless if it doesn't contribute to my self-esteem, my self-respect, my self-worth."

The Scriptural Background of Self-Esteem Theology

As soon as I came to that position, guess where I found myself theologically, scripturally? I found myself in the Garden of Eden before the apple was eaten. Let me explain.

What, after all, is the scriptural background to this theology of self-esteem? It is the story of Creation with which the Bible begins. The psychological or the psychiatric background arises because, in the twentieth century,

Christian theologians have abandoned the doctrine of the human being to a new discipline called psychiatry and to a new breed of professionals called psychologists. And we've said, "Self-esteem deals with the human being, that's humanism. You take care of that. We deal with God. We are not man-centered; we are God-centered."

Well, if you are God-centered, you will also be man-centered. God didn't send Jesus Christ to Planet Earth just for kicks. Jesus didn't die on a cross for the Holy Spirit. He didn't die to save angels. He died for men and women.

Jesus was man-centered, woman-centered, human-centered. God so loved what? Heaven? No. "God so loved the world" (John 3:16). What does that mean? God so loved our mountains and our streams, I suppose? No, it means He loved human beings, doesn't it?

Yes, the psychological background of self-esteem theology comes from Freud, Adler and Frankl. But Jesus had a better idea than any of them. And His idea lay in the teaching of the Old Testament that the human being is created just "a little lower than the angels" (Ps. 8:5). That can also be translated "little less than God" (*RSV*). And what's the rest of this passage? "And dost crown him with glory and honor" (*RSV*). Doesn't that sound a little heretical? Is the human being supposed to have glory and honor? Aren't they reserved for God only? What do you think?

The theology of self-esteem recognized the ultimate value of the human person. And from where do we get this? We get it from Scripture, beginning with Creation, first of all.

Look at the whole concept of self-esteem, at the whole theology of the human person. What was the spiritual state of mind and heart and spirit of Adam and Eve before the Fall? Adam was a prince. And Eve was a princess. We, as human beings created in the image of God (see Gen. 1:26) have royal blood in our veins. That's why no human being should ever be insulted, oppressed, ridiculed, laughed at, mocked, scorned or shamed. Do that and you attack the citadel of the soul. You also attack God Himself whose image each person bears!

So you see, the whole scriptural background of self-esteem theology starts with Creation. But then a terrible thing happened—Adam and Eve fell. And what was the first thing they lost? They lost their glory. They were stripped of their emblems of honor and sent out of the palace, if you will (see Gen. 3).

That event created the crux of the human predicament—that every human being is conceived and born in the condition of Adam and Eve when they were cast out of the Garden (see Rom 5:12). And what is that condition? Alienated from, separated from God our Father. We have the blood of royalty in our veins, but no longer can we claim our regal inheritance until we have been reconciled to the Father. We want glory, we want to get it back, but we don't know how to get it.

How we do get it is through Jesus Christ. In His Incarnation, Jesus Christ honored the human person by inhabiting our flesh and blood (see John 1:14). He took our nature and restored our God-given dignity. Then He took our sin and restored our God-given righteousness. That thrills me!

What's the central theme of the Incarnation to negative-thinking Christians? They say that Jesus was humiliated. Well, of course, there is that truth, and we find it in Scripture (see Isa. 53:1-7; Mark 15:15-20). I do not deny it. He was humiliated by our fallenness, not by our humanness. But now look at the opposite side of the coin. If it was a humiliation for Jesus, He was willing to endure it for our sakes (Heb. 12:2). The truth is He honored us!

Creation. Incarnation. Then we come to the Crucifixion. What does the cross of Jesus mean? It means many things. But first of all, at the simplest level, the Cross means that God would pay the ultimate price to redeem one human soul (Luke 15:7). And if God would send His only Son and sacrifice Him to save even one human life, then once and for all, what is one human being worth? We don't appreciate human beings the way God does.

G. A. Studdert-Kennedy wrote some lines that are appropriate here:

> When Jesus came to Golgotha
> They hanged Him on a tree.
> They drave great nails through hands and feet,
> And made a Calvary.
> They crowned Him with a crown of thorns,
> Red were His wounds and deep,
> For those were crude and cruel days;
> The human flesh was cheap. [3]

It still is cheap!

Get outside of real, authentic Christianity and human beings are cheap. The tragedy is that even within Christianity are those who really do not value human beings as they should be valued. The Crucifixion starts with the fact that God was here to redeem His children.

I believe in substitutionary atonement. What I have learned and what is meaningful to me is that Jesus Christ was my substitute on the Cross. But having said that, what place does the cross of Jesus Christ have in self-esteem theology? *The Cross is central.* Why? For one reason: the ultimate cause of a loss of self-esteem is guilt and shame. What were the two single negative emotions that moved into the heart and soul of Adam and Eve when they were cast out of the Garden of Eden? Those two emotions, resulting from their loss of glory, were shame and guilt.

Now then, all of Scripture, I believe, makes it clear that God faced an enormous problem. His love is so boundless, so deep, so fathomless that in His mercy, God just wants to forgive every single human being, to overlook all our sin and just say, "You are my children. I don't have the heart to send you to hell. I don't have the heart to cause you to suffer. I'll just forgive you."

But if God bowed to such extreme emotion, He would lose His morality, would He not? For if God overlooks all sin, then He really becomes an accomplice to the whole evil enterprise, doesn't He? So what did God face here? He was faced with what you and I are faced with all the time—a contradiction. Let's face it now.

You see, I happen to believe at this point that all truth is contradiction. And I have not understood truth until I've had the nerve to stand right in the middle of a contradiction between the two conflicting elements and resolve them. Jesus was a contradiction: very God of very God, yet very man of very man. What a contradiction! Yet what do you have? Nothing less than the Truth Incarnate. "I am the . . . truth" (John 14:6).

The Bible is a contradiction. The Old Testament stresses law, and the New Testament, grace. How do you resolve them creatively? If you want to save your life, you have to lose it, Jesus taught (see Mark 8:35). What a contradiction! Male and female—together you have humanity; drop one out and you don't. What a contradiction!

In physics, the ultimate truth is a contradiction. In music, it's a contradiction. You take discordant melodies, bring them together, and you have a creative outburst. It is true in all of life. And that's what I'm talking about.

The ultimate contradiction in moral philosophy is the contradiction between justice and mercy. How do you combine these contradicting elements creatively? Every parent has that problem. Do I spank my disobedient child, or do I hold him and love him?

The Cross was God's way of creatively combining the contradictory elements of justice and mercy. No one now can ever come back to the Almighty and say, "You are immoral because you let all those crooked, sinning people off the hook. Cheap grace!" No one can say that, because He can come back and say, "I have born in myself the stripes. I took the rap myself for them."

Yes, "with his stripes we are healed" (Isa. 53:5). So His justice is met in the Cross, and His mercy is expressed in His willingness to bestow the benefits of His Son's redeeming act on any person who by faith trusts in Jesus alone (see John 1:12, 3:16-18, 5:24, 20:31).

> My hope is built on nothing less
> Than Jesus' blood and righteousness;
> I dare not trust the sweetest frame,
> But wholly lean on Jesus' name. [4]

Alleluia!

Yes, the whole concept of self-esteem theology is based in the Creation, in the Incarnation, in the Crucifixion and, finally, in the Resurrection. What does the Resurrection mean? It means that just as Jesus had finished paying the price for our redemption, and now that earthly glory could come to Him, what does He do? He takes off. He takes early retirement and gives the job to us.

He gives you and me the job of doing what? Of being His ambassadors. Yes, we are ambassadors of Jesus

Christ (see 2 Cor. 5:19-20). Can you think of a more glorious title to attribute dignity and value to a person than that? We are ambassadors of God. Wow!

Do you remember the late Frank Laubach? He was the famous pioneer missionary known as the "Apostle to the Illiterates" who taught countless millions to read and write in his lifetime. Frank Laubach was also a great man of God. He cared about people and believed in the worth of all persons. He once said that if you want to know how valuable a human being is, consider a sprinkler head.

A sprinkler head, you say? True, it's not worth very much. You can go to a hardware store and buy one cheap. Human beings are cheap, too. Suppose you get killed. Take a man, a woman and nine months, and you can be replaced.

A person may look cheap to you until you realize his or her value. Take that sprinkler head, for instance. Connect it to the pipes, then let the water flow through, and the sprinkler head makes the grass grow, the flowers bloom and the vegetables flourish. What verse does this remind you of? Why yes, John 7:38 (*RSV*) where Jesus said, "He who believes in me, as the scripture has said, 'Out of his heart shall flow rivers of living water.'" Doesn't that feed your dignity? Your self-esteem? Your self-worth? Of course.

So Jesus in His resurrection left us to get on with the business of being His ambassadors (see 2 Cor. 5:20). But remember, when He was alive on earth, He had a big problem: He could be in only one place at a time. He had another problem as well. He probably spoke a single language, Aramaic, the language of the Jews of His day.

And there's something else. He had only one color of skin. But again, He had a perfect solution. He atoned for our sins. He was resurrected. And then what? He sent the

Holy Spirit so that He, Jesus, could come and live inside of men and women of every color everywhere. Yes, through the Holy Spirit, He now lives in a variety of peoples, in a variety of cultures, and speaks in a variety of languages all over this earth. What a brilliant solution to His impossible problem! And, as part of that solution, you and I become ambassadors of God. Now that's the Christian faith as I understand it.

The Background of Self-Esteem Theology In My Life

Early in my ministry, I became fascinated by the statements of Jesus where He used the words "possible" and "impossible." It was something that Dr. Norman Vincent Peale said in his sermon at our new little drive-in church which drove me to study the possibles and impossibles in our Lord's words. There is a great possibility that God, and not just Norman Peale, was in his words that day, because he said, "If Jesus Christ could stand here today and talk to you, what would He tell you?"

I've never forgotten that question. Every time since then that I go to deliver a sermon, I ask myself, "If Jesus Christ could talk to these people before me today, what would He tell them?" I always start with that thought: What would He tell them?

Then Dr. Peale said, "Would He tell you what miserable lost sinners you all are?" Because of where I was at that point and time, I was nodding affirmatively. I thought, *We've got a bundle of them here today, I'm sure.*

Dr. Peale answered his own question by saying, "No, I don't think He would. I think Jesus would tell you, 'Follow me, and I will make you into fishers of men. You are the salt of the earth. You are the light of the world. Let your light so shine that men may see your good works and glorify your Father who is in heaven.'"

My own strategy changed that day. Until then in a sermon, I was inclined to spend the first 20 minutes making people feel guilty, really guilty. Then in the last five minutes, I would quickly tell them about Jesus and how He died to save them. And that was it. The problem was that I had spent so much time convincing them they were lost, depraved, sinful and wicked that by the time I got to the good news, they couldn't hear it. Or, if they could hear it, they couldn't believe it. I had already numbed them with all that bad news.

I went home and started reading my King James Bible with all the words of Jesus in red letters. Having this red-letter edition proved convenient for me, because I just wanted to find out one thing. *What did Jesus say?* You see, Dr. Peale had said, "Jesus never called a person a sinner." And when he had said that, I thought, "You're mistaken, Dr. Peale. I know Jesus called people sinners. I know He did."

How wrong I was! As I read those red-letter words of Jesus, I found that He never did call a person a sinner. He knew the people He met were sinners. He was aware of this, but He did not condemn them as sinners. Only the holier-than-thou hypocrites received His stinging rebuke.

There's a difference between recognizing that someone is a sinner and labeling that person as such. Rather, we must model a new life positively before such people until they abhor sin and develop a hunger and thirst for righteousness.

The second thing I found was that when Jesus ran into wicked, sinful people, He treated them as if they were terrific. He actually or indirectly complimented them. Look at the crowd He collected around Himself and turned into His disciples. When He came into a town, He dined with someone as notorious as Zaccheus. Why did He do that?

Now, years later, psychologists are still trying to understand what Jesus knew, for there is a psychological principle that explains how people are changed. And Dr. Paul Yonggi Cho, the distinguished Korean pastor, has stated it well: "I am not what I think I am. I am not what you think I am. I am what I think you think I am."

If you want to change a person, you don't tell him how bad he is, you tell him he is the person you wish he was. You say, that's not telling the truth. Well, I don't know. It's what I call "exercising terrific faith."

Jesus did just that. He said to His followers, "You are the salt of the earth" (Matt. 5:13, *RSV*). Wait a minute. What did they do? They abandoned Him at the Cross, didn't they? "You are the light of the world," He said to them (Matt. 5:14, *RSV*). But wait, where were they then when the Roman soldiers hammered the nails into His hands?

No, I'm not what I think I am. I am not what you think I am. I am what I think you think I am!

Suddenly, all these New Testament sayings of Jesus began to say one thing to me: Faith in God is what makes the difference between possible or impossible. As Jesus said, "With men this is impossible, but with God all things are possible" (Matt. 19:26 *RSV*). I have faith in God that you are going to be a good person. So I declare that you are a good person. I claim you in the name of God as someone who is targeted for His redeeming mercy. Faith makes it possible. And so it happens.

About that same time, I wrote a book called *Move Ahead with Possibility Thinking* and, as a result of that book, something happened. People wrote to me and said, "Schuller, I read the whole book, but it doesn't work for me. And if you knew me, you'd know it wouldn't work for me."

Then I realized that something deeper had to be said, and I followed it with a book called, *Self-Love, The Dynamic Force of Success*. And that gave rise eventually to self-esteem theology and *Self-Esteem: The New Reformation*. Possibility thinking and self-esteem theology can both be summarized in this single sentence: The "I am" always determines the "I can."

If I say I am a sinner, I will sin like the devil himself. But if I can say I am redeemed, then I will be inclined to believe that it's possible to live the redeemed life. The "I am" determines the "I can."

Some Problems in Self-Esteem Theology

The problem of perfectionism

The first problem is our problem. There are people who say, "Okay, look at this self-esteem theology that says you have great value. You have great worth. You have a right to rise above poverty." They find fault with all this.

Well, I don't think the faults they find with our position are as bad as the fault in the lives of our critics—the fault of perfectionism. Now follow me carefully. We all are insecure people until we've experienced the grace of Jesus Christ, until we feel ourselves wrapped in the righteousness of Jesus Christ, until we depend totally upon the grace of God. Until then, all of us as human beings are infected with a psychological inclination to be perfectionists. And that means we always have the capacity to find fault with someone or something.

Here's proof. Try this old psychological test: Take a blank sheet of paper, 16 by 14 inches and make a little black dot in the middle of it. Put it on a board and say to a class, "What do you see on the board?" Almost without exception, the class will say, "We see a piece of white paper." A few of them will say, "A black dot." But hardly any of them will see the whole thing, which is a black dot on a piece of white paper.

Perfectionism finds something wrong with every idea, something wrong with every position. There are problems, yes, with the so-called self-esteem theology. But the alternative is more dangerous. If there are people who feel so smug, so contented that they have no sense of guilt, that is a potential problem. But the alternative of coming down heavy on them and preaching a doctrine of total depravity and total wickedness is absolutely unacceptable. That sees only the black dot and misses altogether the sheet of white paper.

I'm so grateful that in seminary I had a professor, Dr. John R. Mulder, who said, "The human being is not totally depraved. Don't ever believe in total depravity. Don't ever preach total depravity. Preach instead the doctrine of total inability." That's the distinction!

If you say a person is totally depraved, totally decadent, totally sinful and there is no value at all within him, that's not scriptural. The real Scripture is that we are totally unable to save ourselves; we are totally dependent upon the grace of God; we are totally dependent upon Jesus Christ. That's scriptural (see Eph. 2:8-9)!

The problem of definition

We come now to a very crucial problem. How do we deal with this doctrine of sin and the so-called doctrine of depravity?

Take these Bible verses: "The heart is deceitful above all things, and desperately wicked: who can know it?" (Jer.

17:9). "For I know that in me (that is, in my flesh) dwelleth no good thing" (Rom. 7:18). What do these and other similar verses mean? They mean that outside the grace of God, all our nature, which is sinful, results in rebellious, antisocial and anti-God behavior.

But the key question is: What is sin? Sin is unbelief. It's that simple. Sin is lack of faith.

Sin, as I see it now and as Scripture teaches, is a human condition before it is a human action. When I was growing up, I didn't learn that. As a little boy, I learned I could not go to movies. That was a sin. I couldn't play cards. That was a sin. And I couldn't swear. That was a sin. If I picked up a pair of scissors and cut cloth or paper on Sunday, that was a sin. If I went fishing on Sunday, that was a sin. And then, of course, there were the sins of stealing, lying, killing and all the rest.

All sin was perceived in terms of human behavior. Consequently, the job of the church was to make a careful definition of what is a sin and what is not. So much energy in so many churches was spent on arguing and debating, "Is this a sin?" "Is that a sin?" "Is this wrong?" "Is that okay?" Incredible!

I'll tell you when and where I changed. When we started this church in Garden Grove, I rang door bells because I found out only four people in this whole unchurched community belonged to my denomination, the Reformed Church in America. But 50 percent of the people in our community belonged to no church at all. So I rang their door bells to find out what were the needs of unchurched people. Where were they hurting?

At one particular house, a woman answered my ring. "Are you an active member of a local church?" I asked.

"Well, I don't belong to any church," she replied, but then she went on. "If you're starting a church, let me ask you, do you believe in original sin?" A surprising question!

I said, "What?" I had been taught it and had had no reason to doubt it.

"Do you believe that every human being is conceived and born in sin?" she asked again.

Now Jesus said, "Be ye . . . wise as serpents, and harmless as doves" (Matt. 10:16). I remembered that as I looked her in the eye and said, "Do you?"

"No, I do not," she replied.

I said, "Oh."

She looked at me and said, "Take a newborn baby. You can't possibly look at that baby and call it a sinner. That baby did not tell a lie. That baby did not kill. That baby did not steal. That baby did not commit adultery. That baby hasn't done a thing wrong. It is as innocent as Jesus. Do you believe in Jesus?"

"You bet I do," I answered.

"Well, that's what I believe," she answered.

"Come to church sometime. You might like it."

I have to say that I never did answer her question. But it shook me up and I prayed about it. I studied and this was the great insight that came to me: Yes, every newborn baby is innocent in terms of action and behavior. But all are born with a human condition and, without exception, that condition is sinful.

What is that sinful condition? It is unbelief. Even as infants have had no chance to do anything bad, neither have they had an opportunity to experience and exercise faith. This lack of faith is the cause of all other sin. I'm sure of that. The condition produces behavior.

We're conceived and born without faith, without any belief. It's interesting to analyze sin, give it that definition and then look at Jesus. Jesus is the sinless Lamb of God, without spot or blemish. Think of that. What does it mean?

It doesn't mean just that He didn't steal or lie or kill or commit adultery. That isn't it. Why, He did some things that many thought He shouldn't have done such as eating with "bad" people.

No, when we read that Jesus was sinless, it means He had perfect, pure faith. That's what it means: perfect, pure faith.

That's why He could say, "If you have faith as a grain of mustard seed, you will say to this mountain, 'Move . . . ,' and it will move; and nothing will be impossible to you" (Matt. 17:20, *RSV*). Even in the Garden, hours before His death, He prayed, "Abba, Father, all things are possible to thee; remove this cup from me; yet not what I will, but what thou wilt" (Mark 14:36 *RSV*). His faith was still unalloyed, perfect, pure.

And on the Cross, He did not lose faith, though He did ask the question, "Why?" (see Mark 15:34). But He did not deny the existence of His heavenly Father. No, never. To the very end, He believed in the possibility of redemption. Unflinchingly, He assured the penitent thief, "Today you will be with me in Paradise" (Luke 23:43, *RSV*). That is pure, perfect faith.

How do you preach against sin in such a way that you don't do the human being more harm than good? If you want to preach against sin and bring about repentance, without which—we all agree—there can be no salvation, then how do you do so positively? Simple. You preach faith. Encourage people to be believers. How. By introducing them to Jesus.

When a person becomes a believer, he has turned his back on sin. And that is repentance, a turning around, a turning to the light. Real repentance is an all-out commitment to believe God with no holds barred. It is total belief.

Somebody said to me, "Schuller, you don't preach the

tough Bible verses. You don't preach the hard ones. Jesus didn't preach an easy gospel. He said, 'If any man would come after me, let him deny himself and take up his cross and follow me'" (Matt. 16:24, *RSV*). You know what Jesus really was saying? "Those who want to be my disciples must have a total belief in God Almighty. They have to be willing totally to deny themselves the protection of the privileged position of persons who never go out on a limb and run the risk of failing for the Lord."

To deny yourself means daring to say, "God, what do you want me to do?" You pray that prayer and the Lord may answer it. And then He'll tell you what He wants you to do. And when He does, you probably won't have time for golf. What I mean by that is that you probably won't have time to play around; you'll have to get to work. Yes, deny yourself. That's what it means.

Then, if you ask God, "What do you want me to do with my life?" you're going to get a dream. And anytime a dream comes from God, it's going to be humanly impossible to accomplish. Do you know why? That's His way of making sure that He's a part of the whole act, and you can't pull it off without Him. No way.

God wants us to operate in the arena of faith, so He always gives us an idea that's bigger than we are. Always.

So, how do we preach against sin? By telling people what a beautiful life they can have if they will become believers, that's how. How do we preach repentance? By helping them to become believers that there's a God who has a plan for their life and that, if they'll pray, He'll give them a dream. And then when God gives them the dream, they need to have the faith to believe that with God's help, it can be pulled off.

Once you've made a commitment to do what God wants you to do, and be what God wants you to be, and go where God wants you to go, I'll tell you what you're going to have to do. You will have to carry a cross!

Success is shaped like a fish. It's beautiful, but if you strip it down, inside you'll find a skeleton. And the skeleton is in the shape of a cross. Carrying a cross isn't all easygoing. Once you've made a commitment to do God's work and God's will, then, with faith, you say, "Okay, Lord, I'll do it." You make the announcement and you begin. Before you know it things are going along. And then, you face what looks like an awful problem, and here you are out on a limb with everybody watching you. Everybody knows what you're doing. And now you're staring failure in the face, and "Oh, dear God, if I fail now, I'll be so ashamed."

Do you know what you're doing? Why, you are carrying your cross. But then what? Then when you have reached the point where you're hopeless and helpless and can't get along anymore and you're ready to cave in and give up, then God comes to the rescue. He does. But not until you have earned the scars that will be the mark of your cross bearing. Then what's happened, you see, is that cross bearing has become constructive. Something God wanted done gets built because you carried the cross. A church. A mission. A ministry.

I say most negative-thinking interpreters of this Bible verse, "If any man will come after me, let him deny himself, and take up his cross, and follow me" (Matt. 16:24) do more harm than good. They produce sick people. They don't build or accomplish anything. How do you preach sin? How do you preach repentance? Put people in touch with God. That's how!

Another question. How do you deal with the commandments? The Bible makes it clear. You're not to lie. You're not to steal. You're not to kill. You're not to commit adultery. You're not to covet. You're not to blaspheme.

How do you deal with the Law in self-esteem thinking?

Our answer is simple. The Ten Commandments are given to us in order to show us how to live in such an ethical behavioral pattern that we will feel good about ourselves. The Ten Commandments are not 10 negative restrictions. They're God's way to the good life. They're God's prescription for feeling proud of who you are and not being ashamed of yourself. You can be sure that if you break any one of these Ten Commandments, you are really going to be ashamed.

It's interesting to know as we talk about self-esteem that the American Psychiatric Association, in a recent convention, found that the single most popular workshop at the convention was a workshop on one word. Guess what that one word was. Shame. Think of that. How does that make you feel? We pastors, evangelists and lay Christians have the answer to the human condition and predicament of shame. Shame entered the world in the Garden of Eden and unless we go back to where it started, we'll never get back to where we ought to be.

So, on the subject of the Law, it's simple. All law is given to us to build our sense of self-esteem and self-respect.

The problem of pride

People ask us what self-esteem theology does to the problem of pride. The Bible say, "Pride goes before destruction, and a haughty spirit before a fall" (Prov. 16:18, *RSV*). So what does self-esteem theology do to arrogance? If you preach possibility thinking and self-esteem theology, aren't you going to produce a whole generation of arrogant Christians?

My answer is this: The easiest thing in the world for God to do is to make a person humble. It's easy for God to take the wind out of our sails. And He can do it after one complaint, one criticism. Or if that isn't enough, after one medical report: "Sorry, it's malignant." Or a telephone call: "Your daughter has been in an accident." It's easy for God to deal with the problem of human pride, that is, destructive pride.

We have to remember something else. In the Scriptures, I see both a positive and a negative pride. And the word in our English Bible does not make that distinction. Genuine arrogance or what we call egotism, what is that? That is a phony attempt to try to deal with an insecurity, that's what it is.

Those people out there in the world seem to have no religion. They're apparently successful. They're the jet-setters, the super rich who drive the big cars and wear the fine clothes. They're cocky, proud, arrogant and really seem to have all the self-confidence they need. Secularists, materialists, they're got it made.

No, they don't! Their self-esteem is shallow. They don't think it's shallow, but it is, because it's based on possessing nice things and nothing more. Their self-esteem is also passing, because it's superficial and external. There will be a time when they cannot have another face-lift. There will be a time when they no longer are physically attractive.

When something happens, then what? All the money and beauty in the world can't bring a loved one back. As they walk from an open grave, they leave behind a son or a daughter or a wife. And their self-esteem is gone. Why? Because it's shallow and passing. You see, any sense of pride that doesn't relate itself to the grace of God is shallow and passing. Yours and mine is found in our relationship to Jesus Christ. That's why it is real and eternal.

I have nice things myself. After all, I haven't taken a

vow of poverty. Nor have you. And I wouldn't advise you to take such a vow, because the Lord needs all the money He can get. Of course I have nice things, but my self-esteem is not based upon my clothes or car or house. No, it is based upon the grace of God.

What we are talking about is positive pride, healthy pride, pride that is rooted in a divine call. Whether your divine call is a call to redemption, to salvation, to a holier life, to high and holy service, your humility is guaranteed. I'm proud that I'm a Christian, but I can't take any credit for it. Jesus saved me. I'm proud that I'm a minister. But, at the same time, I'm truly humble because I'm called to it. It is all God's doing.

Perhaps you understand now what I'm saying when I assert that real self-esteem is that wonderful feeling within yourself which is the presence of Jesus Christ through the Holy Spirit cleansing you of sin, removing all guilt, taking away all shame and putting you in such a position that you know that you and the Almighty are good friends forever. That's the greatest thing in the world. Nothing can top it or touch it.

The problem of individualism

Another problem. There are those who say self-esteem theology produces a very self-centered individualism. They say that if you preach this kind of gospel, you're turning people into very strong individuals. And that militates against brotherhood or solidarity. After all, we are supposed to be our brother's keeper.

Yes, this kind of gospel that we preach does produce rugged individualism because we believe that the dignity of persons is an individual matter. I find my self-esteem, not just in my community relationships, not just in the collective support that I get from people, but I find it most importantly in the solitary decision that I alone made when I accepted Jesus Christ as my Lord and Saviour and personal Friend.

Christianity is an individual thing. We're not saved collectively. My contention is that the Bible is clear that every human being is responsible for accepting his own salvation. He's responsible for making his own decision. He's not saved just by becoming a member of a church. He's not saved just because he lives with a group of Christians or because his father and mother were Christians. Being born into a Christian family doesn't make him a Christian.

Put a pear tree in an apple orchard and it's still a pear tree. Yes, self-esteem theology produces rugged individualism. But I think that's exactly what we need. I also think it's theological and scriptural. And ultimately, I think it's for the betterment of the human race if that strong rugged individualism is baptized by the Holy Spirit in the power of Jesus Christ. That's the corrective measure that keeps this rugged individualism from becoming rampant selfishness. That's the redemptive element. So we've got a redeeming corrective element built into it.

The problem of narcissism

Finally, people say, "Well, this self-esteem theology leads to narcissism. If you really build your church and tell people they're great, they're wonderful, God loves them and they can be fantastic, you begin to preach a self-esteem faith." Some will say that's narcissism. They couldn't be further wrong in their judgment.

Narcissism comes from Narcissus, the mythological Greek character who suffered from insecurity until the mirroring water reflected his beauty. Narcissism is finding a phony self-esteem based upon something materialistic.

Oh, look at the shape of my nose, isn't it pretty? Look at the style of my hair, isn't this beautiful? Don't I have a lovely profile? I don't, but you do maybe. At any rate, the point is, narcissism always seeks to satisfy the problem of an adequate self-esteem through a materialistic image. Self-esteem faith finds it in the grace of God and in my relationship with Jesus Christ as one of His redeemed children, an ambassador of the faith.

This strong rich doctrine of the human person is the basis for my emphasis on self-esteem. The story of Creation tells us that God made man in His own divine image. Though scarred by sin, that image is still present in every human person. God has made us "a little lower than the angels" or, in the words of the *Revised Standard Version,* "little less than God" (Ps. 8:5).

When God's masterpiece, human persons, willfully chose to abandon faith in God and walk away from His fellowship, God entered this very human nature He had made and came to us in His Son Jesus. The Incarnation was a tremendous tribute to our potential greatness. Christ died for us while sharing our nature (see Phil. 2:5-8). That same nature was resurrected to deathless glory. And our destiny is to be like Him (see 1 John 3:2).

Since all this is true, I believe it is the most exciting calling in the world to invite human persons to believe the incredibly good news that God loves them, He forgives them, He wants their companionship and He restores them to the glory He intended each one to have from the beginning. Whatever the understanding of the gospel may be to some, to me it is good news—astonishing, mind-blowing, heart-quickening, hopeful, redeeming good news.

Notes

1. I'm not particularly crazy about the words "self-esteem theology," but after all, no matter what language you speak on Planet Earth, all human language has shortcomings, frailties, imperfections. I happen to choose language that, to the best of my knowledge, relates to scriptural truth and, at the same time, translates into the cultural idiom so that we can talk and communicate with non-Christians in our society and in the other disciplines.
2. A position created by Sigmund Freud.
3. The first verse of "Indifference" from *The Sorrows of God* by G. A. Studdert-Kennedy, copyright by Harper & Row, Publishers Inc.
4. Written by Edward Mote. Public domain.

The Good Shepherd statue—
a beloved landmark on the campus.

Chapter 7

DYNAMIC LEADERSHIP: THE CRYING NEED

There is no substitute for dynamic, aggressive, positive, inspiring leadership! Almost without exception, the lack of success means the lack of effective leadership. And the reverse is true. Great success is the result of great leadership.

Some years ago I returned from a visit to the Taegu Presbyterian Hospital in Taegu, Korea. I have never in my life seen a more successful Christian mission in operation than this work that was going on under the dynamic leadership of Dr. and Mrs. Howard Moffett. More than 150 churches in the area of Taegu have been started and nourished by the ministry of this hospital. And all of Korea is aware of this exciting ministry.

The hospital itself stands as one of the great medical centers of the world. Multistoried and fully equipped with the latest modern medical devices, the hospital stands as an inspiring example of doing something in a big way, with a spirit of excellence. Many millions of dollars have been invested in this ultramodern missionary venture.

I also think often of the Christian Medical Center in

Vellore, India, a fantastic success story which gives great honor and glory to the enterprise of Jesus Christ on earth. At Vellore, just as at Taegu, the secret of success is dynamic leadership. One person, Dr. Ida Scudder, inflamed the minds of people and got them behind her amazing project.

It is thrilling to see something done *right!* Too often, Christian enterprises have been guilty of doing too little, too modestly and too late. We are not always like the old army general who explained his successful mission in this classic sentence: "We always were the firstest with the mostest!"

Leadership Is the Key

Leadership is the key to church growth. If the church is really to succeed in its mission of witnessing effectively to the unchurched world in the twenty-first century, we must develop dynamic, aggressive and inspiring leaders.

And what is leadership? Leadership is thinking ahead, planning for the future, exhausting all possibilities, envisioning problems and dreaming up solutions to them, and then communicating the possibilities and the problem-solving ideas to the decision makers. *This* is leadership.

In any institution, the leader is the man who is thinking ahead of everyone else. He is not living in the past but in the future, for leadership draws its inspiration from future projections and not from past accomplishments. The leader is alert to movements, trends and evolving developments. He is literally thinking longer thoughts than anyone else is—and expressing them more effectively!

Leadership Is Local

Who is the leader in the modern American congregation? As we look for the answer to this question, we shall uncover some pretty unhappy situations. And we shall offer some suggestions on who *should be* the leader in the local church.

In our consultation with many ministers from different denominations through our Institute for Successful Church Leadership, we have discovered a real leadership crisis in the modern Protestant Church. There is confusion as to who really is supposed to be in the leadership role.

Some ministers assume that the leadership of the local church must come in the form of ideas, theories and practical suggestions from their denominational executive officers. In such instances, the pastor is often not the dynamic and creative leader that a local situation demands for a successful mission. The local pastor who looks to a national executive officer for leadership is seldom the dynamo that a local church needs for exciting forward movement.

It is obvious that national directors of denominational bodies cannot be in touch and in tune with every local situation. How can they possibly be expected to be effective leaders for each local church? The social, spiritual and community needs vary drastically from one community to the next. Consequently, the leadership role must not be detached from the local setting. Those who head the administrative work of major denominations may be the official or unofficial "bishops" of the local pastor, but except in rare instances they should not attempt to be the proxy leaders of the local congregation.

We find other ministers who expect that leadership is vested in the heads of the theological seminaries. Somehow, a local pastor expects that ideas for effective churchmanship should be forthcoming from the theological schools. It is our contention that the role of the theological school does not afford a sensible setting for inspiring local church leadership.

The theological seminary must necessarily deal with such weighty matters as theology, church history and other top-level projects. Again, the theological professor is prone to be lost in his own mental world of academics and tends to be detached from the heartbeat and the soul throb of the people who live within the radius of the local church. Generally speaking, a local pastor who goes to a theological seminary and expects to receive inspiring leadership for his church program is looking in the wrong direction.

Leadership Is Full Time

Perhaps the bishop—or whatever title your church uses—of the diocese or the district or the synod should be the inspirational leader. Is this where the root of leadership is to be found? The bishop, like a national executive director or a professor of a theological seminary, can doubtless provide much needed wisdom and valuable direction. But the local bishop cannot be the leader of the local church.

Leadership is a full-time business. A local institution needs a full-time leader who can be thinking, planning and selling his ideas; a man who can be solving the problems that stand in the way of the successful achievement of local goals.

Is leadership then to rest in the local church board or in the local congregation? We find several churches that are struggling alone and labor under the illusion that the congregation is to be the "corporate leader." These churches with a strong congregationalism allow no major thinking, planning or promoting to be done without congregational approval. If the pastor and the church board feel they need to buy new hymnbooks, they would expect to call a "congregational" meeting for the approval for such a decision.

I have yet to see a church with such a system of government that is really roaring ahead with fantastic success! In this type of system there is no room and no authority for strong, inspiring, centralized leadership. And whether we like it or not, this kind of leadership is the key to successful church development. Any dynamic, progressive and enthusiastic pastor will find his style being cramped, his energies draining away and his dreams turning into despair if he thinks he has to "sell" his plans and his dreams to a negative-thinking congregation.

Is the church board then the corporate leader of the church? Perhaps the board is the "corporate" head and the pastor is the "errand boy" to carry out the church board-prescribed duties? To answer this question, let's look at how effective modern business operates while, at the same time, remembering the words of our Lord who said, "The children of this world are . . . wiser than the children of light" (Luke 16:8).

In a growing, modern American industry you will find a board of directors. This board, for the most part, consists of wise advisors who are part-time thinkers. They meet occasionally to approve major propositions of their leader. They are a consulting group that the leader uses to test out his ideas before they are publicly launched. When they approve the ideas of the leader·they hired to dream dreams and then to plan and execute them, they look upon their role as supporters—to sell the decision to the community that needs to get behind the program.

In such a case, who is the leader? Leadership does not rest with the board of directors. Leadership rests in the hands of full-time executives who are hired by the board to think ahead, plan ahead and envision great possibilities, as well as ways in which these possibilities can be profitably exploited and ways in which potential problems can be solved. Leadership then rests in the hands of full-time, salaried people.

If I were a capitalist financing an enterprise, I would insist that the unchallenged leadership be placed in the hands of full-time thinkers and planners. As a pastor heading up a church, I insist on the same.

There will be no great forward renewal in the Protestant Church until we recognize that dynamic and aggressive leadership is the key. Leadership definitely does not belong in the hands of part-time thinkers. So the place of leadership logically and naturally rests in the lap of the minister and the salaried staff leaders in the church!

Leadership Is Responsibility

Leadership is an enormous responsibility that cannot be irresponsibly placed in the hands of people who do not put the church first in their lives. And no matter how dedicated the members of a local congregation are, the church does not take first place in their lives. The same can be said for members of the church board.

The most dedicated elder, deacon or trustee—with rare exception—considers the church to be the third priority in his life. His business, career or profession is generally first interest, with the welfare of his family second. The church comes third—and perhaps not that high. In many instances, his hobby takes third place and the church has to settle for fourth in his order of priorities. But the local pastor places the church foremost in his life!

Let there be no dodging of this issue. Pastor? Do you

hear me? You should be the spark plug. You should be the inspiring commander leading the troops up the hill!

I recall that when I was a seminary student, working part-time in a local church, the pastor told me: "Never forget, Schuller, that you are a servant of the church and not its master. The consistory (the church board) is the leadership group. They do the planning and the deciding. You do the work. They will tell you what to do. Carry out their orders faithfully and you will be a successful pastor."

I was enormously impressed by this misguided advice. As I look back on it, I remember attending board meetings in that church where the board was the leadership group and the pastor their "faithful servant." I recall sitting in a board meeting where two hours were spent discussing whether or not they should buy a new sump pump for the basement of the church. It is incomprehensible that 25 minds could spend two hours wrestling over such a petty decision!

Leadership Is Thinking Big

Big things happen to big-thinking people. Nothing big ever happens to little-thinking people. Important movements are started and carried out by big people who are able to make vital decisions swiftly and move forward with confidence and assurance. This can only happen with positive leadership in control.

Leadership Is Organization

In the Crystal Cathedral, the leadership rests in the hands of the pastor and his professional staff. The church board approves the basic policy and then expects the ministerial and professional staff to take over the job and move it ahead with maximum effectiveness.

Let me illustrate how this works.

In the early days of our church, I presented the budget to the entire congregation for its approval. It was a terrible mistake! There was always *some* member who could find *some* fault with *some* item in the budget. There is always going to be someone in the church who doesn't appreciate the music and doesn't want the money spent to buy a good organ or to build up a top-notch choir.

What we were doing was simply creating a public platform for negative thinkers. We quickly abandoned the method.

Our budget is now prepared by committees. In a large, multi-established church such as ours, a full-time salaried person is usually the liaison person on each committee. I am the minister who virtually controls the publicity committee. It has always been so, except for a two-year period when we lacked the bylaws to give me leadership power. Then a negative-thinking minority in the church succeeded in manipulating appointments to the publicity committee so that one of their friends who opposed advertising was made chairman. As a result, for that period of time I couldn't get a dime to advertise.

Since then a new set of bylaws gives me, as chairman of the board, power to appoint committee chairmen. I insist upon this. So I have since had control of publicity. It is an area where I am capable, so my leadership is not challenged.

The minister of education is the staff man on the Christian education committee. The minister of youth is the staff man on the youth committee. The business administrator is the staff representative, along with me, on the finance committee. So it goes. A professional salaried member of staff is in close contact with each committee.

Meanwhile, as the president of the corporation and chairman of the board, I, as a senior minister, am an ex-officio member of all committees and appoint the chairmen of all these committees and present them to the church board for their approval. By appointing the committee chairmen, by being an ex-officio member of each committee, by being the chief of the staff presiding over regular staff meetings, I am able to maintain leadership control over the entire operation of the church, working through the church board, committees and staff.

It is our sincere belief that this is the only way to organize a church for successful leadership. In a church with a smaller staff, it simply means that the senior pastor would attend more of the committee meetings himself instead of entrusting the flow of leadership into committees through one of his staff members.

Does this mean that the senior minister is a dictator and that he and the staff, who are hired to run the church, are the big bosses? Not at all! The senior minister is not a dictator for the following reasons:

1. He is hired by the church board or the congregation.

2. He reports to the church board and the board reserves the right to overrule his recommendations.

3. He appoints the chairmen of the committees, but the board must approve these chairmen. And, in our church at least the chairmen of the committees are always selected from the board itself.

4. The minister can only *recommend* and *launch* the project. Obviously, the success of any program can be effected only by loyal, hardworking and generous-giving laymen and laywomen who pick up the ideas of their leader and make them work!

I have often said, with utmost sincerity, "I have never done anything in the Crystal Cathedral. The people have done everything!" And they have! I have done a lot of possibility thinking, a lot of possibility planning, a lot of mental problem-solving—and a lot of talking. But it's the board that makes the decisions. And it's the board that disseminates possibility thinking throughout the congregation to infect the entire membership with the inspiring conviction that the ideas that have been adopted are tremendous.

Great things will happen in a church where big-thinking lay people will say to their pastor, "Pastor, we want you to spend all of your time dreaming great dreams on how our church can become the greatest mission for Jesus Christ in this whole territory! And, Pastor, show us how we can get behind your big dreams and make them succeed. We will (1) be praying for you through the week while we are earning the money to pay the bills to make this dream come true; (2) we will also welcome training to equip us to do the actual work of the church as lay evangelists, teachers, and counselors!"

Leadership Is Leading

Pastor, be an analyzer, be an organizer, be a climatizer—and you will be an inspiring leader. *Analyze* the needs and potentialities of your church and your community. *Organize* the program, the staff and the plans for making the church move ahead. *Climatize* the people through your positive and inspiring sermons so that they will want to get behind your dreams and make them come true.

You, pastor, must be the leader, under God, reporting to the board! That's God's call and command to you!

Where does leadership rest in your church? The tragic fact is that in a majority of churches we've seen in our

Institutes, leadership has been surrendered to property. The size of the structure and the location of church property sets the pattern for everything they do. Leadership—that is, the thinking, programming, planning, goal setting—is not in the hands of the church board nor the congregation, nor is it in the hands of a bishop or a denominational leader, nor is it in the pastor's hands. All are prisoners of the property that they own—or rather, that owns and controls them! The shoe must never tell the foot how large to grow!

This means God Himself has lost control. For God can think through a brain but God cannot think through a brick! So great dreams are never born here—"We wouldn't have room to park the cars," "We couldn't seat the people," etc., etc.

Ninety percent of all American churches should relocate! That's the impression I have after examining the Self-Study Guides of thousands of Protestant churches!

"It's time that the leadership be changed!" I must often advise pastors. "You take command. You have the freedom to sell that property! Release yourselves from bondage! Break loose from the chains that bind you. Break forth into the freedom of dynamic leadership! God cannot be the leader of a church if the creative imagination of human beings is blinded and bound by glass, stone, plaster and dirt."

Many pastors have followed our advice. Church properties have been put up for sale. Extensive acres of land in prime locations are being purchased. And the pastor, the board and the congregation are now being inspired by God to do something great! God is in command again!

Leadership of the church is not to be placed in the hands of part-time administrators or people removed from the scene of action. Nor is leadership to be controlled by a piece of real estate, a bank account, a treasurer's report or a denominational manual.

Leadership is to be in the hands of a living human being who is constantly thinking, constantly praying, constantly reaching out and constantly surrendering himself to the Holy Spirit of Christ. That, my big-thinking, possibility-thinking pastor, is YOU! Now make up your mind to be the leader. Assume your responsibility and build a great church for Jesus Christ!

Chapter 8

WHAT MAKES A TRULY GREAT CHURCH?

Years ago a fellow clergyman asked me: "How many members do you have in your church, Dr. Schuller?"

I answered, "You just made three mistakes in that one question. First this isn't a church—it's a mission. Second, it's not *mine*—it belongs to Christ. Third, we don't have members—they're all ministers and only a few get paid."

Read through this chapter and you'll understand why I answered as I did. For a truly great church is first of all a mission!

I was trained in Reformed theology. For my M.Div. thesis in Western Theological Seminary in Holland, Michigan, the faculty approved my project to prepare "a scriptural and *exhaustive, theological, topical* index to the four-volume *Institutes of the Christian Religion* by John Calvin." I had no idea how big a job it was going to be! Nearly 300 pages long, it at least made me familiar with John Calvin's theology.

I discovered then that the theology of the Protestant reformers was, to some degree, reactionary. Calvin's definition of the church was "a place where the word is proclaimed, sacraments administered, and discipline maintained." The definition ignores emphasizing the most important aspect of the church—which is "a group of joyful Christians happily sharing their glorious faith with the despairing souls of their fellowmen who have never known the joy of Christ!"

The Church

Now let's see what constitutes a great church and then lay down the pattern for organizing a great church!

The Church is a corporate group of happy Holy Spirit-inspired Christians who allow themselves to be minds through which Christ can think, hearts through which Christ can love, hands through which Christ can help. In that sense, the Church is the living body of Christ, *helping* hurting people in a local community. And nothing is more exciting than to be a part of the Body of Christ in its caring, sharing love.

If you were to come to the Crystal Cathedral on an average Sunday, you would see magnificent buildings, remarkable crowds—and you would witness inspiring services of worship. You would probably leave the church enormously impressed, commenting, as many visitors have: "What a great church this is!"

The truth is, of course, that beautiful buildings with spacious grounds do not necessarily mean that the happening is a great church. My particular job as senior pastor is, hopefully, to deliver messages that will bring great crowds to church on Sunday morning. And as the leader, it is my job to organize the institution in such a way that this enormous crowd of worshipers becomes a true and vital church.

By all means do not allow yourself to be confused by

the anti-organization people. They love to say, "The church is an organism not an organization." The truth is: *every organism God creates is always organized!* The nose always is on the head! or else the creation is a chaotic mess.

I am the first to declare that a great crowd of happy Christians gathered in a place for public worship does not make it a church! It might be a "Preaching Center." In another case it might be an "Evangelism Center." In still another case it might be a "Camp Meeting," a "Bible Conference," a "Missionary Rally" or a "Charismatic Conference Center."

There are in America today not a few dynamic organizations where large crowds of Christians gather in one place once a week—or more—to sing or pray or study the Bible. Often these large assemblies of people are loosely referred to as "churches." Part of this confusion is the result of the different schools of thought that train the Protestant pastors.

There are in America educational institutions called "Bible Institutes." Historically they have been efforts to extend beyond his lifetime the work of an evangelist, a person whose really only single concern was to "save souls." He had little interest in the nurture of these souls other than to "put a Bible in their hands."

Hence Bible institutes emphasized evangelism—how to get people saved, which usually meant getting them to come forward and kneel at the altar in a public service. Further courses taught there would be on song leading, prayer life, personal witnessing and Bible study. From the perspective of the typical nineteenth and twentieth-century traveling evangelist this was all the education a person needed to go out and "preach the gospel."

Then there are the training centers called theological

seminaries, most of whom belong to the American Association of Theological Schools. Every main-line American Protestant denomination has these training centers for ministers. The thinking behind the theological seminaries is that it is not enough just to be an evangelist and Bible student. A pastor must also be knowledgeable in the philosophy and psychology of the people to whom he ministers.

As a Christian leader he must be interested not only in "converting the lost souls"—but also in building their faith and life and applying their faith to society. That means, of course, offering instruction in the Bible. But far more than Bible knowledge should be offered. A knowledge of Christian history "after the book of Acts until our own time" is important too! Also courses in Systematic Theology as well as Biblical Theology!

So the minister's role is to be more than an evangelist. He is to be the builder and chief architect of a church. And the true Church is the Body of Christ!

The Pattern

The metaphor of the Body of Christ is our pattern for shaping, molding and organizing the local church. A statue isn't a living body. It only looks real! So it is that many large assemblies only "look like real churches."

How do you turn a statue into a live human being? By putting into its hollow shell three systems: the blood vessels, the skeleton and the nerves.

How do you turn a "crowd gathered to hear a great preacher" or "a great crowd gathered in an evangelism tent"—how do you turn these "statues" into "true bodies"? By checking all three "systems"!

The body

The blood circulatory system of the church is evangelism. But first, we require a body to put it in. After the first six years of working in this community, I succeeded in securing land for a church site. Next we completed arrangements with an architect for a walk-in, drive-in church. Then, between 1955 when we held our first service of worship and 1961, we managed to build a congregation of nearly 1,000 members, raise the money for and erect a magnificent structure seating that many people.

The circulatory system

Phase One was completed: the basic body was shaped and sculptured. We were now ready for Phase Two: to put in the system of blood vessels. So, the first person we added to our staff was the minister of evangelism. His job description was and is today: "To recruit, train and motivate laymen and laywomen to be lay evangelists of the church." And my assignment to this man was "to think in terms of adding people to the membership of the church and know that you are succeeding as long as people who have not been active members of any other church are being won into a lively membership of this church! You are, on the other hand, failing when the only people who join this church are Christians transferring from other churches."

To this minister I said, "If you really recruit and inspire and cultivate the lay people to do the job, we will have so many persons accepting Christ and joining this church that you will be kept busy the year around conducting classes, training new Christians and new potential converts in the faith and work of the church."

And my words came true. We have been adding an average of 700 members a year, two-thirds of whom were not active church members elsewhere!

As senior pastor, it is my job to *attract unchurched people into the sanctuary on Sunday mornings* through sermons *that do not sound like sermons,* but which sound like helpful and inspiring messages. Hopefully, I will lead them to an awareness of a faith in God and a faith in Jesus Christ which is the only means of joy-filled living.

I make a strong personal appeal for commitment. And I use all the powers of persuasion that God has given me to inspire people to join the pastor's classes. Here, in a controlled classroom situation, our minister of evangelism and his associates are able to lead people step-by-step to a knowledge of the faith that saves in life and in eternity. These pastor's classes are conducted one right after another all year around.

So a great church is a church that has a healthy blood supply system: new blood must be constantly generated in the form of new lives that are continually being transformed by an act of Christ. A church where Christ is at work reaching into human hearts is a living church. Unless there is a steady flow of new blood in the form of new conversions, the church will degenerate into a comfortable club. That is the beginning of a dying institution.

The skeleton

But to have a large building filled with great crowds of people, and to have them converted to the Christian faith, is still not a great church. A skeletal system, as well as a blood circulatory system, is required. Converted people must become educated Christians. If evangelism provides the blood vessel network in the Body of Christ, then education is required to furnish the skeletal structure.

The second staff man added to our church was the minister of education. His job was and is "to recruit, train and motivate lay people to be the teachers in the church." As he began work, I told him that it would probably take five years to organize an effective educational program in the church.

The prediction proved to be accurate. When we celebrated our fifteenth anniversary in 1970, he was able to report that we had more than 300 church school teachers and youth sponsors in active service.

So far, nearly 3,000 adults have received thorough Bible instruction in our training program. We believe an *inspired* congregation must also be an *informed* congregation. An intelligent body is a body that has backbone and can stand up against alien ideologies and theologies.

In keeping with the training and tradition I inherited from the perspective of the theological seminary, I believe that a program of Christian education demands more than Bible knowledge. Early in my ministry I was impressed by spokesmen and writers who talked about the "church of the laity." I observed, however, that none of these nationally renowned writers and theorists offered a program to really train the laity.

In a lecture I delivered early in my ministry I said, "The problem with the church is we do not take the training of the laity seriously." The proof of this is the lack of material to teach laymen and laywomen on how they can become the "ministers in residence" in the local church. Further proof of our historic lack of interest in training the laity to *be the ministers* is seen in the absence of a national institution that would have arisen had we really been serious about this job of turning out educated lay leaders. The American Association of Theological Schools is an institution that, if nothing else, is a monument to the seriousness with which denominations viewed the training of the clergy.

I outlined, therefore, to our minister of education a plan to organize in our church a "theological seminary for the laity." It would, like classical theological seminaries, offer courses in Bible, Church History, Theology, Philosophy, Psychology, Comparative Religions, as well as courses in Practical Theology, such as, counseling, witnessing, teaching.

Rev. Kenneth Van Wyk, our first minister of education, caught the vision and organized what may well have been the first "seminary for the laity" to offer such a full range of classes. We called this lay training organization C.A.L.L. or Center for Advanced Lay Leadership. The faculty was drawn from across Southern California. Our local goal was to have no less than 1,000 trained lay persons. We require 220 units for full qualification. Vigorous lay training continues to grow to this very day.

And so we are building the skeleton! My greater dream is that this concept will spread until we see in America such centers for lay training across the country under a standard-setting institution like an "American Association of Accredited Lay Training Centers." I have been talking about it for 20 years and am pleased to hear the idea being discussed more and more!

The Nervous System

Now add the nervous system. After acquiring property and buildings, after adding a minister of evangelism to build the membership and after adding a minister of education to train these members, we were now ready to add a minister to care for the daily needs and hurts of these members of its body! So we added the minister of family and parish life. This is the nervous system!

As the mind can be occupied with lofty thoughts—only to have a pinprick in the finger divert the attention of the entire brain to the minor wound, so a large church must be so sensitively organized with caring and concerned lay people that no lonely member can remain unattended in a moment of pain. So our minister of parish life was challenged with the job description: "to *recruit, train,* and *motivate* the laymen and laywomen to do the pastoral work in this growing body."

The nervous system is beautifully supplemented in the Crystal Cathedral by dozens of sharing and caring groups. I'll let one of the small group leaders from our church describe this exciting ministry:

"Brothers and sisters in Christ are practicing love and compassion on one another first, before extending it to the world around them. Each family fellowship group has a unique personality and is made up of individuals in varying degrees of spiritual growth. Sometimes the group succeeds and sometimes it fails, both individually and together, but with God's help they keep working together. At each meeting there is prayer, Scripture, a quiet time and sharing time. The blessings that come from such sharing times are many:

We are learning how to lose ourselves in others.

"By freeing ourselves from spiritual problems and by gaining a healthy love and respect for ourselves, we are becoming liberated. Getting ourselves off our hands frees us to lend a helping hand to others, and every time this happens in a group, we call it a modern-day miracle.

We are learning how to listen deeply.

"Too often conversations become monologues rather than dialogues. Too often we 'tune in' and 'tune out' at random. But in a small sharing group, everyone in the circle gets his turn to talk. The shy one no longer has to fight the aggressive talker. Everyone listens as each person takes his turn. Shy, frightened persons learn how to open up and reveal themselves as they grow in trust.

"We learn to hear the silent words of the soul as well as the spoken words of the lips. Persons who have never prayed aloud learn to utter their first child-like petitions to God. Every time this happens in a group, our eyes are wet with joy.

We are learning how to love the unlovely.

"Since no two people are exactly alike, each group is made up of a variety of different individuals, some with peculiar idiosyncrasies that one might ordinarily walk away from. But in small groups, we stick it out if we wish to stay in the group, and eventually we learn how to unlock the hidden blessings in the person we judged as unlovely. We learn to accept people just as they are—as God was willing to do with us when we first came to Him.

We are learning how to leave our mistakes at the foot of the cross.

"Confession and reconciliation are good for the soul. Freed from guilt through forgiveness, we can proceed with God's next assignment rather than waste needless energy on unrepented mistakes. Praying companions make this easier and remind us when we tend to forget.

We are learning how to discover God's plan for our lives.

"Through searching the Scriptures and by sharing collective insights and actual experiences, God can reveal to His modern-day disciples His step-by-step plan for our lives. One man feels led to change jobs; another feels challenged to stay where he is. One couple feels led to get involved with teenagers, others to start a blood bank, adopt children, take in foster children, help welfare families, repair missionary machinery in Mexico, provide clothing for an orphanage, counsel persons in need through phone calls or through letters received from our television and radio outreach, or volunteer their services in various programs and activities within the local church.

We are learning how to lean on the power of the Holy Spirit.

"The Third Person of the Trinity is no stranger to the people in small sharing groups. We have learned to depend on His supernatural power during the traumatic or everyday experiences of life. Accidents, alcoholism, blindness, bankruptcy, cancer, death, divorce, drug addiction, heart attacks, mental illness, runaways, suicide and unemployment have all been experienced and lived through by real people surrounded by real, live fellowship groups— undergirded by the power of the Spirit working in and through people.

We are learning to lead others to Christ.

"Each member of a group makes reports to his group every two weeks, telling of his day-to-day encounters with God—God's assignments, His corrections, His blessings, His guidance, and His revelations. Talking about Christ becomes so natural and so easy. It finally becomes second nature to share these vital experiences with unchurched neighbors. This often helps to open the door of their hearts so that Christ can come in.

"Small groups are certainly one way to The Way. They help us, the human Body of Christ, become more deeply aware of the Body's many parts—hurting when others hurt, rejoicing when others rejoice, lifting when others are down, supporting when others are weak, loving when others are discouraged.

"It works! Garden Grove has tried it and has seen it work!"[1]

The Goal

It is the goal of the Crystal Cathedral to have a membership made up of persons won through evangelism and whose lives have been changed through the life-giving power of Christ. They will have been educated through our adult education program, and they will be held together as one caring, sharing and loving community by the nervous system of our church.

Your church in your community may not have the potential for a large membership, but your church must have the blood circulatory system of evangelism, the skeletal system of education and the nervous system of trained laity caring for its fellow citizens in Christ, if your church is to be a true Church: a Body of Christ leading, loving and lifting your community.

And the church that is truly the Body of Christ is the kind of an institution that will never be out-of-date! It is the kind of a church that will be as modern as the twenty-first century!

Note

1. Mary Lee Ehrlich, "Modern-Day Disciples," *The Church Herald*, (Garden Grove Community Church, October 22, 1971), pp. 12,13.

Chapter 9

ARE YOU GROWING INTO YOUR MISSION?

Is the future of the Church in America strong? I believe it is. In fact, I believe the Church has a fantastic future! Why? Because the Church is recognizing two important needs: the need to be a mission and the need to grow into that mission!

"But," you say, "the Church is in decline." And you cite, as an example, the fact that church membership—particularly in mainline churches—is declining.

True, the Church in recent decades has been in decline. To understand why this is so, we need to understand some of the major reasons for this decline that began in the midtwentieth century.

Until the advent of the Second World War, the United States of America was oriented toward small towns and cities. The institutional church was represented largely by the "First Church Downtown on Main Street." Unfortunately, you would find a First Presbyterian Church on one corner, a First Methodist Church on another corner and a First Baptist church on a third.

False Assumptions

After World War II, America moved into the age of suburbia. With the new rise of suburbs around major cities in our country, Protestant leaders of all denominations realized we were now facing a new opportunity to develop new churches that avoided the mistakes of the past. But, in formulating basic policy for church planning, they made certain assumptions that, unchallenged and universally accepted for several decades, proved catastrophic for church extension and development.

What were these assumptions?

One: Large churches are bad news

Church planners assumed that the ideal size for a church was approximately 500 to 800 members or about 150 to 250 families for the ideal church. "Ideal" because this was just the right size for one pastor to handle effectively.

But why did church planners assume that a large church, possibly one with several thousand members, was ineffective? America at that time was still in the tycoon era. All large institutions and establishments, with rare exceptions, were generated, motivated, managed, administered and promoted by tycoons. Their enterprises— Ford, Chrysler, McCormick, Goldwyn and others—even bore their names.

The same sort of tycoon administration and management was at work in the huge churches that existed in our nation until this time. And the problems of tycoon-centered churches were obvious. When the tycoons died, the churches for the most part turned out to be huge, empty auditoriums. So church planners hastily assumed "large churches are bad."

Ironically, in the industrial and business world, stock-holders, though seeing the shortcomings of tycoon management, did not consider breaking up or shutting down their large industrial enterprises. They saw positive values in hugeness and used creative imagination to eliminate the negative aspects of great size. Companies with complementary strengths merged together, creating larger markets, pooling resources and achieving greater success for all concerned. Most importantly, team management was born, replacing tycoon management. As a result, large companies across America today are headed by teams of competent senior executives, whose names, unlike those of their predecessors, are not household words.

But churches reacted differently and negatively to tycoon management. Their solution? Consider all big churches to be bad news and don't plan for any large churches in the future!

So what is the result of the false, unchallenged assumption that big churches are to be avoided? The result is that denominational leaders in church planning formulated a variety of goals based on this premise: If, for instance, the ideal church is 500 members, then only an acre of ground is needed. The sanctuary can be planned to seat 300 or 400 people. A few classrooms and one office will suffice.

So across the country in all the new suburbs, property was secured—in the early developmental stages—of one acre on an average, occasionally two or three acres and, rarely, perhaps five acres. As a result, new Protestant churches sprang up across the country designed to be small. And for the most part, they struggle and limp along today.

When I was graduated from seminary in the early

1950s, I accepted an assignment with a small church in Chicago. As pastor of that small church, I found I simply did not have a program that appealed to the masses. We had only a Sunday School with one adult class, a young people's group too small to be exciting, too few competent musicians to have a good choir and nothing for single adults or young college kids or divorcées. *If only we had several thousand members,* I thought, *we could have large and effective groups for every type of person.*

So even then, I saw the large church as the most effective church in the mission of evangelizing unchurched people. That's why, when I was given that opportunity to come to California in 1955 to begin a church on my own, I leaped at the opportunity. Now, some 30 years later, I remain convinced of the advantage of the large church today and feel it is the church for the twenty-first century.

Two: One pastor is an ideal arrangement

This assumption is most unintelligent. The average ordained pastor is not a 10-talented man. He may be a good preacher—or a good pastor—but he is generally not strong in both areas. He may be a good pastor but not skilled in organizational work. His appeal to the youth or to the educational department of the church might be strong or weak. Perhaps he is a good pastor and even a good preacher, but very ineffective as a promoter and as a financial planner. Or perhaps his strength is in counseling and in no other area.

That intelligent church planners could assume that "a single-pastor arrangement is ideal" seems incomprehensible. Yet this is what must have been assumed. A congregation of 500 to 700 members worshiping in a sanctuary seating 300 and built on one or two acres of ground could expect to generate only enough income to support one full-time minister, perhaps a full-time secretary and some part-time help with a little money left over for missions.

Three: A church should be "in community"

For the church to be "in community" meant ideally that it should be located in the center of a square of developed land. The tragedy of this assumption was that untold thousands of newly developed churches in the midtwentieth century were sited off the beaten path, leaving masses of persons in surrounding communities unaware of their existence.

Four: A square mile of homes
Will support a church

The assumption that a church should be "in community" was related to another unchallenged assumption that a square mile of newly developed suburban homes would adequately support a church. Church planners, watching new suburban homes spring up by the hundreds after World War II, assumed that 1,000 new homes would be enough for one large church. Certainly then, one square mile of approximately 2,000 to 3,000 homes would be more than enough to support a single church.

But this assumption was false. Half the people in any community were already committed to some faith, leaving about 1,000 uncommitted families. These, for the most part, were the disenchanted or disinterested who couldn't care less about the church. The odds of winning them were stacked against success.

Church planners also wrongly assumed that, if there were one Protestant church in that square mile, every Protestant residing in this square mile would attend that one church. They forgot that some loyal denominational followers would go outside that geographical area to a church of their own denomination, even driving a half-dozen miles or more to get there.

Five: Parking is not
All that important

Pastors of new churches complained of having to buy additional land to meet city planning commission requirements of one off-street parking space for every five seats—or something of the sort. So pastors prepared elaborate cases for planning commissions arguing that "one parking space for every five persons was unnecessary. After all, did not great churches through the years succeed with parking only along the curb?"

So it was not uncommon to see many new churches develop in the midtwentieth century with no parking provisions whatsoever. We were slow to discover that if a church were to grow, it must have surplus parking.

Six: Preaching and pronouncements
Are effective communication

On the assumption that churchmen can communicate effectively through one-way methods, prominent church leaders in their national and international assemblies preached their sermons in the form of pronouncements. This method may have worked in the Roman Catholic Church 30 years ago. And it may have been effective in many Protestant churches a generation ago. But today we no longer assume that we can communicate with people effectively through monologue.

Dialogue has replaced monologue. Why?

Because we now recognize that one-way communication is essentially demeaning. It assumes that the party making the pronouncement or giving the sermon is the more enlightened, intelligent, informed, brilliant or sensitive party—hardly a compliment to the man on the receiving end of the pronouncement or sermon. Consequently, the pronouncement form of communication establishes polarizations, creates chasms and establishes a mental climate where effective, warm, meaningful dialogue becomes a virtual impossibility.

So if we want to succeed in communication, we will avoid the one-way approach. Rather, we communicate through the witnessing approach. An enthusiastic sharing of what God is doing is the way to communicate with people and change their lives. We may witness or we may ask questions. The question approach builds bridges where dialogue becomes genuinely constructive. What a contrast to the pronouncement approach!

The successful communicator today attempts to put every communication objective in positive terms designed to stimulate positive emotions in the hearer. Then, if he "sells his idea" by stimulating those positive emotions, he knows he will have not only a solid convert, but a happy and enthusiastic Christian as well. The result? A Christian who has investigated, questioned and come up with satisfying answers he is thrilled to pass on to others.

So you see, successful selling is nothing more than communicating to people a truth they weren't aware of before!

Seven: Mainline denominational labels Impress people

My denominational affiliation is the Reformed Church in America. When we began the Garden Grove Community Church 30 years ago, many of our new church pastors felt that, if we had a name like "First Reformed" corresponding, let us say, to "First Presbyterian" or "First Baptist," we would really impress unchurched people.

What we did not realize was the obvious: *unchurched people are not impressed by denominational names.* If they were impressed by such names, they would already be members of those denominational churches.

Eight: Great churches give 50 percent Of their income to missions

Almost all new churches started in suburban America were made to feel that they were selfish if they didn't strive early to give more and more to the denomination's national headquarters. In church after church, pastors labored without secretaries, mimeographing their own bulletins, to save money for missions. Yet I have never found a denominational executive who did not have secretarial services.

The denominational home offices skimmed off the first meager profits from their new branch offices instead of urging them to concentrate for the first 10 years on "reaching every unchurched person in the community—your first mission!" National headquarters stunted the growth of their young by demanding too much too soon. So it's no wonder home offices today are lacking in income. Better to have 10 percent of the mission dollar income of a large church than 50 percent of the income of a small, stunted church.

The Result of These Assumptions

The real result of these assumptions was the loss of the Church's regional power bases. During the midtwentieth century, the large old churches downtown declined, and the downtown along with them. Yet no master plan was prepared for replacing these strong centers of power with new, equally large or larger power centers in the newer suburbs. By default, suburban churches were designed against largeness.

Too few church consultants, if any, really understood the enormous value of the large old church on Main Street or the three vital functions they served:

They formed a strong financial base. The largest and usually the wealthiest churches generated a mood of financial strength, security and confidence to the regional group of denominational churches: "Old First will back us up!"

They were sources of enormous psychological power to the smaller churches and to struggling pastors in the region. They served as "psychological cathedrals," providing a sense of security to all small churches in the area. Smaller congregations which could denominationally identify with large Old First felt a sense of belonging to something bigger and stronger than themselves and were sustained by it.

These Old First churches were centers that became reservoirs of human resources for great lay leadership. Here were found the lay leaders who spearheaded great lay movements: the building of youth camps, the underwriting of religious radio and TV programs, the launching of evangelistic crusades and many other major projects.

Though they were the sturdy base blocks in the regional denominational foundation, these large churches were undervalued. So with the dying out of Main Street and its large churches, together with the development of suburban churches *designed against largeness,* a weakness penetrated the American Church. By the 1970s, Protestantism discovered it was without power centers in many regions. Younger churches and pastors became discouraged even as the pastors of Old First Church downtown became discouraged.

In this state of affairs, the established Church developed an inferiority complex, declined and tended to be judged as a dying and ineffective institution. Predictions were heard that the Church of the future would be the underground church or the church in the home. Such irresponsible predictions neglect the obvious: *only an established church with buildings, people, staff and programs can form a base of operations for generations to come.* Eliminate that and you eliminate the base of operations for the future.

The tragedy is that the unchallenged assumptions which shaped church extension in the midtwentieth century, U.S.A., were all false assumptions. Why? Because they violated the fundamental principles of successful retailing. We'll talk more about successful retailing later in chapter 9. But for now, remember always to challenge an assumption, particularly a negative one that suggests you think small, design small, build small. To accomplish big things for God in the twenty-first century, you need to dream big, plan big, build big!

Grow or Perish!

So where do we begin? We begin with a question: *Do you and your church want to grow?* Are you sure? A law of life that applies to churches as well as to anything else is that "where there is no growing, there is dying." The implication is clear: the Church must either grow or perish.

Where there is growing, there is dynamic living. But tragically, too many churches really do not want to grow any larger than they already are. Why? For the answer, let's look at the types of churches that do not want to grow—and why.

An entrenched lay leadership

One of the no-growth types is the small church with entrenched lay leaders who fear they will lose their positions of power if they win the dynamic leaders in their community. Forming the power structure of the church, the old guard fears they may lose their positions of power if new blood comes in the membership of the church. They will not allow the church to grow because they consider their own positions threatened.

Here is a story that has unfolded too often. Some young pastor comes into a community to begin a new church. Beginning with no members, he is eager to receive whatever support he can secure at the outset. He enthusiastically reaches out and welcomes in gratitude the first men and women who step forward to offer their help. And, as in most such cases, those first people offering their help are men and women who have never before held positions of influence or leadership in a church.

I think of one particular congregation represented in our files of hundreds of churches whose pastors have come through our Institute for Successful Church Leadership. Let's call this the Case of Church 127. Located in the suburb of a great midwestern city, this church organized with 43 charter members. A church board was formed with 12 officers—elders, deacons and trustees. Not a single one of these 12 men had ever been a member of a decision-making, policy-setting board of directors before. Not a single one among this group demonstrated anything higher than a notch above failure in private life.

Now suddenly, the power of this church was in the hands of 12 men who felt strangely and terribly important. But they lacked the vision, imagination, courage and determination that makes for qualified and dynamic leadership. Because they were both inexperienced and insecure, they were natural obstructionists to their young pastor. He enthusiastically won the interest of unchurched people who then attended his worship services, only to receive a cold shoulder from the entrenched charter church board members.

The chairman of this board was employed as an attendant in a gasoline station. He looked upon the school superintendent who visited in church one Sunday as someone who certainly would be elected to the chairmanship of the church board if he should ever become a member of the congregation. After the frigid nonwelcome he received, it is not surprising that the school superintendent never joined the church. Nor did the village doctor, nor a successful salesman, nor a dynamic insurance executive. All were made to feel unwelcome by entrenched lay leaders who feared for their positions. The truth is—they didn't want to grow.

Unfortunately, this is not an isolated incident; it is all too common. In too many churches, an entrenched lay leadership, fearfully enjoying a first taste of power, refuses to receive with sincerity, any new member who is considered a threat to the present power structure. They do not want their churches to grow.

So again I ask, are you sure you want to grow? If you do, and your lay leaders do not, a condition exists hindering growth. You must demonstrate strong leadership, and the congregation must face up to its insecurity. Through a renewed discovery of Christ, they can become willing to open up to new members.

A negative piety

What are the symptoms of a church infected with negative piety? Afraid that they might lost their purity, fearful that somebody might come into their ranks who is not truly born again, members of this church—made up of superpious, holier-than-thou, narrow-minded persons—do not dare for their church to grow. And shockingly, there are hundreds of such congregations in our country.

Somehow the Church must discover the power of the Holy Spirit to do His converting work in human life. It is amazing how successful the Church has been in creating obstacles, building boundaries and carving chasms between the community of Christians and unchurched people.

By contrast, how refreshing to live and work with Christians in a church relationship who look only for a sincere love for Christ and a warm commitment and devotion to Him as a criterion for membership. Beyond all doubt, extreme, narrow-minded piety, with its man-made regulations and restrictions, has been a weapon used by the devil himself to keep potential converts out of the Christian Church.

A "right size" mentality

Another type of church that refuses to grow is the church that labors under the we're-big-enough-already theory. Tens of thousands of pastors and lay leaders still believe the unchallenged assumption of midtwentieth century church planners that 150 families is "just the right size." That an arbitrary numerical figure should establish and control the program, policy and future of any church is surely an idea devised by the devil himself!

To use an arbitrary figure as the ideal size for a church is as unnatural as to take an "ideal" size shoe and bind it permanently on a young child's foot, so the foot will never become larger than that "ideal" size. Just as the feet of Chinese women generations ago were deformed by the crude and inhuman practice of foot binding, just so is the congregation of a church, forced to remain small by such a preconceived, growth-restricting concept, doomed to remain shrunken and withered. Eventually, it dies!

One thing is certain: *a church must never stop growing.* When it ceases to grow, it will start to die. And when it stops growing, it will cease to hold its dynamic leadership. Its staff members, if it is a multistaffed church, will look for other positions which offer a challenge, adventure and excitement. Dynamic, effective, energetic and successful laymen, as well as professional churchmen, gradually drop away from a nongrowing situation. And finally, the church realizes that, in losing its dynamic leadership, it has allowed the seeds of death and decay to be planted.

A fear of growth

A last type is the church that literally has a fear of growth. Of course, growth will mean problems. Perhaps the lovely sanctuary with the stained-glass windows will become too small. "We certainly wouldn't want to sell it, would we?" Or, "We certainly wouldn't want to get involved in having to build a larger sanctuary. That would mean *raising money!*"

Sure, growth does produce problems. But these problems are the very challenges generating the energy and vitality that mark an institution as being *alive.* Where growth problems do not exist, death lingers near.

Fear of growth rises also in the minds of some pastors. There are not a few churches that are led by insecure ministers who really do not want the church to grow for fear they might have to add additional staff ministers to the organization. And, indeed, there are not enough ministers who have learned the skill of working in a multistaffed situation. But certainly any minister who honestly searches his heart and concludes that he does not really want his church to grow for fear he will have to add additional staff ministers and perhaps share his glory, his weddings, his funerals and his baptisms—such an insecure pastor must come to stand afresh before Jesus Christ and surrender himself once more to Christ as his Master, his Lord and the Leader of his church.

Now, are you sure you want your church to grow? Believe me, it can, unless you are in some place with a declining population. There are very few churches that we see in our Institute for Successful Church Leadership that do not have growth potential! Consider the pastor of a beautiful New England church who attended our Institute. His church's old colonial chapel was a community landmark in the old downtown square. It was and is a historic landmark. It was and is a magnificent example of pure colonial architecture.

Unfortunately, the growing population in the city offers fantastic opportunity for this church to grow, except for one thing: the existing edifice is a growth-restricting problem. The church already conducts two services of worship and each is filled. They obviously cannot grow as long as they continue to use this beautiful structure. As a result, the church board has virtually adopted a no-growth policy. The question was addressed to me in a counseling session: "Dr. Schuller, what should we do?"

Our suggestion was to retain this magnificent facility as an inspirational place of worship in the city center. Retain it as a chapel for weddings, small funerals, special baptismal services with recorded devotional programs to be played in the sanctuary throughout the week, with the doors open for tourists and residents to enter for inspiration.

Meanwhile, the congregation was encouraged to move its major church operational and functioning plant to a new piece of property approximately one and one-half miles away. Here on a new 10-acre parcel of land, a large sanctuary could be built with a large educational and recreational plant, a dynamic youth center, generous off-street parking and the physical capability to accommodate a maximum membership of 4,000 people in the next 20 years.

When considered this plan produced fantastic excitement and energy. When adopted it provided an enormous future for this church, giving the congregation a twenty-first-century church while still ministering in the twentieth century. Wisely recognizing the certainty that no potential for growth means great potential for death, they chose, not to perish, but to grow.

Yet, you say, one tree doesn't make a forest. True, but more and more other possibility-thinking pastors and churches, faced with the same challenge to grow or perish, have also chosen to grow. In the special section following this chapter, you will find the exciting case histories of 12 of these future-minded, growth-minded churches as told by their own enthusiastic pastors.

And, in the balance of this book, after the special section, are several practical chapters chock-full of sound principles and advice on how your own church can grow. For unless you grow into your mission, you will decline until you become a mission field.

THEY MADE THEIR DREAMS HAPPEN

I am excited about the great possibilities within you and your church. Why? Because results-generating, excellence-oriented principles of church growth and management are bringing about a revolution in the American Church. And you and I are a part of it.

Pastors and churches of every communion all across this country are making their dreams happen by applying in their own communities the dynamic leadership fundamentals taught over the last 15 years in our Institute for Successful Church Leadership. By combining great faith with great ideas, these amazing men and women are achieving great things for God.

Now they share with us their challenging experiences in establishing some of America's most exciting twenty-first-century churches. As you read their thrilling stories, you will be moved by their joyous enthusiasm and will be given a vision of the future for your own church as well.

"THE VISION KEEPS EXPANDING"

Thirteen years ago my wife Vivian and I, together with a decision-making couple from our congregation, attended the Robert Schuller Institute for Successful Church Leadership. When we went out on Saturday evening at the conclusion of the Institute with some friends I ate food which upset my stomach the whole night. At 7:30 the next morning I told Vivian I was just thankful for one thing, that I didn't have to speak that morning.

In a few minutes the phone rang and Wilbert Eichenberger said, "It is a fantastic morning, Jim! How would you like to be on national TV with Dr. Schuller?"

I thought: Turn obstacles into opportunities! "Sure, Ike, I will see you in an hour." That confident decision cleared my mind and filled me with strength. What I shared that morning was used by God in astonishing ways.

When I returned home would my goals be so great I would be sure to fail without God? Fourteen years before I had been the founding pastor of a congregation near Purdue University which numbered a thousand members when I returned from Garden Grove. Three hundred professors, a force of business and professional leaders, and a host of university students filled the sanctuary twice every Sunday. This was certainly enough. I had earned my Ph.D. two years before and was leader of a strong congregation in a strategic educational center. But I had no further goals and our congregation had no clear sense of direction.

Find a need and fill it, find a hurt and heal it. Set goals beyond goals. Suddenly I recognized a need in our congregation which I had tried to ignore, for I regarded it as a problem. Many people in this large congregation in times of need could not find the help they needed.

My staff and I were overwhelmed with our counseling load. Where there is a problem there is a possibility. To my mind came the dream of members within Covenant becoming equipped to shepherd flocks within the congregation. I portrayed the need and invited people to join me. One out of every 10 Covenant members became willing and able to care for others. This concern has generated strength and enthusiasm through the parish in amazing ways. Once we determined as a congregation to meet the needs of people, a host of persons began coming into this fellowship with its promise of receiving help.

This vision awakened us to the needs of people within our community. But how could we help those families in the blighted areas of our county who are victims of life? An eminent problem and a determination to find the solution brought the big idea to my mind of challenging families in

Covenant to become Samaritans. A Samaritan family seeks to share the faith and love of Christ with a distressed family until that family is restored to effective living. The witness of the families whose lives have been lifted from despair to faith is one of the most powerful signs of hope in our community.

A congregation whose people genuinely cared for people grew quickly to be the largest among the more than 100 Presbyterian congregations in northern Indiana. But many of our members still looked upon growth negatively.

I had initiated goal setting among pacesetting leaders as Dr. Schuller had taught us. Possibility thinkers saw the thousands of people within the range of our witness who were unchurched, and the goal was set of actively extending the faith and love of Christ to those who do not have this hope. We set clear objectives for building the program, the lay leadership, staff and facilities necessary for reaching that goal. And we reached all objectives, but the notion of building expansion aroused criticism. Resistance to growth formed at this clearly defined point.

We went ahead and challenged the congregation to provide space to meet the needs of people who were coming to share in the spiritual vitality and enthusiasm of a vital congregation. A significant building effort was achieved, but even before it was finished intense crowding of the parking and sanctuary raised serious problems. The congregation was challenged with the goals of doubling the membership, staff and facilities of Covenant during the next 10 years. Robert Schuller's Institute for Successful Church Leadership awakened this dream within me and within a continuing stream of our decision-making laymen who attended the institute. Consequently, we have achieved each of our goals.

Now a life-challenging vision has captured the whole

congregation. The hope and strength this effort promises to awaken in human lives is a constant inspiration and joy to us. This expanded horizon came into view for me through the influence of Dr. Schuller. He had put this life-changing awareness deep into my mind: Confidence for courageous world-changing effort is generated when we set our lives upon an objective which encourages others and demands of them that faith which only Christ can give.

The creative force of the personality is alerted into intelligent bold action when challenged to the sort of effort that

- helps people who are hurting,
- makes ourselves and others into better people,
- helps to solve serious human difficulties, and
- will be done only when we do it.

Every life needs that kind of supreme effort to enjoy the best that life has to offer.

Ten years ago, as the membership of Covenant continued to boom with enthusiasm, and unchurched people came in greater numbers, I saw two needs:

- A need for the faith of all persons participating at Covenant to be deeply enriched, so as to remain strong and vital, radiating to the world.
- A need for opportunities for growth so that people could realize the strength of the Christian life.

The result of meeting these needs would be that enthusiasm and encouragement extended to one person could be reproduced with major impact in the lives of many others.

With the incentive of possibility thinking, I entered into a style of New Testament discipleship and challenged a few laymen with possibilities for personal growth and outreach through business, profession and community. This group of disciples now numbers 150, and its members are now leading, beginning and extending small supportive fellowships throughout the community. This Discipling Fellowship is extending the strength of the Christian faith into countless lives, inspiring a life-style which multiplies through people in a dynamic way.

With the success of this endeavor I am asked to visit congregations and hold seminars across the country to share in the dynamics of discipleship. It is inspiring to have a national and world vision. It is the basic incentive of possibility thinking which sees a need and meets it, finds a hurt and heals it, that has carried us into this exciting opportunity for training lay leadership in outreach and spiritual growth. My book, *The Shared Adventure: The Dynamics of Discipleship* has recently been published. This also is the result of possibility thinking.

Covenant has witnessed dynamic growth through possibility thinking during the past four years. All the facilities that were built through the vision and the incentive Dr. Schuller initiated and encouraged are now filled to capacity, and we are looking forward to providing space for children in a Sunday School that is already filled beyond capacity and for parking where the unchurched can find access to the Sunday morning celebration. The attendance and participation in all phases of the ministry are dynamic and growing.

An exciting music and worship opportunity has been developed with 95 people in the adult choir and 400 children participating in choirs. Adults involved in study/teaching fellowships are growing dynamically. The small-group ministry continues to challenge more and more people.

We have now established a wellness center that promises to open the promised abundant life to ever-expanding circle of people throughout this area. We initiated a TV ministry with a significant outreach. The ministry to junior and senior highs and college students is the most exciting ministry I have ever witnessed. We have been privileged to develop a strong professional staff with strong lay leadership. We now conduct a National Growth Seminar at Covenant twice a year in which many churches from across the country participate.

The vision keeps expanding. We are thankful for the challenge that Dr. Schuller continues to give us.

—JAMES R. TOZER, *pastor, Covenant Presbyterian Church, West Lafayette, Indiana.*

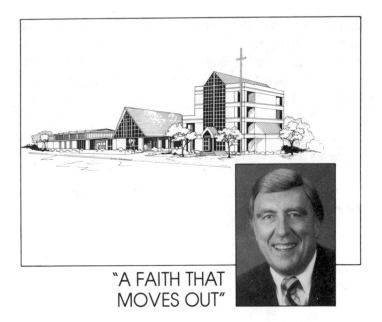

"A FAITH THAT MOVES OUT"

With God all things are possible" (Mark 10:27). I am now serving my thirty-fifth year of pastoring Concordia Lutheran Church in San Antonio, Texas, and I pray that verse may serve to illustrate my ministry and way of life.

At Concordia Church we have sound evangelical belief that appeals to people in any era, a solid faith anchored in the Word of God and trusting for salvation through Jesus Christ. We have a faith that moves out to meet needs and heal hurts. Concordia seeks to minister the gospel to the whole person serving, witnessing, caring, singing, exalting God, giving careful attendance to His Word and doing all of this with contagious joy and gladness in the Holy Spirit.

While this ministry has grown into one of the largest, most inspiring and positive-thinking churches of our Lord Jesus Christ in America today, we are both one of the smallest and one of the largest churches here in Bexar County. We have organized Concordia Lutheran that way. While thousands attend the two services every Sunday morning, we have the schedule structured in such a way that people who like small churches can attend the evening service at 7 P.M. And extending our congregation's ministry even further, we broadcast nationally on cable and locally on TV with an inspirational weekly program entitled "Breakthrough."

Symbolic of Concordia's attention to the whole person is our recent erection of a beautiful four-story ministry building, dedicated to the proposition that the human person is body, mind and spirit and needs to be ministered to in an holistic fashion. Our new ministry building has a large well-equipped nursery, a beautiful bookstore, a foyer and lobby for fellowship, and a lovely chapel for small services and weddings, as well as a TV production studio.

The ministry building also houses offices for our many staff members in TeleCare, an around-the-clock telephone ministry; offices for Lutheran Social Service workers who deal especially with unwanted pregnancies and problems of the elderly; office space for psychologists who are subsidized by the congregation to meet the rising counseling demands; and a wellness center with a library, VCR viewing areas and space where people in the healing fields are present for advice and counseling. The fourth floor of this building includes a large banquet and fellowship hall where virtually every week a seminar or workshop of some kind is held to meet needs and heal hurts.

Senior citizens are ministered to at Concordia with an active program under the direction of an associate pastor, providing fellowship and inspiration for these "Keena-gers." At the other end of the age spectrum, Concordia serves some 500 students in a booming Christian Day School.

Hundreds of members enjoy sports at Concordia. Our teams compete in an organization known as the San Anto-nio Sunday School Athletic Association, comprised of teams from churches of various denominations all over the city. We consistently field more teams than any other church. For the last 10 years, we have won more league and city championships than the next three churches com-bined. However, winning athletic contests is not the goal of our program. All the coaches of our youth teams are chosen for their abilities as Christian leaders who use praise and patience as they seek to mold Christian charac-ter while guiding these teams.

Our adult athletic program is as solid as the youth pro-gram. We use all our sports programs as outreach, always inviting nonmembers to participate in the hope of having them "come to play and stay to pray."

Scouting, too, is a part of life at Concordia. And so are busy groups, such as "Innovators" for singles 18-21, "Pacesetters" for singles 21-35, "Saints Alive" for mar-rieds 21-35, "Celebrators" for marrieds 35-50, "Motiva-tors" for marrieds 50-65 and Alcoholics Anonymous, among others.

We have grown from a handful of worshipers to over 4,000 members in a relatively short time, making it hard to believe that 34 years ago, no church—just a farm—stood on the site that is now the thriving Concordia campus. Those first years were hard ones, yet so rewarding. We began with 37 people and a small parsonage that doubled as a site for Sunday School classes and for other instruc-tion. Now on an average Sunday, some 3,000 members of all ages attend Concordia worship services.

Thankful as we are for the organization and the Christian fellowship, the teaching and preaching of the Word of God is the most important business at Concordia. No one becomes a member of this congregation without knowing first the Christian confession and posture of the Lutheran Church.

Beginning with a chance meeting in 1971, Dr. Schuller and I became fast friends. I was in California representing our church as vice-president at a district convention in Southern California and was invited to attend briefly part of a seminar being conducted by Dr. Schuller at his Garden Grove Community Church. Since both of our churches had been included in Billy Graham's "Great Churches of Today," an affinity sprang up. Since then, we have had numerous contacts, and I have had the privilege of speaking at Dr. Schuller's institutes and seminars on several occasions.

I have sent many of Concordia's lay people to various seminars at the campus of the Crystal Cathedral for personal and leadership development, Bible training and church management.

I would like to add my "amen" to the principles that Dr. Schuller has so clearly enunciated in this book. Among the most prominent in my mind is the principle that "believing is seeing." Even the world can say "seeing is believing," but only those of true faith can say "believing is seeing." And much of what has happened in great churches today has come because of great belief, which then issues in great visualization, action, implementation and realization.

Another principle that Dr. Schuller emphasizes enthusiastically is that *we* don't build the church, *God* does. But we can remove the growth-restricting obstacles that prevent God from doing His work. There is no one who better defines those growth-restricting obstacles than Dr. Schuller does today.

Furthermore, though I have always been a goal setter, until I had the chance to trade thoughts with Robert Schuller, I never had set my goals as high and as broad as I do now. His emphasis on how to set your ideas successfully are eminently worthwhile.

Dr. Schuller himself often quotes the words of William P. Merrill: "Rise up, O men of God! The Church for you doth wait, her strength unequal to her task. Rise up, and make her great!"

Indeed, your church can have a fantastic future! God bless you.

—GUIDO MERKENS, *senior pastor, Concordia Lutheran Church, San Antonio, Texas.*

"BELIEVE IN THE IMPOSSIBLE"

The principles of Robert Schuller's Institute for Successful Church Leadership have profoundly influenced my life and ministry here in Salem, Oregon at The People's Church.

This church was officially formed in 1952 in a rather humble fashion, meeting in rented facilities upstairs in a downtown business building. The church then purchased a vacated older church building which it subsequently added to and remodeled. Later the church purchased land, relocated and built a new church that had an auditorium and education facilities for 700, but had only 59 off-street parking places.

Shortly after the church moved into its new facilities, the pastor who had led in this relocation was killed in a plane crash. An associate pastor assumed the leadership of the church for the next two-and-a-half years. I arrived to pastor the church in July 1967. I found the building as it was when the congregation moved in—large areas yet unfinished and one entire area only framed-in that had been closed off. My immediate task was to solidify the congregation, then numbering about 200.

In some moments of discouragement I learned a few valuable lessons. One day I was complaining to a pastor friend of mine who had moved to Oregon from California shortly before I had. I said to him one day, "Don't you think the people in California are more progressive than Oregonians?"

He replied, "No, people are just like their leader. They will follow positive leadership if they have it."

I went home that day realizing that any lack of growth was not the fault of the people whom I had been chosen to lead, but was due to my own lack of vision and enthusiasm. That was a turning point in the life of the church.

Shortly after, I was invited to a luncheon in Portland where for the first time I met Dr. Robert Schuller. He talked about an Institute for Successful Church Leadership which he was going to begin. I received the information and had the privilege of attending the first Institute he conducted. I felt the study-guide he had us prepare in advance was one of the most valuable things that happened. Even if I had not attended the Institute, just involving our church members and leaders in the preparation of the study-guide, the taking of pictures where you would build a church if money was no problem, and the dreaming and goal setting that was required opened up many new possibilities.

The principles I received at the Institute became the catalyst for a life-changing experience. I had an associate pastor ask me, "Have you always been like this (positive) or did Schuller change you?"

I told him that I felt that I had always been a positive, happy person, but Dr. Schuller helped me to define my motivation into clear goals and procedures. I found that there is not one principle given at the Institute that in some way does not apply to all local situations.

We began to experience solid growth in our church. For two consecutive years we were honored as "Oregon's Fastest Growing Sunday School." During this time it became apparent that we were not going to be able to get the job done and complete the vision that God has given us in our present facility, even though it was relatively new. There was no way, without tremendous capital expenditure, that we were going to solve our parking problem.

It was while I was attending the Institute for Successful Church Leadership and thinking about my own situation, that, with a personal word of encouragement from Dr. Schuller, an idea came to me at three o'clock one morning. I had been inspired by the messages and workshops at the Institute and had been excited that day with the possibilities of reaching our city for Christ. I was having trouble sleeping because of the excitement I felt.

Let me digress a moment. One day in Portland, Oregon, a few of us, about 12, had been invited to meet Dr. Schuller for a few minutes as he was traveling through the city. During the time we were together, he was speaking and suddenly stopped and asked one of his associates to write down what he had just said. He stated that our session was not being recorded, and he didn't want to lose the thought that God had just put in his mind. That made me very conscious of the fact that God does speak to us, that He has given us a mind for Him to think through and that we need to be sensitive to the fact that those creative ideas that come to our minds have been placed there by God. I knew that, but that day the reality of that great truth became a part of my life-style.

Back to my sleepless night. I had seen so many of my friends in the pastorate have difficulty in presenting the idea for relocation and had witnessed some sad things happen to the harmony of the local church. I wanted to have the right direction in how to present such an undertaking to a congregation who already had sacrificed much to get where they were and who were in a building that had been made possible through the dynamic leadership of their pastor who had been killed.

Suddenly I had an idea. I got out of bed and wrote down what proved to be a God-directed plan for presenting what needed to be done. I prepared four ideas to be presented on two overhead projectors. One had the idea for growth, and the other had the approximate cost of what that growth might cost. These ideas ranged from staying where we were and maintaining what we had to starting a branch church, to buying up property to build a parking garage and, lastly, to relocate. The cost of relocation was stated only as "total commitment."

There were several who spoke that evening. I can't recount them all, but finally a man whom I had previously misunderstood as a negative thinker stood up and said, "To build this church where we are now meant we had to mortgage our homes, we couldn't buy a new car, we had to sit on run-down furniture, and now I think it would be a dirty shame (at that point I silently prayed, 'Oh, God, please shut him up!') if we don't let the next generation do the same thing." I must say that man has been one of the greatest supporters of our expansion through the years.

The congregation voted that evening on all four proposals at the same time and 93 percent of the congregation voted to relocate. That was the most emotional night of my entire life.

From that meeting in 1971 to move-in day on January 1, 1978, was a long, long time. We had made the announcement and through a miracle we located the property. By another miracle we were able to purchase it. We made that second announcement and prepared to sell the property we were now using.

I had determined the same faith that would see a new facility built could see the present church facilities sold before starting the new project. Those were difficult days of waiting. Building costs were going up monthly, and still nothing happened. Some got discouraged and thought that it would never happen and left the fellowship.

About the time of my deepest discouragement, a church from out of state called me to pastor. It seemed like a great opportunity. They had just purchased 30 acres and were anxious to relocate. It seemed like a way out for me.

Dr. Schuller came to Salem about this time to speak to another group. They asked me if I would introduce him, and naturally I was pleased to do so. As we talked together, he asked me, "How long have you been in Salem?"

"Eight years," I replied.

He answered, "Are you going to throw away an eight-year investment and go start over? You stay here and build that church for God, for if you don't, nobody else will!"

At that moment, he shoved a coin in my hand and said, "Take that and build that church for God."

I put the coin in my pocket and later that night I read the words inscribed upon it. On one side were these Scripture verses:

"Be still, and know that I am God" (Ps. 46:10, *NIV*).

"If God is for us, who can be against us?" (Rom.
8:31, *NIV*).
"I will not die but live" (Ps. 118:17, *NIV*).
On the other side was this prayer:
"Thank you, God . . . for solving so many of my
problems in the past. Please God, help me
today. I need you and I trust you. Amen."
The miracles of finance, property sales and construction costs are stories in themselves. But on January 1,
1978 we moved into the 45,000 square feet of our new
totally finished and furnished facilities. With an attendance
on opening day greater than I could ever have dreamed, I
stood up that morning and, for the first time in public,
pulled that coin out of my pocket, read the Scriptures and
prayer, and preached on "The Coin That Built a $2-Million
Church."

When I first went to the Institute, I was the only pastor on staff with one part-time secretary. Today we have
six full-time pastors and three other full-time ministry
directors with an office staff of seven to assist. On the first
Sunday of 1983, we moved into another new education
building that has now given us a total of 67,000 square feet
for ministry. Our budget has grown from $50,000 to $1.4
million annually. Our missions budget alone last year
expended over $300,000. Each summer on a weekend in
July we sponsor an outdoor Jesus Festival that attracts
10,000 people. Our parking has been increased to handle
600 cars off-street. God has used us, I believe, as an inspiration to other churches in our area, and some very positive things are happening in many churches in our city.

Dr. Schuller has helped us see the real meaning of missions, the value of advertising and promotion and the need
for lay involvement. He has also encouraged us to dream
big and to believe in the impossible.

I highly recommend that before any church considers a building program, or purchases property for relocation, they attend the Institute. The placement and design of our buildings and the property that was purchased all reflect the influence of the Institute. We have been able to secure over 13 acres on the second busiest street in the state of Oregon. We also have secured and paid off totally an additional 122 acres on the opposite side of our city. We feel that this investment is going to turn into another miracle in the future of our expansion.

The People's Church story is not finished. We have been pleased with people of great vision. We have done some things that have not succeeded, but there has been a willingness to try. I believe if any church will take and apply the principles that are outlined in this book, they will succeed for the glory of God.

This is the day of the church. Why not yours? Why not where you are? Why not now?

—DENNIS DAVIS, *pastor, The People's Church, Salem, Oregon.*

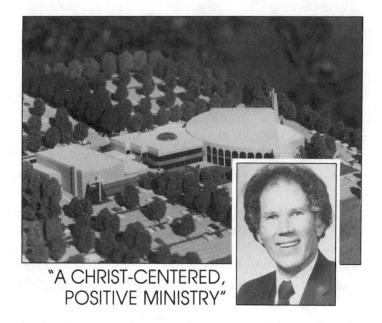

"A CHRIST-CENTERED, POSITIVE MINISTRY"

Preceding the launching of New Hope Community Church at the 82nd Drive-In Theater in Portland, Oregon, on October 14, 1972, my best friend and wife, Margi, and I sat in the prayer chapel on the fourteenth floor of Dr. Schuller's Tower of Hope. We were attending the Institute for Successful Church Growth where Dr. Schuller was delivering the material that is in this splendid book.

In the last message Dr. Schuller said these words, "The greatest churches ever built in America have not even been started yet. Someone here will build a greater church yet, with seven days a week of activities! It will be a sensation for Christ."

I believe that New Hope Community Church, operating in one of the most unchurched cities in America, Portland, Oregon, is well on its way to becoming one of these churches that Dr. Schuller prophesied.

At this writing, New Hope Community Church has 3,000 members, 80 percent of which were completely unchurched before being reached by this ministry for Christ. In an average week more than 4,000 people's hurts are being healed and dreams are being built in this Christ-centered, positive ministry. Christmas, 1986, the church that was started with no people and no outside support will be in its spectacular 3,000-seat sanctuary with its 110-foot cross towering over the main shopping center and freeway system in Portland. In 13 short years this church has gone from the humblest of beginnings to being one of the largest in the Northwest.

While there are many principles Dr. Schuller teaches that are now in practice at New Hope Community Church, there are four that stand out immediately.

The first is positive, need-meeting sermons. The sermons that are preached are ones that give people a tremendous psychological, spiritual lift. We preach self-worth and self-esteem. We begin by letting people really know and experience that God loves them, forgives them and restores their lost dignity. And because they have been restored through Jesus Christ, they can feel good about themselves and begin to build right relationships in their families and with one another.

The positive message we preach creates the climate of love in which people are healed, set free and grow as persons and in their relationships with one another in devotion to God. The gospel sets people free. Free from sin, free from condemnation. There is phenomenal personal growth that happens to the people who attend New Hope and when this happens to them they get so excited they tell all their friends and bring them to experience the faith, love and hope of Jesus that they've experienced.

Second, we offer many need-meeting ministries. One of the secrets of building a successful church that Dr. Schuller has been underlining and proclaiming for years is, "Find a need and fill it. Find a hurt and heal it." Seven days a week, 24 hours a day, New Hope is committed to going where the people are to minister to their needs. This healing of hurts and building of dreams is done through a variety of people-meeting-people fellowships that help individuals weather the turbulence and stress that life brings. Any of these need-meeting ministries are, by themselves, larger, much larger than many churches.

Each ministry becomes a point of entry that brings unchurched people into the church. Some of these need-meeting ministries are: New Life Victorious, a ministry for alcohol- and drug-dependent people; the Positive Singles Ministry; Blended Family Ministry; Grief Ministry; *"New Hope at Night,"* a nightly radio program with counselors responding to the calls with loving prayer; Separation Survival; Divorce Recovery; Counseling Ministry; Music Ministry; Junior High Ministry; Senior High Ministry; Young Adult Ministry; Special Education Ministry; Marriage Enrichment Seminars; Prayer Ministry; Men's Ministry; Women's Ministry; Successful Leader's Ministry and many others.

The principle that New Hope has followed from day one was to find a need and do a good job of ministering to that need. Then as the church grew, we found another need, matched it up with the right leadership and started ministering to that need. So with the years of growing success has come the multiplication of scores of need-meeting ministries. We believe that the best is yet to come.

The third principle we use is that we recruit, motivate and train lay people for meaningful ministry. New Hope

Community Church has been building an army of lay ministers and "unleashing them" throughout the greater Portland area. New Hope has 350 lay pastors who are trained, equipped and supervised and who meet weekly for reporting and motivation. Then they go out and lead more than 200 Tender Loving Care groups that meet weekly in circles of love. In an average week there are close to 2,000 people attending one of these dynamic cell groups where discipling, evangelism and shepherding takes place. Out of the lay pastor ministry have come many pastors and staff people who are reaching out to an unchurched and hurting world.

Then fourth, we have a shopping center location. Accepting Dr. Schuller's vision to be like a major shopping center, New Hope Community Church and its leadership accepted a vision to find a piece of property that would be a spot of natural beauty on a lush, green hillside. It should offer accessibility to a major freeway system and be within 15 minutes of 100,000 people. We wanted a piece of land that would be highly visible along the freeway to thousands of people who would pass by every day. It needed to be at least 10 acres or more where we could have parking for thousands. The property would need sewer and water so it could be developed.

Do you know where New Hope Community Church is located today? It is one block off a major exit right along Freeway I-205. It is directly across the freeway, towering over the top of Clackamas Town Center with its 175 stores making it one of the major shopping centers in the entire Northwest. More than 50,000 people drive by the church every day.

It is our dream that New Hope Community Church, the church for the unchurched thousands in Portland, Oregon, will be a church of 10,00 people by 1990, multiplying to many times beyond that by the turn of the century.

I want to live my life doing things that I have to depend on God to accomplish—things that require all I can give plus a whole lot of God's power.

—DALE E. GALLOWAY, *senior pastor, New Hope Community Church, Portland, Oregon.*

"EXPECTING BIG THINGS
FROM GOD"

I love the Church. I was brought up in the Church and have always been involved in it. So I have always wanted the best for the Church, and I get deeply hurt watching many congregations suffer and struggle so intensely.

Within the Church are power struggles, uninspiring messages, unsingable hymns and unenthusiastic worship. For over five years, I traveled and visited literally hundreds of congregations and found that many of them are unbelievably discouraged. Some are slowly dying. Many are actually dead.

Following college graduation, I was invited to be a youth director for a Lutheran church in Burnsville, Minnesota. In that church was life, vitality, spirited worship and a vision for exciting ministry. As part of my educational leave in 1975, I attended the Robert Schuller Institute for Successful Church Leadership in Garden Grove, California. I didn't know very much about that ministry, but I had been told that an extraordinary ministry was taking place there.

Everything I had heard about Dr. Schuller's dynamic ministry was correct, and my love for the Church grew even more as I experienced firsthand his vibrant ministry. What impressed me most was the warm, friendly, positive, enthusiastic climate that surrounded every part of the ministry. Certainly all the principles of successful retailing, goal setting, possibility thinking, inspiring preaching, exciting programming and enthusiastic publicity were stimulating. But the ministry also showed that without the proper climate, it would be difficult, if not impossible, to move ahead in mission.

The most profound part of my experience at the Institute occurred on Friday morning. The lecturer was interrupted by a messenger who announced that Walt Kallestad should come to the office for an emergency phone call. The words penetrated like a sharp knife. I ran to the phone and received word my two-year-old son, Patrick, had wandered outside the home in which we were staying and had fallen into their swimming pool. By the time he was found, he was blue and unconscious. They told me the paramedics were working on him and were rushing him to the hospital. I was to meet them there.

Tears streamed down my face as I hung up the phone. In a daze, I started out to my car. Then someone tapped me on the shoulder and asked what the emergency was all about. It was Dr. Schuller himself.

Through my tears, I told him what happened.

He looked me in the eyes and asked, "Do you believe in miracles?"

I stammered, "yes."

"Then let's pray for a miracle for your son, Patrick," Dr. Schuller offered. He put his arms around me and prayed. After the prayer I sensed a new peace and hope within me.

As I headed for the hospital, Dr. Schuller went into the session and asked the 500 pastors present to pray for Patrick. Prayer took priority over program. And that is an important key to the success of the Garden Grove ministry, I believe.

The miracle happened! After about an hour, Patrick's attending physician ran out of the emergency room and said, "Boy, are you lucky. Your son had his lungs filled with water when he arrived and it just seems to have disappeared. He's calling for his mommy and daddy."

During the remainder of the day, many called from the Institute and offered anything and everything. We felt so loved and cared for. My wife, Mary, and I agreed this is what a church should be like.

Throughout the Institute, Dr. Schuller kept saying the keys to successful ministry are:

1. Find a need and fill it.
2. Find a problem and solve it.
3. Find a hurt and heal it.

Dr. Schuller and his congregation were practicing what they preached. During the final morning of the institute, Patrick was released from the hospital and we all went to church for the closing communion service. Dr. Schuller reached out to hug us as we approached the altar. He held Patrick as we and the other 500 pastors there shed tears. A miracle had transpired and we were all witnesses to God's incredible greatness. I left the altar that day dedicated to build a church as loving, caring, friendly, warm, inspiring, positive and faithful to mission as that church.

My love for the Church had now been connected with a vibrant vision as a result of the Institute. I wanted a church that really cared, one with dynamic Bible studies and educational growth opportunities, one with something for everyone. I could clearly see a church with a vision for mission—totally inclusive, not exclusive—committed to evangelistic outreach and growth.

I needed to become as tooled and equipped as I possibly could for the ministry, so I made the decision to attend Luther Theological Seminary. On our way home from the Institute, we drove through Arizona to visit my wife's family. As we drove through the northwest part of Phoenix, where Community Church of Joy now exists, I turned to my wife and said, "Wouldn't it be great to start a church here someday?"

In God's great prompting and providence, following my preparation at Luther Seminary, I received a call to Phoenix. It was a dream come true for our family. A fantastic opportunity for mission and ministry was located right on the edge of one of the fastest growing cities in America.

I couldn't wait to build a church, applying all the positive church growth principles I had learned from the Institute. I just knew that building a great church was going to be the most happy and exciting adventure I had ever been part of.

The first Sunday came. My congregation was four years old and had approximately 90 worshipers and 260 members. I gave my first "inspiring" message. Bubbling over, I stood at the door greeting people after the service. One member came up to me with a scowling face and grunted, "Whose side are you on?"

I was taken aback and flippantly responded, "God's side." My questioner stomped off.

The next Sunday I was notified there was a fist fight in

the parking lot. Two of my church officers were actually punching it out!

Things got worse. My work was criticized. Several did not like the fact that I wanted the church to grow and reach out. They argued over how much of a raise to give me. It was a mess.

As the weeks passed, the problems grew. My messages continued to be about God's unconditional and nonjudgmental love. They were geared to build positive faith and a spirit of joy. Several people left the church. They didn't want any part of this possibility thinking. The success for the first six months was phenomenal for we "grew" from 260 members to 100. I figured that in about six months we could just close up the place. I was devastated.

One evening when the temperature skyrocketed to 120 degrees, the church caught fire. I rushed to my car and, clutching the steering wheel, I cried, "God, what is wrong? I had this inspired dream of a great church but it's all falling apart. God, I need you. I can't keep on without you. You take charge and if anything great happens, I will give you all the credit. I promise." A ton of weight was lifted from my shoulders in that moment. A new desire and spirit were placed in my heart.

Slowly things began to turn around. It was difficult to build and shape a church around the very principles of possibility thinking, but I kept going pursuing God-inspired, God-given goals. Inch by inch, we began to move forward. Now today, seven-and-a-half years later, we have over 2,500 members and a budget of $1.3 million.

Our youth ministry has grown to over 450 active juniors and seniors. We have a singles ministry, a vibrant music ministry, care and counseling for the sick, suffering and hurting, numerous Bible studies and educational classes. Our preschool and Sunday School are overflowing with children developing as leaders. We have a senior citizens ministry, a prayer ministry and a small groups ministry. Our new member orientation has about 600 per year who attend classes, then join the church. And we have a good solid staff and organization of well-equipped volunteers to handle these vital ministries.

We most definitely have not arrived at the end of our dreams. We have only just begun. I believe that the best is yet to be for our congregation and for the entire beautiful Church of Christ. Everyday I claim the words from I Corinthians 2:9: "No eye has seen, no ear has heard, no mind has conceived what God has prepared for those who love him." *(NIV)*.

I thank God for what Dr. Robert Schuller has meant to me and my ministry. He has helped me grow in dreaming big dreams, setting big goals, planning big plans and expecting big things from God. My friendship with him is a special gift from God, and I look forward to that friendship and partnership in the ministry for many years to come.

—WALTHER P. KALLESTAD, *senior pastor, Community Church of Joy, Glendale, Arizona.*

"CAPTIVATED BY A VISION"

Christ Community Church of Spring Lake, Michigan, has become a creative center for Christianity—a people joined together in a common faith in Jesus Christ, a mutual trust in the grace of God and a shared vision of the exciting possibilities for ministry as we move toward the twenty-first century. We are a people encircled by the love of God, touching the world God loves.

We have opened our life together to the fresh winds of the Spirit, allowing Him to shape us into an instrument of His grace for the healing and wholeness of all who would join us in the pilgrimage of faith. We have been captivated by a vision; we are driven by a dream; we are a people in process, seeking to become what our name implies. For the past decade and a half, Christ Community Church has been a place of dynamic ministry and explosive growth.

It was not always this way, however.

In 1970, the First Reformed Church of Spring Lake celebrated its centennial, and with it 100 years of stable congregational life and steady growth. A handful of Dutch settlers had organized the church in the days when the village was a bustling lumber center. The parish consisted of 200 families and its growth had plateaued for a decade. There was much to celebrate then—faithful pastors, competent and committed leaders, loyal support. The centennial was celebrated.

The cause for celebration however lay more in the past—for what had been—rather than for what lay ahead, for all was not well in 1970 for the First Reformed Church of Spring Lake. Membership was on the decline, our youth were moving away from the church, the median age of the congregation was rising. The First Reformed Church was participating in what appeared to be the slow demise of the parish church.

There was, in 1970, deep concern for the church's future and sincere prayer for renewal. But, there was no clue that the First Reformed Church was on the threshold of becoming Christ Community Church, vibrant with life and empowered by hope.

And then it happened! Without warning, without plan or program. Suddenly, with a spontaneous eruption of spiritual life and power, with a new vision and a dream, a 101-year-old village church was reborn.

Every church is unique—with its own special circumstances which make it what it is. So it is with Christ Community. Two significant factors came together and the result is a story overflowing with God's providence and grace.

The first factor contributing to the rebirth of this parish

church was an invitation to me by the congregation of First Reformed Church to return as their pastor. Now this was a significant risk in love on their part, for my life was in shambles. My marriage was broken, I had three small children to care for, I was in difficult financial straits, having just completed four years of post-graduate study in Europe, my future was extremely cloudy. I returned to First Reformed Church to become their pastor once again and found the congregation had become to me the mediators of God's healing grace.

At that time, Dr. Herman Ridder was president of Western Theological Seminary in Holland, Michigan. He suggested to the Spring Lake elders that they send me to the Institute for Successful Church Leadership. The 1960s had been not good years for the parish church. The despairing question I heard over and over when I returned from Europe in 1970 was "Will the church be alive in '75?"

My elders saw the wisdom of Dr. Ridder's advice. They encouraged me to go to Garden Grove. I was ready to go, but I didn't want to go alone. I encouraged others to join me and, in April 1971, nine of us attended the Institute. That was the second significant factor.

I remember the opening session of the Institute as though it were yesterday. We were in the chapel at the top of the Tower of Hope. Dr. Schuller was speaking: "Some of you are here saying, 'Okay, Schuller, I'm here. See if you can make a believer out of me!'"

I thought, "How does he know what I'm thinking!" I was full of suspicion, misgivings, doubts. But I was there.

Our experience at the Institute changed my ministry and transformed my people. By the time we boarded the plane for home, we could have flown on our own power. It had happened to all nine of us. We had become believers.

We returned to our congregation open and full of hope,

ready to let the fresh winds of the Spirit reshape us into instruments of grace. With positive ideas to build in Spring Lake a creative center of Christian faith, we became a catalytic core, literally turning the church upside down.

The eruption of new life was spontaneous; the climate was one of supportive love. It was a beautiful, joyful, amazing experience for all involved. In dramatic fashion right before our eyes, God worked a miracle! Renewal broke out with a passion, initiating a dynamic movement that is still alive and well—and growing. By God's grace in the power of His Spirit, it had happened! We dared to dream the impossible dream—and God made it happen.

After 101 years, the First Reformed Church became Christ Community Church, a name suggested by Dr. Schuller because of the positive image it created in the minds of those outside the church walls. The name gave us a new sense of identity and projected into the community a new image. Involved in that name change was more than painting a new sign. It involved the willingness of an old, established village congregation to die in order to be reborn. That willingness to let go of the past created room for new life, not by rejecting the Reformed heritage that was ours, but rather, in gratitude for that heritage, setting it free to be shaped by the demands of Christ's mission today.

"Find a need and meet it; find a hurt and heal it," we had heard Dr. Schuller say. So we set about building a staff who would create a program to heal the brokenness of the human situation, to mediate the grace of Jesus Christ. We added a second person, then a third and a fourth. We heeded Dr. Schuller's advice, "You don't do it when you can afford it, you do it when you cannot afford not to!" With staff came program—a need-meeting ministry; and with a ministry to meet human need, growth followed.

Growth took place in many forms: We beautified our grounds, installed glass doors that opened up the sanctuary to the outside, began a daily five-minute radio ministry, greatly increased our advertising budget, purchased adjoining property, added a second morning service and then a third.

"Worship Is Celebration" was printed on our Sunday bulletins, and so it was. Strong preaching and an excellent music program combined to make Sunday mornings a dynamic center that energized the whole life of our community.

The renewal gained momentum; the growth necessitated added services until the facilities could no longer handle the growing numbers. The church erected a new building, and on the day we moved in, CBS-TV cameras were there to capture it on film for a feature of our ministry in the Sunday morning series, "Look Up and Live."

Statistics can never really tell the story, yet numbers do represent persons touched by our ministry. In 1971, as we made our way to California to attend the Institute, our total community numbered 678. We are now at 3,000. During the decade of the '60s, the total budget for our church was $60,000. Today it is over $500,000. In April 1971, I was the "staff," along with a part-time secretary. Now we have four ordained ministers and seven part-time persons engaged in various facets of the ministry, plus a four-person support staff. In 1971, the median age was over 50. Now 14 percent of the congregation is over 50, while 65 percent is under 35.

A traditional midwestern congregation deeply rooted in the Reformed faith has been reborn. In a village of 3,000 with 40,000 persons within a 10-mile radius, a congregation of 3,000 has grown. And there are more prospects today than when we began.

In the years following our dramatic appointment with destiny in Garden Grove, we continued to send our people to the Institute. About 40 persons have been exposed to the dynamic, positive principles for growth presented by Dr. Schuller. We have learned well the helpful lessons of his ministry and, having come to a totally different setting, have adapted those lessons to our own situation. We are a living demonstration of their universal applicability.

Joy reigns at Christ Community Church. A positive spirit of hope and confidence in the limitless possibilities for ministry is evident.

An air of excitement and an openness to new forms of ministry continues. Having just gone through a thorough self-study and reflections of where we have been and where God is calling us to be, we are ready to move into a new phase of dynamic expansion of ministry as we move toward the twenty-first century, convinced that the best is yet to be!

—RICHARD A. RHEM, *pastor, Christ Community Church, Spring Lake, Michigan.*

"WE ARE A PEOPLE WITH A DREAM"

We nearly lost Dr. Schuller in San Antonio, Texas, on that September day in 1983, and he *loved* it. My husband/co-pastor picked up Dr. Schuller and Ike Eichenberger early Tuesday morning to go to the airport after a successful speaking engagement the night before on the importance of leadership in American churches.

With rush-hour traffic causing delays in making the flight, Jim exited the airport off-ramp at a high speed, as a 16-wheeler, making equally good time on the access road and refusing to yield at the yield sign, approached on Dr. Schuller's side of the car. In a hair-raising race, Jim scooted in front of and past the huge truck, braking in time to get in line for departing flights. Dr. Schuller punched the car roof hard, almost creating a sun roof, as he shouted in that famous booming voice, "I *love* it! I *love* it! You didn't give up *leadership*!!" The rest of us were scraping ourselves off the floor of the car.

Give leadership to our start-from-scratch ministries is what Dr. Schuller had encouraged us to do years before. Based on his advice, plus an understanding of our natural and spiritual gifts, skills, interests, education and experience, we began with the two of us as co-founding pastors, along with Lizz and Katy, our two daughters and one unchurched person. We chose the bar of the Ramada Inn as our first "sanctuary" because of its key location, easy identification, accessibility, visibility, ample parking—and because the bar was the only room for rent that had windows. The hotel was horrified at the idea of a church in its bar and, at first, refused to rent to us. But we explained that we were targeting for unchurched people and they would probably not feel uncomfortable in this setting. Besides, the bar wasn't allowed to open until noon on Sunday. We'd be out by then!

So we began the inch-by-inch-anything's-a-cinch process toward the dream God had given us of a 20-acre campus and a concept of ministering to the whole of a person's life needs, all targeted to the unchurched. George Gallup's most recent, most extensive poll on religion in America revealed that over 90 percent of Americans believe in God, 52 percent percent believe that Jesus Christ is divine and a majority desire Christian education for their children. In our target area of North Central San Antonio, 80 percent of the 100,000-plus people living there are unchurched. These people are primarily business and professional people, a unique target market. We directed our efforts toward them, assuming that they have needs in their lives that they would like the church to meet.

But how do you communicate from the church to

unchurched people? You don't put two lines in the church directory of Saturday's newspaper. They don't read the church news. We contacted an advertising agency to pose the opportunity of reaching people who weren't looking for us. They extensively interviewed us to understand our theology, philosophy, purpose and goals. Then the agency produced a logo reflecting our values, an ad to be placed near the comic strips—which most people *do* read—or in the business section to reach our target market of primarily business and professional people and a brochure reflecting our identity, purpose, direction and opportunities to meet needs for direct mail and handouts.

The ad agency designed a telephone market survey that was implemented by the congregation. Our "congregation" then consisted of the advertising woman who had now joined the "church," which until that time had been the unchurched person and two pastors. Using every fifth phone listing in the prefixes of our geographical target area, we asked whoever answered the phone whether they currently participated in a church. Only the unchurched people were asked to respond to our brief questions.

Naming our new church was a direct result of polling unchurched people. We asked them, "If you were invited to church by a friend, which of these names would most appeal to you: Good Samaritan Christian Church, New Life Center, Town and Country Christian Church, San Antonio Christian Church or Christian Life Center?" The list of names was chosen to offer selections which were biblical (Good Samaritan), contemporary secular-sounding (San Antonio) and contemporary Christian (Christian Life Center.)

We were extremely surprised by the name chosen by unchurched people—San Antonio Christian Church. The choice was overwhelming—97 percent. The next question on the survey was "Why did that name appeal to you?" The consensus answer: "If I were to return to a church, I would want it to sound old, stable, secure—as if it had always been there."

Our expectations had been that unchurched people in our target market of business and professional people would enjoy meeting in a neutral, even secular setting like a hotel. Instead, we found that they value land and building because of the stability and longevity they represented. We expected they would enjoy a contemporary worship service—soloists instead of choir, no preaching robes, informal service, totally contemporary music for congregational singing and special music. We found that pioneer types (Peter Wagner's church-growth language) were attracted to these elements, so we were able to build up a large core group. But homesteaders—the type of people who help a church shift gears from a small, informal group to a larger, more stable organization, required a blend of contemporary and traditional. This blend meant a musical balance of gospel hymns, such as "Amazing Grace"; classic hymns like "God of Glory"; and contemporary hymns such as "Come to the Waters"; as well as occasional praise music, such as, "The Horse and Rider." These examples represent an even larger group of ideas and experiences than we expected. We thought unchurched people would want the church to be "different," but we found that our target market of business and professional people wanted the church to blend traditional values and experiences with a contemporary attitude of openness and warmth.

In the beginning, the services we offered were limited, but we found we could offer breakfast, teaching from the Bible, relationships, partnership groups, counseling, occasional seminars and, most importantly, a *dream*. We basically had nothing to sell except a personal relationship with God through Jesus Christ, and a dream. A great idea for God, a great idea from God. That was enough for some people; it was not enough for us.

The dream is a church for the unchurched where we attempt to meet all of life's needs. Believing that all of life is holy, all of life is one, San Antonio Christian Church began in a bar with one unchurched person in the belief that "like would draw like" and aimed at a 20-acre campus that would someday include a church building for worship and education; a Christian Life Center for therapeutic counseling and preventive seminars, retreats, information, a Christian school—grades K-12, plus a day school and a retirement home with nursing assistance.

We were a long way from that dream and we understood that attracting the first 20 people would be the hardest effort, then breaking the 50 mark. The most difficult of all would be growing past 100 adults in attendance. After that, we could move past 400. We could then determine our size on the basis of what type of ministry we wanted to offer and what styles of management the pastors were willing to change to.

In three years time we have grown and have begun building, but our growth has been backwards and our building is not bricks and mortar. Though we have grown numerically from one person in the congregation to over 200 people, our primary growth has been in staff, assets, operating revenue and ministries. Numerical growth has suffered through each geographical move we have been forced to make: from the bar, which we outgrew, to half of the hotel's ballroom; from the ballroom, which was expensive, to a downtown church; from the church, available for evening services only, to a small church building, freed up through a merger of congregations; from the church building, too limited, to the cafetorium and classrooms of a centrally located high school. Eight moves in all, due to being shuffled from place to place within the hotel and within the downtown church.

Only now are we able to provide a firm foundation for growth. The high school was chosen due to its visibility, accessibility, abundant parking, central location and spaciousness and identity as a familiar landmark in the city. Our next move is anticipated within 18-24 months to our own land and buildings.

We miscalculated how drastically the lack of a permanent location would affect the ministry and it took us a couple of years to understand and believe that unchurched business and professional people, if they decide to return to church, want a moderately traditional church with stability and credibility. In the beginning we preached in suits instead of robes, sat informally around small tables and held loosely structured services with all contemporary music. Eventually, we evolved into preaching robes, a robed choir, more traditional music, semicircle seating and a more formal worship service—all due to feedback from the business and professional unchurched target market telling us what communicated best to them. This change in worship proved to be over-adjustment even to the people who had suggested it and the better blend was expressed in a robed choir, ministers preaching in suits, semicircle seating and a balance of contemporary and traditional music in a structured service with a sense of informality and warmth.

Our backwards growth is reflected by the fact that we now have a staff large enough to take the church into a significantly larger size, while it may seem out of proportion to our current size. San Antonio Christian Church now has four ministers, a director of music, an administrative assistant and a pianist. Half of the staff is part-time until resources can provide full-time salaries.

Another reflection of backwards growth is that almost $1 million is accumulated for purchase of land, as cost of land in North Central San Antonio is approximately $132,000 an acre. These assets are the result of two mergers with older, smaller congregations: the University Christian Church with eight people and the New World Christian Church with 18 people plus one pastor. Our operating revenue, in excess of $150,000 for 1985, has brought us from a mission church to a giving church.

Our ministries have expanded into a full program of Christian education for children, youth and adults; mission efforts; special programs and retreats throughout the year; choir; training for the laity and partnership groups.

Building has come not in the form of bricks and mortar yet, but in the form of people, core group, systems, foundation and credibility. Organizational behavior theory maintains that how an entity is begun is basically how it will stay for 20, 30 years and more. Fine-tuning may be done, additions may be made, but dynamite can alter direction only minutely. Therefore, the beginnings of a church are crucial in terms of what direction is set by the foundation—the constitution and by-laws, understanding the nature and purpose of the church; by the systems created—who makes decisions, what are the lines of communication and of command; and by credibility—image in community consistent with real behavior, ministries actually helping people, land and buildings to represent stability and longevity.

We are a people with a dream. For a while, all we had was a dream; then we attracted other dreamers; then we began to actualize the dream. Our people are survivors. They liken our movement to the Hebrews' trek across the wilderness—many hardships, unchartered course at times, but worth all the risks for the kind of relationship with God and with people that we know we can bring to unchurched business and professional people in North Central San Antonio. Our dream is based on Luke 10, the Good Samaritan experience, to increase love of God and love of neighbor by touching all aspects of people's lives.

—JAMES B. SCOTT AND MOLLY DAVIS-SCOTT, *co-pastors, San Antonio Christian Church, San Antonio, Texas.*

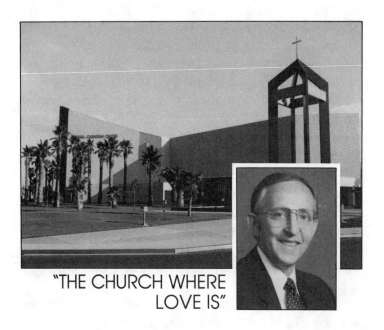

"THE CHURCH WHERE LOVE IS"

In 1970 while I was pastor of Evergreen Christian Center in Olympia, Washington, I attended the Institute on Successful Church Leadership sponsored by Dr. Robert Schuller and the Garden Grove Community Church. It was an experience that put legs under my ministry.

Dr. Schuller's principles of church growth put into context what I had already believed and felt about the ministry of the local church. I heard for the first time from someone else the concepts that had been forming in me over the first 10 years of my ministry. I went home to a building program that was already underway in Washington's capital city with a fresh understanding of Christ's words, "I will build my church" (Matt. 16:18).

On the way back to Olympia by car, my wife and I stopped at a church in Oregon on a Sunday morning. An effort was being made to build a new building through that congregation. The pastor made a statement that was to affect me in my desire to carry out the principles learned at the Institute. The pastor said to his people, "We don't want to use the people to build a great church; we want to use the church to build a great people."

When I drove up in front of my church, a 30,600-square-foot building under construction, I somehow knew it would not be large enough in a short time. The sanctuary would hold 700 persons, with a gymnasium for an overflow of 250 more. Adequate rooms were being built for Christian education, including a new Day Care program.

Let the statistics speak for themselves. In 1970, the average Sunday attendance was 428 with an income of $174,839.64. The move to the new facilities took place in the middle of 1971, and the average attendance was 469 with an income of $207,285.53. In five years time the congregational attendance increased by 675, and the income increased by $792,959.47.

When I accepted the call to pastor what was then called Bethel Temple in Sacramento, California in May of 1978, the church in Olympia had 5 percent of the area population in services on Sunday morning, numbering approximately 2,000 in attendance.

Could it be done again? Most of my friends said, "No!" They thought my move to Sacramento was foolish. I told them God was in it. I knew He wanted me to go, although I could not understand it. I believed in Dr. Schuller's theory that you should plan to stay a lifetime in a church. That was my desire. God had other ideas.

Did the growth patterns of the '70s manifest themselves in Sacramento in the '80s? Most assuredly, only greater!

The name of the church in Sacramento was changed to fit a more "community" approach to the ministry of the local church. Although the name "Bethel Temple" was known in the community, it was identified with a Jewish synagogue on numerous occasions. We needed to make a new statement to the community. This was not easy to achieve.

The church had been in existence since 1917. A 1,500-seat sanctuary greeted me in 1978. But, it was half full. Empty seats stared me in the face. I had not seem empty seats for some time. It was a shock. You could shoot a cannon through the sanctuary on Sunday night and not hit anyone. What could be done? Apply the principles of Successful Church Leadership, of course.

The name was changed to Capital Christian Center. A new sign appeared in front. A motto was chosen by the congregation which went in the advertising and on the letterhead, "The Church Where Love Is." The church began to grow. New faces were seen week after week. Many accepted Christ and were baptized. The membership classes produced excited participants in the ministry of the local church.

In 1978 there were approximately 750 worshipers and a budget of $600,000. We had 13 acres of property with no opportunity for expansion at that site. We had to add a worship service in the morning to accommodate the people coming. Stack parking was instituted to get the cars off the street. A 575-car parking lot was transformed into a 1,000-car parking lot. The attendance grew to 2,500 and the income increased to $2 million. I knew we were going to have to move this congregation to larger facilities. Here was an opportunity to put to the test the principles learned at the Institute. We had to have an accessible location, excess parking, an appealing facility, and a good deal of exposure, preferably on a major freeway.

It was then that a miracle took place in Sacramento. A 63-acre building site became available on that major freeway. A developer made it available to Capital Christian Center as a gift! A $5 million miracle was in hand. How could the people vote down my program? We had a miracle! The church voted to sell the facilities they had occupied for 20 years, relocate at the new site, and in general, touch Sacramento for Christ.

The old facilities sold for $4 million. The church was able to lease them back through the construction period of new facilities. Construction began in 1982 on a 3,000-seat sanctuary, a 300-seat chapel, a full gymnasium and complete education facilities to handle the Christian Day School, the two-year Bible School, as well as the Sunday and Wednesday evening programs of the church.

On April 1, 1984, a proud and happy congregation moved to its new home. Almost 200,000 cars per day pass the beautiful and practical facilities of Capital Christian Center on Highway 50 in Sacramento. In seven brief years attendance has risen from the 750 level to over 5,000 on Sunday. The income has increased from $600,000 to approximately $5 million. The Day School has 920 students and more buildings will be erected soon to take care of waiting lists in each grade. Twenty acres will soon be developed for a full athletic complex, including a football bowl that will double for large outdoor community events such as the Fourth of July patriotic musical and fireworks display.

Dr. Schuller has said, "Protestantism must experience a revival of possibility thinking, a belief that we are co-workers with an Almighty God who can accomplish anything that would be a great thing for His cause in this world!"

That is our belief. The most important part of the New Testament Church is the rate of conversion, new people being added to the Church. Acts 2:41 says it well, "there were added *unto them* about 3,000 souls." Then in chapter 4, verse 4, another 5,000 is mentioned. Soon you begin to read the word 'multiplied' in the book of Acts. The result seems to be amplified in Acts 4:21, "All men glorified God." These great affirmations of Scripture should take care of the small-church mind in our midst.

I believe the concepts of Dr. Schuller's ministry that have helped me the most are in the following areas:

Facilities. As the size of a family increases, or as the children get older, it is necessary to add on to the house or secure a larger one. Too often the size and shape of our church buildings determine the size and shape of our congregations.

Staff. The next big obstacle to growth in a church of 300 or more is the lack of help. There must be a diversity of ministry. The senior pastor must share the responsibilities of the church. Limitations of time, energy and skill must be realized. One of the beautiful things about the larger churches today is the teamwork of a multiple staff. I have 15 pastors working with me.

Delegating responsibility. Following close behind the need of developing a staff is the need of delegating responsibility. This lies in the area of paid as well as volunteer help. Here is a big question: "Can I give someone a job and let him do it?" It may not be done just the way you would do it, but give a person the right to be themselves. Creativity and productivity is stymied when we feel we have to walk behind those working with us to make sure they do it "our way."

Equipment. The importance of good, well-planned equipment in our buildings is invaluable. It is most difficult for people of any age to hear what we have to communicate if they are not comfortable. In a larger church there seems to be no end to the demand for equipment.

The power of plans. The present condition of your church reflects the vision and planning, as well as the work, of somebody. The future condition and size of your church will reflect the same. There is no substitute for organized planning. Take a look at your annual reports. Is there anything there that says to the people, "This is the way we should be going?"

Concentration. Have you ever been watching a football game on television and with a groan, observed a player drop a beautiful pass? The announcer then says, "He lost his concentration. He could have caught it but he wasn't concentrating." Are we doing those things that really build the work of God? What could we chop off in order to concentrate on the most vital?

The Leader. People like to follow someone who knows his direction. There are risks involved, but that is the challenge of leadership. Someone has to be willing to take those risks. It would be easier by far to follow, but someone has to be out in front leading the way. Paul told Timothy to "stir up the gift of God, which is in thee" (2 Tim. 1:6). The gift of leadership must be exercised, not shunned. The leader that is captivated by his assignment, who really knows he is where God wants him, will have untold fulfillment and happiness. The "greener grass elsewhere" idea has no place in the life of the leader.

When we dedicated our $14 million complex in October 1985, Dr. Schuller was our guest speaker. He spoke on "Faith," the theological term for "Possibility Thinking." It is faith that moves mountains, forges rivers, achieves the impossible. I am grateful for the influence of the life, the books, the institutes and the inspiration of Dr. Robert Schuller. The stories that are being written around the world of what the church is becoming, can be written in part because of his influence.

—GLEN D. COLE, *senior pastor, Capital Christian Center, Sacramento, California.*

"CATCHING A VISION
FOR GROWTH"

I am eager to share my thoughts about this book, an important map for me in my leadership of Saint Paul's Church. It has been a very important tool as I looked at the possibilities within this very vibrant and caring Christian family.

I accepted the call of the vestry of Saint Paul's Church in December 1978 and came here with a great deal of enthusiasm and resources on how to lead a parish. What I was to discover is that they were not adequate to strengthen this ministry. I was classically trained and had 11 years pastoral experience in college ministry and parish work. I also had a strong background in counseling.

What I remember reading early on in my work in Walnut Creek was a paper written by the Alban Institute which indicated that the most effective pastor could only work well with 150 persons. I had a congregation of 700 and realized that my life with most of them would be highlights—personal crises, weddings, baptisms. This premise troubled me, yet I did't know then the most effective way to minister to this family.

At the end of my first year, I felt as if I was looking through the lens of a sophisticated camera with no clue how to focus it. At the same time I wondered what kind of continuing education I should take that year.

For some time I had been watching "The Hour of Power" on TV. On one telecast, Dr. Schuller interviewed Wilbert Eichenberger, who was for many years the director of the Institute for Successful Church Leadership. "Ike" spoke about an on-campus seminar which would be held in January, 1980. I found myself writing down the address and soon I was enrolled in the seminar. When asked about where I intended to take my continuing education, I often sidestepped the issue, because Bob Schuller was not normally well received in my tradition.

So I made the journey to Garden Grove and, yes, I was amazed, challenged and renewed in my ministry. I came to respect the work of the Institute, especially the leadership of Dr. Schuller. Supporting his ministry during those four days was Ray Lindquist, former pastor of Hollywood Presbyterian Church; Robert Merkle, director of counseling at the Crystal Cathedral; and Peter Wagner, a well-known authority in the arena of church growth.

To be in that community of faith was so powerful! The content was biblically based, and it caused me to look at how I had been giving leadership to my ministry. For the first time I understood in my heart Ephesians 4:11-13 where St. Paul speaks of equipping God's people. I heard from Ray Lindquist the necessity for bringing a definite commitment to the preaching ministry. I had long stood in a liturgical tradition which I felt could carry the worship. Ray asked us to consider the possibilities that renewal could be part of our preaching. It was a new beginning for me in praying and preparing my Sunday messages.

The four days were turbulent and yet encouraging. The lecture on the seven basic principles of retailing were revolutionary but accurate. I was wisely given solid counsel by the staff at the Institute to marinate and reflect on the principles I had learned. Unfortunately those words went unheeded. I came home with a tremendous enthusiasm and drive and began to force-feed my leadership team—vestry and staff. Some liked the diet, others became nauseated and some could not stand the fare. My impatience and insensitivity led to some bitter moments for me and members of my parish family. I made many mistakes and most of the mistakes were colossal. It has been difficult for some of our folks and for me.

As I look back at that moment, were I to do it again, I would take greater care in my initial equipping of people in the principles the book promotes. I would spend more time in assisting people to understand my focus and the direction in which I was intending to go. What is clear to me is that our journey since January 1980 has been a tremendous growth experience for this community.

I have the privilege of working among very talented and committed people. They are bright, caring and have strong feelings about the direction we should be going. They want caring leadership that has vision and a clear purpose. What I have been able to do is the result of their catching a vision for growth which would have as its primary goal a deeper relationship with our Lord. I believe that Dr. Schuller's book is a vast and comprehensive navigational tool for one who is considering or is committed to growth. The book will create an environment which is supportive of change and renewal. It does a thorough job of plotting a challenging and reasonable course for action.

To be specific I must say that the chapter on successful retailing is succinct and appropriate for the church community. At first I realized that some people are distressed by the concept of treating our work as one might consider a business enterprise. Yet we are the retail outlets of our denominations. We are the environment where lives are touched and people are renewed. We are the community where support is available to those in great need. In order to meet those needs, we must then investigate our leadership style and make a strong commitment to the biblical concepts of growth and the care of the Body of Christ.

Let me illustrate. With a community of 700 persons, I felt called to develop a lay ministry of pastoral care. If the research of the Alban Institute was correct, then I certainly was not doing the best job of caring for this community. I was able to train 12 people to launch a ministry of pastoral care. After a year of "general practice" they branched out into more specific ministries in our parish and in the community. They were most effective in assisting me with acute pastoral crises as well as doing a very solid job of ministering to shut-ins.

Another development of this ministry was a pilot project in our diocese using lay persons to take Holy Communion to those who could not be in table fellowship with us. Eucharistic Ministers carry the consecrated sacrament each week to those unable to attend. The care and love of our Lord which they bring to those who cannot be with us is vital and gives life to the words of Ephesians 4:12 *(NEB)*, "to equip God's people for . . . service."

Another area of concern was our worship life, especially since we stood in the liturgical tradition where formality and structure can be intimidating and forbidding. Much care has been taken to develop a worship life which will be inviting to newcomers and those not familiar with our liturgical tradition. Again the book challenged me to look at our worship style and try within our liturgy to develop worship which will be positive and inviting.

I also read George Gallup, Jr. and David Poling's book, *The Search for America's Faith.* In it they suggested that the great churches of tomorrow will be built with great worship. That made sense to me in light of what I had read earlier. Coupling these two themes encouraged me to look closely at renewing our worship, a necessary move in building a stronger parish family.

I also felt that our ministry would be blessed if we as a community committed 10 percent of our operating budget to missions and outreach. This commitment began to bear a sturdy harvest. Saint Paul's had had for many years a strong outreach commitment. We were able to strengthen this mission by giving a tithe from our operating budget.

I want to emphasize that *Your Church Has a Fantastic Future!* has been for me a navigational instrument. Dr. Schuller sets a course which needs to be experienced. What is equally valid is that the course and direction can be altered. The principles are primary and substantial if you are willing to consider the renewal of your church family.

Here at Saint Paul's we have strong resources and vision. We are on the threshold of our second century of service. Our first five-year plan has been nearly accomplished. We are now looking at where the Lord is asking us to be next year and the years to come. We have chosen to risk and take action in the name of our Lord.

—STEPHEN MCWHORTER, *rector, St. Paul's Episcopal Church, Walnut Creek, California.*

"REACHING OUT TO THE UNCHURCHED"

A s co-founder of a youth group in Park Ridge, Illinois called Son City, I readily knew and understood the concern of my teenagers desiring a ministry that would reach out to their parents who had been disinterested in traditional churches.

About that time God began to burden my heart to reach out to adults, in a fashion similar to the way teenagers were ministered to through Son City. The big question was, "Could it really be done?"

During my college years, I attended a church growth conference in California led by Dr. Schuller. Coming from a small denominational background, I was overwhelmed by what God had done in that area. The time spent on the West Coast affirmed in my mind that it could be done, and that God was indeed calling me to begin a ministry to the unchurched community.

I began to receive encouragement from co-workers and from a professor who also had a deep love for the church. And I felt reaching out to the unchurched community in a creative way could be honoring to God if it was led properly.

In 1975, a handful of believers who weren't quite sure where this new beginning would take them, ventured out on faith and began a church dedicated to reaching the unchurched person in a contemporary way. Willow Creek Community Church began in a rented movie theater with about 125 people. Today our church continues to grow and enjoy the abundant grace of the Lord. With over 6,000 people in attendance on Sunday mornings, the church now operates from a 113-acre campus in South Barrington, Illinois with a full-time staff of 35.

Since its inception, Willow Creek has adhered to a two-pronged philosophy of ministry. On Sunday mornings, drama, multimedia, contemporary music and practical spoken messages are used to present the ageless truths of Scripture at an introductory level easily understood by unchurched people. The low-key evangelistic environment of these Sunday services stands in marked contrast to the worshipful atmosphere of the Wednesday evening services, where believers gather together for singing, communion and in-depth expository teaching.

—REV. WILLIAM HYBELS, *pastor, Willow Creek Community Church, South Barrington, Illinois.*

"THE WILLINGNESS
TO RUN A RISK"

Seven years ago, our Baptist church in Fort Myers, Florida, was desperate for space. We had three worship services every Sunday morning, three Sunday Schools and still no room to grow. Trying to park at the church was like trying to stuff sardines into a can. We were feeling the effects, as every time we grew, we would back off and then regrow to that same point.

A committee was formed to project needs and growth patterns. After trying to find a way to salvage our old location, the committee suggested that we relocate to a larger property. This recommendation brought great unrest in the church, and I truly feared a split in the membership. Here we were strangled by the lack of space, and half the church did not want to go along with what I, too, saw as the only possible solution.

When it finally came to a vote, we voted to relocate on 20 acres of land that were available three miles away. The vote was by a slim 54 percent majority. I felt miserable, wondering what would happen now.

At that time, I received a sample copy of a new religious periodical. In it was an article on church growth, following and continuing a long interview with Dr. Robert Schuller. What he said in the article came like cool water to a thirsting man. He said, "Every church has a dictator. It is the property. The property dictates what you can and can't do." I knew this statement was true. I had lived with it for the last five years and had tried to "Mickey Mouse" a solution again and again.

Schuller also made the bold statement that 90 percent of the churches in America would have to relocate in order to succeed. I tell you, this was music to my ears. Here I was in a possible split of loyalties, staggering under criticism, doing the only thing I knew to do, and Dr. Schuller comes along and says, "Go for it. It's the only thing that can be done."

In the same magazine, there was an advertisement for Dr. Schuller's seminar on church growth. In desperation, I asked my congregation if I could attend.

What happened at the seminar was the beginning of a new life for me. I believe I was theologically born again when I was 15 years of age. However, this conference gave me a "new birth" of outlook and philosophy and made my faith come alive in a way I had never experienced before.

Just what did I learn that was so revolutionary? I learned *first* that true faith is not just the recitation of beliefs and the proper agreement with sound doctrine. It is also the *willingness to run a risk!* Being a conservative by nature, I knew that risking had always been very difficult. But I became convinced that unless a man would take a risk under the leadership of God, he did not have much faith at all. In fact, before the conference was over, I had determined to put into practice one of Dr. Schuller's mottoes: "I would rather try something great and run the risk of failing, than be afraid to try anything at all." I came home determined to give it my best shot. I had even built up courage enough to go for a million-dollar project.

The *second* life-changing thought was that we must set goals and develop a strategy toward reaching them. Things do not just happen. All things do not come to those who wait. Instead, they come to those who venture forth in a specific direction. "Where there is no vision, the people perish" (Prov. 29:18). I was beginning to see a dream take shape in my heart and mind.

The *third* major lesson I learned was that of "possibility thinking." In order to reach our inspired goals, we must come up with a list of possible ways to approach them. Then we must try out each possibility until we find the one that will work. I made a list of 10 possible ways to obtain a million-dollar building fund.

1. One person could contribute $1 million
2. Two people could contribute $500,000 each.
3. Four people could each contribute $250,000
   and so on.

When I got down to about number seven, it was looking possible:

7. One thousand families could each contribute $1,000.

As I listed the possibilities, even my most skeptical conservatives had to admit, "Well, when you put it that way it does seem more possible."

An important side benefit of this possibility thinking was the effect of creating a positive faith-filled atmosphere in the church. People will rise to a positive challenge much better than they will proceed under negative criticism or threat or guilt motivation. Again I determined to go home and positively reinforce the faith and direction of those who were willing to run the risk of progress. I vowed not to take any potshots at any who were in disagreement or fearful.

The positive emphasis has taken hold on everything we have done. My sermons, our programs everything has been on the note of building up, instructing and encouraging, rather than threatening or criticizing. This emphasis in itself has given us a new congregation and a new spirit that is beyond price.

So many other bits of wisdom were given during the seminar. Much of the philosophy was caught. But I can say that everything Dr. Schuller told us works. He said, "You never have a money problem, only an idea problem. Ideas will attract people's participation and they will want to help by giving." This is so true! And our own experience soon confirmed it.

Dr. Schuller said, "People want to share your dream; big dreams attract big men." How true this has proven to be! God has brought people out of the woodwork almost from the moment I arrived back in Fort Myers from the conference. Some of the greatest men and greatest thinkers in our area have literally flocked to be a part of this dream.

When I arrived home from the conference, I was pleased to discover that my church leaders had only been waiting for me to get the faith to go ahead. They were used to risk. They have to run it every day in their businesses. Perhaps they understood faith better than I did.

Five of them had purchased five more acres of property contiguous with our land, so that we would never become space-locked again. They were ready to go for it, once I could get the vision and courage to try.

We began to plan something in the area of a million dollars, plus the cost of the property. I told our architect what Dr. Schuller had said, "If it doesn't sizzle, it will fizzle." He put plenty of sizzle into the design, brought it back, captivated our imaginations, and said, "It's probably going to cost $3 million." I dared not balk at this point. If I had determined to run the risk of a million, what was 2 million more? Well, before the project was over, it ran $6.5 million, counting the property. But miraculously, the first $3 million toward it was paid in cash.

This project came to a beautiful fulfillment, and we are now ministering to nearly 2,000 people every Sunday. I believe that before long there will be a capacity crowd of 2,800. We are already trying to anticipate future needs before we are faced with them, as Dr. Schuller has taught us to do.

Of course, buildings are only a tool. For us, it was a first necessity. To continue to minister effectively, much more is required. Here again, Dr. Schuller's sound advice has given me direction. He said, "Find a need and meet it, find a hurt and heal it. Make this the strategy of ministry." Jesus said, "If you want to be great, offer service" (see Mark 9:35).

We try to put this into practice in everything we do. We want to serve the different needs of our community. Along with the proclamation ministry of God's Word from the pulpit and the teaching ministry of the Sunday School, we now have an outreach to single adults. We have over 300 single people to whom we are ministering every week in their loneliness and need for direction and spiritual strength. We provide a full-time counselor to the troubled people in our community. We minister to senior adults and young people and children in various ways. We've only just begun, but the pattern is there. Find a need and meet it, find a hurt and heal it, and through meeting people's immediate needs, lead them on to Christ who can meet their greatest need.

And, by the way, our God Himself is such a tremendous, advanced planner. He must have known all along that our new location out in the boondocks would become the hub of activity for Lee County. One mile further out from us, Westinghouse is starting to build 32,000 executive homes. The woods behind us are coming alive with houses, as the city moves out toward the new international airport that has just been completed. I'm so glad we dared to try and follow our God!

At age 50, I have become a dreamer—not a day-dreamer, but someone who realizes that without a vision, God's people and God's work perish. The way God gets His work done is to give someone a dream and to help him fulfill it. I had never seen this in Philippians 2:13, until Dr. Schuller pointed it out so eloquently. "For it is God who is at work in you both to desire (dream) and to do (accomplish) His good pleasure" (author paraphrase). God gives us a dream and helps us to fulfill it.

We are now dreaming toward the future. The church family is beginning to pray about goals and sort through possibilities for reaching these goals. Is this now, after all, what the walk of faith is all about? How much more exciting and meaningful life can be when we grasp this concept and when we are grasped by it!

—JAMES O. HOLBROOK, *pastor, McGregor Baptist Church, Fort Myers, Florida.*

"A BIG HEART AND A BIG FAITH FOR GOD"

Ten years ago, I heard Dr. Robert Schuller say at his leadership conference, "The greatest churches in the world are yet to be built!" That statement triggered much excitement in my heart and mind as I began to think about all the great churches in the world.

I began to ask, "Why not?" God is certainly not limited to doing things just as He has in the past. God is capable of doing more than He has ever done, if somehow He could infuse a person's life with wisdom, faith and determination to do something significant with his life through a local church. At that point something very dramatic happened for me, and the story of Prestonwood Baptist Church is but the unfolding of that thought stimulated by Dr. Schuller, his life, his books and his remarkable success for God.

In 1977, I went out to a new part of Dallas and looked at a piece of vacant property. That property represented what was going to become one of the most significant corners in our city. The eight-and-a-half acres cost $500,000—more than any other church in our denomination had paid to start a brand new church.

I had never started a church before. I did not know how to do it. Minister friends advised me not to start a church in that part of our city because "people in that part of Dallas don't go to church." I was already pastor of Northway Baptist, a church in Dallas that had become very successful and had grown to over 4,000 members in a short period of time. It was located 10 miles away.

The task from a human perspective seemed more than I could possibly ever do. But this question kept coming to mind, "What does God want me to do with my life?"

Even though I was pastoring Northway Baptist, I began the "Prestonwood Dream" in 1977 with a small handful of people meeting in a rented gymnasium. I stood to my feet in that first service and said, "I believe that God is going to build one of the truly great churches in America, beginning today! Will you join me in this great dream and vision and work for God?"

On that first cold Sunday in February, 1977, 25 people joined hands with me and said, "Bill, we'll help you accomplish this great work for God."

For two years I pastored the Northway Baptist Church and this brand new church, Prestonwood Baptist Church, preaching twice each Sunday in each location, four times per Sunday. In January 1979, I resigned my comfortable growing church to take this small group of people in far North Dallas as their permanent and full-time pastor.

One-hundred-and-fifty people were present to worship on that Sunday in January 1979. Now, seven years later,

we have a beautiful 4,000-seat worship center, two services on Sunday and a combined worship in excess of
5,000 people. Our annual receipts are in excess of $9 mil-
lion and we are adding over 1,600 new members per year.
For the last four years we have been recognized as the
fastest growing Sunday School in the Southern Baptist
Convention of over 38,000 churches. Our staff includes 18
ministerial associates with a total of over 90 on our entire
staff. We have built additional buildings and purchased
additional property and now have a combined asset value
of over $30 million.

The beautiful thrill about this story is that "We've Only
Just Begun." Our visionary plans include doubling again in
the next five years in every area of church-growth life. We
are in one of the most beautiful and dynamic cities in
America, and we are confident that God is calling us to this
challenging task of building one of the truly great churches
in the world today.

Let me share some of the beautiful principles God has
used so effectively to inspire me through the leadership
and ministry of Dr. Robert Schuller.

We are committed to reaching the unchurched. We
believe that there are over 100,000 unchurched people
within a 15-minute radius of our church location. I ask,
"God, is it asking too much to help us reach at least 10
percent of these unchurched people in our community?"

Our church leadership and staff believe that this is just
the starting point, and our goal is to reach 10,000 in worship attendance by 1990. We are confident that this is a
realistic goal and would be great for God in every way. We
are right on schedule in accomplishing this goal, and daily I
pray, "God, what is our next challenging goal beyond the
10,000 when it is reached?"

Although we are proud of our beautiful worship facilities and buildings, we are not married to the buildings and are willing to do anything necessary to provide programs and facilities to reach even more in the years ahead.

This basic commitment to reach the unchurched reflects itself in everything we do as a church. My messages are based on my understanding of the needs of people. At times there are some who suggest that I be deeper and more theological and exposition-oriented in my Sunday morning preaching. I continue to feel pressed by God to bring messages relating biblical principles to the practical areas of people's needs and frustrations. God is using this to help us reach unchurched people; we probably reach more non-Baptist people than any church in our denomination in the city.

I am certainly proud of our denomination, but I am aware that unchurched people couldn't care less about becoming a part of any denominational institution. They are hurting and are anxious to find someone and some place that can help them today with their daily frustrations.

Our commitment to the unchurched has also affected our style of architecture. The colors are warm and the style is comfortable, open and inviting. The worship center suggests dignity with informality and spontaneity. It is a place where people can feel comfortable meeting, visiting and enjoying the smiles, greetings, warm handshakes and sense of God's presence.

We are committed to the principle of visionary and creative planning. I often look at our committees who are making major decisions and say, "If money was no object, what would we do for God in this situation?" It is amazing how that attitude lifts the eyesight and the vision of the people as we think in terms of the resources of God being a channel through people whom He can trust. Dr. Schuller has often said that big ideas attract financial support, and that has been proven repeatedly in our church as we have challenged our people to do something big and great for God.

A year-and-a-half ago we started a television ministry. We announced to the church we believed that it was God's will to do so. We did not know where the fund would come from, but we did know we needed a million dollars. At the close of one of our services a man came forward and said, "God has impressed me to give a million dollars to the church for this new ministry." Although that is most unusual in terms of the amount, it is not unusual in terms of the kind of support that we have been able to gather for our creative and faith-stretching ideas that have become realities week after week.

I am confident that there are no limits with God and that He is anxious to show His power through the faith and commitment of His people who are willing to plan and to trust with a big heart and big faith for Him.

We are committed to aggressive and well-planned goals in every area of the life in the church. Church growth is no accident. Goals must be specific, aggressive, God-honoring and always based on the needs of people. Whenever staff members suggest a program, I always ask, "What need will this meet in the lives of people?"

Goals remind us how to pray and how to evaluate the progress of God's work in our lives. Before we ever develop our budget for the year I ask our staff members to give me their spiritual and numerical goals as they have planned for the new year.

We constantly analyze every area of the life of the church. For the past five years our church has had an average of 39 percent growth rate annually which means, if that growth rate continues, by the year 1990 we will have over 30,000 members in our church. If our growth is only 15 percent per year, we will have approximately

12,000 members by 1990. We set goals in every area in the life of the church—worship service, Sunday School enrollment and attendance and church membership enrollment. Keeping these aggressive goals ahead of us reminds us of what we have to do in terms of providing space and leaders to implement the success of these goals.

We are also committed to making our church visible as is suggested so often by Dr. Schuller. We have become visible by choosing an outstanding location which is a heavily traveled intersection of the rapidly growing, far North Dallas area. We also become visible through our regular mass mail-outs which we develop regularly throughout the year in an attractive way to advertise our church and its programs. These are well designed, tastefully done and sent to 70,000 to 80,000 residents to attract attention to our church and its interest in their needs. We also advertise regularly in the newspaper about our church, its ministries and especially our TV program that reaches throughout the North Texas area to thousands of homes. This gives our church and ministries exposure as well as visibility.

Two years ago, we developed another program to attract visibility and attention to our church through a special concert ministry called "Saturday Nights in Dallas." We invite major Christian artists from all over the nation each month to perform and have attracted thousands of unchurched people and other prospects to our worship center. Many of these have come back to participate in our regular Sunday worship services and eventually determine to make their commitment to Christ and become a part of our church.

We are committed to giving people encouragement and hope about the daily problems of life and to affirm them as valuable human beings whom God loves and wants to redeem and to use in a special and significant way. Losers can become winners, and failures can become successes as they learn the beautiful relationship of faith in Jesus Christ. The spirit of Prestonwood is definitely one of positive excitement about God and the possibilities in the lives of every individual. There is a natural and beautiful change in lives that are extended and committed to Him.

Prestonwood is committed to the premise that Christian involvement in ministry is more important than membership on a church roll. I sincerely believe that where there is genuine faith there is a desire to serve Christ in some form of personal ministry. We continue to provide opportunities through special programs, outreach opportunities, committees and ministries so that people can feel a part of the Prestonwood spirit. We believe that until they begin to serve they never really grow in their faith. So we must take initiative to provide opportunities for them to serve. When our new members join each week we always show them how to get involved in some form of ministry.

We are committed to helping people feel at home and welcome whenever they come to worship. Our greeters, ushers, parking committee and entire membership respond aggressively, enthusiastically and warmly to one another each Sunday as they meet. I am confident that the atmosphere of worship starts when we enter the church grounds, and the spirit of faith, love for Christ and desire to help and love one another is an ingredient that the world cannot duplicate. Worship should not only be serious but fun and enjoyable, and people should feel a certain spiritual excitement whenever they meet to worship.

We are committed to many aggressive and creative outreach programs to reach unchurched people. We have Bible studies in country club bars, movie theaters, cafeterias, schools, recreation buildings and many other off-site locations. Once a month we have a breakfast at a nearby country club and invite well-known sports achievers and business achievers to share their testimonies of personal faith to attract the unchurched. We have an annual 10km run which attracts several thousand people on a Sunday afternoon and then we encourage them to hear one of our own members, Dr. Ken Cooper, founder of the Aerobic Center in Dallas, to share his personal faith. We should use every creative means possible to attract people so that we can share the wonderful good news of Jesus Christ.

There is no limit to what can be done if you believe that the sin and the need of man can be met only through personal faith in Jesus Christ. G. Campbell Morgan in *The Great Physician,* said Jesus assumed the same about every person—that they were all lost and needed to be saved, yet He never used the same method on any two individuals. Then Dr. Morgan said that most Christians have reversed that. We are not convinced that all are lost and need to be saved, so we try to use the same method on everyone. We must be creative and aggressive in finding new and innovative ways in communicating the wonderful good news of Jesus Christ to a hungry world.

We are committed to sharing with others the principles of leadership that we have learned. Because of Dr. Schuller's influence in his Leadership Institute, we have developed our own Annual Leadership Conference which is attended by nearly 500 pastors and church leaders throughout America. We are convinced that God wants His churches throughout this great country to be great for Him, and we are committed to assisting others in any way that we possibly can.

Our plans for the future in the area of leadership and church growth include developing a Church Growth Center where pastors and staff can come and learn not only from our own staff, but also from outside professionals.

Giving assistance and guidance to others in the area of counseling, leadership, growth principles, time management, preaching, outreach and promotion is a real goal for our Church Growth Center.

We are committed to seeing our new satellite network, Discovery Broadcasting Network, become an even greater assistance to churches. Our goal is to have over 2,000 affiliates on-line with our network and to assist them through series of programs developed to help pastors and their churches. By providing seminars, lectures, concerts, outstanding Bible scholars and workshops, we can help churches of all sizes be more effective in reaching people, in strengthening their outreach and in supplementing their own programs.

In conclusion, we are committed to the significance and importance of prayer. The Bible says, "With God all things are possible" (Matt. 19:26) and that we should always pray and not faint (see Luke 18:1). The Bible says, "My house shall be called the house of prayer" (Matt. 21:13). We realize that the best human ingenuity and creativity will fail if it is not undergirded by God's presence and power.

We are also aware that limited human ability can be greatly successful if it has been transfused with the power of God and His Holy Spirit through prayer. We believe God wants the best for both. We plan hard, believe big, work aggressively, but we also regularly spend time asking God's wisdom, guidance and strength in all the planning.

I am still convinced that the greatest churches in the world are yet to be built. I want Prestonwood to be one of those churches!

—BILL WEBER, pastor, *Prestonwood Baptist Church, Dallas, Texas.*

Chapter 10

SEVEN PRINCIPLES OF SUCCESS

Much as it may offend many leaders in the Christian Church, the truth remains that the parish church is in the business of "retailing religion." We define retailing as "bringing the goods and services to the consumer," in contrast to wholesaling which packages products or ideas but doesn't deal directly with the customer. In that sense national church headquarters and theological seminaries might be called wholesalers, while the local church is the retailer. So we had better discover the secrets of successful religious retailing!

In the 1950s, the era of church extension, Protestant churches moved into the suburbs to build their new small churches on too-small pieces of ground—snugly hidden from the masses of people on the move in their swift cars. In this same period, the business retailers moved from the downtown Main Street, now dead and defunct, into the suburbs to lease space in exciting new retailing developments called "shopping centers."

The birth and rise of shopping center retailing is one of the phenomenal successes of American business in the twentieth century. All successful shopping centers meet the basic principles for successful retailing, which are as follows:

One: Accessibility

Shopping centers are located at major highway inter-changes or at the junctions of major streets or highways. Logically, the first thing a businessman needs is a good road to his place of business. It is obvious that the best product cannot be sold and will not be bought if people can't get their hands on it! So, in putting the church within the heart of the community rather than on a well-traveled artery, the church was violating a fundamental principle of retailing—accessibility.

Two: Surplus Parking

A second principle for success in retailing is surplus parking. Forward-thinking planners talked about "ample" parking. And it is obvious from my review of hundreds of Self-Study Guides from hundreds of churches across America that very, very few churches have *ample* parking. By ample parking, we mean off-street parking spaces for the faithful members of the church who could be expected to attend on an average Sunday.

Successful retailing, however, demands far more than *ample* parking. Successful retailing demands SURPLUS parking! With the development of shopping centers and their acres of *surplus* parking, modern Americans became used to this convenience. And as they have become spoiled by easy parking afforded by the shopping centers, they have become more and more disenchanted, impatient and irritated by the parking congestion they find elsewhere, including that in their own church settings.

Now, the *faithful* had, and still have, a high tolerance level. But if an unchurched person decides to visit a church on a particular Sunday and drives up to the church only to see the entire parking lot filled, with cars parked along the curbs in every direction, the odds are that this person will simply drive on. His body and mind are conditioned by his life-style throughout the week.

In the middle of the week, if he decides to go out to a restaurant for lunch and heads for the Red Lion, only to find the parking lot filled with cars and all the curb spaces taken, he will anticipate that the restaurant is "jammed and service will not be too hot." So he simply moves on to the Black Bull and pulls into the parking lot where there is an empty space.

His behavior pattern, shaped by parking as he knows it in the business world, is not going to change radically on Sunday when he comes shopping for a church—unless he is deeply committed. And the unchurched person whom we ought to reach is not deeply committed at this stage! Surplus parking is an absolute requirement for successful retailing.

To any pastor, I make this firm declaration: if your church does not have surplus parking, you are hurting. You are paying a high price for this lack of parking! It would be much cheaper for you to buy additional property, to build a high-rise structure or to sell out and relocate on larger property. It would be less expensive for you to do this, with a 20- or 30-year loan, than it would be to struggle along in a dying way as you are today!

We faced this problem in our church when our 10 acres became too crowded for two services. Our parking lot was entirely filled with 700 cars, and cars were parked along the curbs. We believed that we had to have surplus parking. As a result, we were determined, if need be, to build a high-rise parking garage. We discovered this would cost $5 a square foot. At that rate, we concluded it would be cheaper to buy an adjoining 10 acres of ground zoned for costly commercial purposes. We did secure 10 additional acres at a cost of a million dollars, or only $2.50 a square foot! And we have all the frontage rights, street rights and air rights as well.

As soon as we purchased the additional acreage, we increased our parking to 1,400 cars, and the growth of the church with this additional *surplus parking* was phenomenal. Attendance rose astronomically! We discovered that many older people had stopped attending church *regularly* when they felt they might not be able to find parking space. Many of the faithful began to become *less* faithful when they began to worry about finding a place to park. Surplus parking, I repeat, is an absolute requirement for successful retailing in America today.

I feel so strongly about surplus parking, I would say it is the number one criterion that must be met in order to grow. The truth is, you need surplus parking before you need pews! You may have a beautiful sanctuary, with marvelous pews and a gorgeous organ and a fantastic choir and an exciting preacher, but if people can't park their cars, they will never stop and come in.

The opposite is also true. If there is surplus parking, they will stop their cars, they will attend services, and a certain percentage will remain if the program is effective. The first thing you need, before anything else, is surplus parking! Get them to park their cars, put their keys in their pockets, and you have them for a Sunday morning!

Three: Inventory

The third principle for successful retailing is inventory.

The Garden Grove campus provides ample parking for all.

If I am out shopping for a shirt, I inevitably head for a particular department store. Located in a shopping center right off the freeway, it's easy to get to. I know I can always find a parking space without driving around and around. And I know they will have the shirt that I want: the neck size, the sleeve length and the color. Time is too valuable to waste making a trip only to find they don't have the goods. Customers go where the business has a reputation for having a wide inventory range.

This is precisely the problem of the small church. Too many persons find that the church, small and beautiful, "just doesn't have what they are looking for." Perhaps they are single adults in their 20s and there is no program for them. Perhaps the church expects them to join the *one single adult* group which includes people in their 40s and 50s. Or the unchurched family is suddenly beginning to get interested in finding a church that has an exciting youth program. The church that is large enough to have the inventory to meet almost every conceivable human need is a church with a fantastic future!

Four: Service

The next principle for successful retailing is service. Accessibility, getting to the place; surplus parking, providing a modern convenience; and a good inventory—all of these are principles for successful retailing. But ultimately the service department is what will make the retailers succeed year after year. If you purchase an item and find out that the business will let you down when you need it serviced, the odds are that you'll be slow to go back there. They may lose you as a customer.

Does your church give good service? Remember, you have to have the service. And, in the churches, that means a trained laity. You can't have a successful church without trained lay people.

The job description of our key staff men is *to recruit, train and motivate the lay people* to call on the unchurched, to keep calling on people after they've joined the church, to telephone and counsel the people who have problems, to do the work of education. That's what is often called the "enabling ministration." And it's also called service!

Five: Visibility

Your church needs visibility. You have all these things: accessibility, parking, inventory and trained service people. But you have to have visibility, too. People who need what you have also need to know that you're in business and that you've got the product.

If they don't know you're in business and don't know that you have what they need and want, obviously you can't help them and you're not going to grow. This means, among other things, that you have to advertise. It's amazing how the Holy Spirit can use advertising power!

How much of your budget is spent on advertising? Please notice that we are discussing principle 5. After all, you can't advertise unless you've got the product and the inventory first. And you can't over-advertise.

I don't think there's a church in America that spends more on advertising than we do. Personally, I've had a lot of exposure, press coverage, television interviews, radio time—all of these. No church buildings have been more photographed than those on our campus in Southern California. But we know we are not over-advertised.

Some years ago I took an airplane from New York to Los Angeles and then took a limousine from the International Airport to the Disneyland Hotel in Anaheim. From the hotel, I took a cab to my home in northwest Santa Ana. I didn't know the cab driver, and as we were driving along the Santa Ana Freeway, I thought, "I'll have a game with him."

So I asked, "What's that building over there with the cross on top?"—pointing to our church tower.

Do you know what he replied?

"That's a Catholic hospital," he said.

"How long have you been driving a cab?" I asked further.

"Seventeen years."

"Where?"

"Right around here in Anaheim and Garden Grove."

Imagine that! A cab driver in our immediate area for 17 years, and all along he thought our church was a Catholic hospital!

I tell that story often, and at one of our Institutes a young minister taking a cab back to catch his plane home decided to play the same game with his cab driver.

"What's that big building with the cross on top?"

The driver told him, "A mortuary!"

Unbelievable!

Visibility—they've got to know you're there, know what you are and know that you have what they need and want.

Six: Possibility Thinking

Even if you already have the other five principles operating for you, you still need possibility thinking in your church leadership.

What is possibility thinking? It's having the right value system, asking the right questions and making the right decisions. You see, once your value system is straight and clear, you simply reduce it to the right questions. Then decision making is easy.

In our case, our value system is service to Christ and our fellowmen. And we've reduced our value system to three questions. Let's say somebody in our church gets a great idea. On our church board it is heretical for anyone's question to be: "What will it cost?" Why? Because we're not in a profit-making business. That's not our value system.

But we do ask three other questions:

Would it be a great thing for God? If we get an answer yes, we move to the second question:

Would it help people who are hurting? We ask this because if we think it will only be a great thing for God and will not really help people who are hurting, then it is probably a pie-in-the-sky, pietistic, heavenly-minded-but-no-earthly-good idea. Besides, if it doesn't really meet a practical human need in the here-and-now, we probably won't be able to sell it anyway. We will not be able to make it go.

If we get a yes answer to those first two questions, we ask the third question:

Is anybody else doing the job? If they are—forget it! Help them, cooperate with them, but don't compete with them. That is, unless they are doing the job in a clumsy, ineffective way or they don't want to cooperate with you. Then, if you know you could come in and do the job right, okay, do so.

Those three are the only questions we ask. That's possibility-thinking leadership.

After we get the right answers to these three questions, what do we do? We make the necessary decisions and go on to find solutions to the problems involved. That's possibility-thinking leadership.

Remember, indecision can fatigue you to the point where you will not be able to think or dream up solutions to problems. I believe it is better to a make a wrong decision than to make no decision at all. Why? Because if you make a wrong decision and learn from it, you will make another decision—a better one.

You dream, you make a commitment. You dream, you make a decision. That's possibility-thinking leadership. Believe it is possible. Inch by inch, anything's a cinch. And all you need to get started are ideas, good ideas.

Seven: Good Cash Flow

Although money is never the first problem to be faced, it is obvious that to succeed in retailing you need good cash flow. I want to say something at this point about financing: *don't be afraid of debt, but understand what debt is!*

Let me illustrate this point from my own experience. When I left Western Seminary and went to my first pastorate in Chicago, Illinois, I lived in the church parsonage. It was heated with coal, and when October came, I needed coal for the furnace. One of the men in the church said, "Well, it'll take about five tons of coal to get you through the winter. At $15 a ton, that's $75."

I didn't have $75 so I called up the coal yard and asked, "Will you deliver five tons of coal?"

"Yes."

"Will you charge it, please?"

"Oh, we don't charge coal."

"You're kidding!"

"Oh, no, not at all. Guess you'll have to borrow it from the bank."

I hung up.

At the bank, I asked, "Would you loan me money for coal?"

"Oh, no," the banker replied, "we don't loan money for coal." What he didn't say, and what he meant was, "You're only 22 years old and you're new at all this, so you don't know any better." Then the banker said, "I tell you what, Rev. Schuller. I'll loan you money for coal this time, but never again."

"Why not?" I asked.

"Well," he explained, "you will burn up that coal. If you don't pay us back our $75, what do we get in return? Nothing—it's all gone up in smoke."

That banker then gave me some of the soundest advice I've ever received: "Never borrow money for coal. You want to borrow money for a car—for a house—come to us. And all we will say is, 'Can you make the monthly payments?' If you've got the cash, or the salary coming in to make the monthly payments we'll loan you money on that house or car.

"Then if you can't pay the mortgage back, we take the house or the car and sell it. If there's any money left over after we get paid, you get it. We call that equity.

"But," he went on, "never borrow money for the gasoline you put in your car. Never borrow money for the tires you put on the car. Never borrow money for the spark plugs. *Never borrow money for coal.*"

Now that's a fundamental principle. We borrow money for this church, but we don't borrow money for coal! We borrow money for everything that has collateral, nondepreciable value. But we don't borrow money for our television ministry, for interest on the capital debt, for salaries or for utilities. That's coal money. That's gasoline. That's tires.

Before you borrow money to expand, build up your

income to the point where you can afford to borrow the funds. This means that you must build up your cash-flow base so that you can at least be sure you can pay the interest and the utilities of the expansion. If your cash flow is built so you can handle these items, then you can expect the added crowds that come—because of the expanded service—to take care of the capital depreciation of the principal.

Follow these procedures, and your net worth will go up! And then you will not really have any debts. You will have liabilities, but you'll also have a positive net worth.

Raise men and you'll raise money!

Waldo Werning, perhaps the foremost authority on church funding, said it: "Raise men—lift them up! Inspire their spirits! And they'll support your ever-increasing cash needs!"

What I have told you here is, in essence, the financing cash flow of the program we use in this church, and it's been successful. But to achieve the same success, you must also maintain these same disciplines. Do so, and you'll find the solution to your church money problem and cash-flow problem.

It is true, by the grace of God, that some churches are enormously successful without meeting these basic retailing principles. it is also true that no church can be permanently successful by ignoring these fundamental principles of successful retailing.

I have sometimes described the Crystal Cathedral as "a 20-acre shopping center for Jesus Christ." We are located right near a freeway interchange, with acres of surplus parking, with the buildings and the inventory in the form of a program and service designed to meet almost every conceivable need that an unchurched person might seek and expect from a church.

We have not been without our critics. But the truth is, our church program has continued to grow by leaps and bounds while those who have criticized have declined astonishingly.

We are not trying to prove to anyone that we are right. We are only trying to help every other minister in the Church enjoy the same success for Christ's glory that has been ours in His happy work!

ELEVEN ATTITUDES THAT HINDER GROWTH

Let's take a look now at 11 growth-restricting attitudes that are holding back Protestant churches in America today. Based on our Institute's research into static and declining churches, we find 11 attitudes that are preventing many churches from moving ahead. Check these attitudinal obstacles to church growth and see if any of them exist in *your* church.

One: Church Growth Just Happens

Most churches that fail do so simply because they never really planned to succeed! They held the false idea that growth and success "just happens" without cause or effort by the church and its leadership.

The spirit of comity that began in the cooperative Protestant ecumenical movement did so with the best of intentions. As new suburbs were developed across America, Protestant churches of the main denominations agreed that, at all cost, we should avoid mistakes of the other generations—such as having four different denominational churches on four corners of a downtown interchange.

Now, with new cities being developed across the country, we had a great and grand opportunity to start new churches, placing them a mile apart. This sounded wonderful. The only problem was that denominational planning then assumed each church had one square mile of free territory. It assumed that competition is always sinful and destructive. It overlooked the fact that competition is frequently a creative and fruitful goal and causes pastors and lay people to really get out and work!

One minister in our community said to me when I came to start our church, "Schuller, starting a church here is like shaking ripe fruit off a tree. I'm the only church in one whole square mile." When he opened his first unit, it was quickly filled with people. He was overwhelmed by 200 people crowded into an auditorium which seated 150! Immediately he was struck with the false illusion that this was easy and virtually effortless. Unfortunately, that church—quite predictably—failed because of his attitude at the outset.

There should, indeed, be no hostility, proselytizing or undermining of another church. But the cooperative spirit that causes any church to relax becomes failure-prone. I frequently tell people that "I work as if our church were the only church of Jesus Christ in all of Orange County and the salvation of all the souls depended upon us alone."

Now I know full well that there are hundreds of beautiful and wonderful churches in the county that are proclaiming the gospel as effectively, and many more effectively, than we are. But if all churches took the attitude that they, and they alone, were responsible for the whole county, the entire unchurched populace would be so overwhelmed by the dynamism, the energy, the vitality of the Body of

Christ in its witnessing movement that conversions would take place by the thousands!

Two: Detachment from The World

It is still true that too many pastors talk a different language from the man in the street. The pastor's vocabulary is theological, academic and overly orthodox.

One need only look at the average hymn language and understand how meaningless much of the theological language is. "Seraphim and Teraphim" are familiar words from an old, old hymn. But what in the name of seraphim do these words mean to unchurched people?

Assuming that we successfully bring unchurched people into our Sunday morning services, will they understand what we are talking about? If they are biblically illiterate, will they understand the biblical terminology? And if they fail to understand, will they not turn off?

Three: Boredom

Many churches are so dignified they're dull! The music is dull, the messages are dull, the architecture is dull; there is no excitement in the air! The worship service might be described as sleepy, quietly meditative and a perfectly tranquilizing arrangement guaranteed to produce yawning and boredom.

There is absolutely no excuse for the bearers of the good news of the gospel of Jesus Christ to be anything but enthusiastic, exciting and dynamic! If the gospel is truly preached, it will be preached as *exciting* good news! Good news is never dull. If a service is dull, there must be no good news. If there is no good news, there must not be any gospel!

Four: Negative Emotions

The pastor who emphasizes fear, hate and anger instead of faith, hope, love and joy has an emotional problem! If the congregation needs to hear sermons that stimulate the negative emotions of fear, hate and anger instead of responding enthusiastically to rejoicing sermons that stimulate positive emotions, such a congregation is neurotic! The parishioner who does not leave church complimenting the pastor unless the sermon has been delivered with a red face and glaring eye must be a sick person! We cannot expect people to rush in to overflow the churches that generate fear and anger.

Five: Denominational Success

I know a minister, pastor of a Methodist church, who started his young congregation in a growing suburb and organized with a membership of 157 persons after five months. It was so exciting that he said to me, "It's a thrilling work!"

I asked him, "How many of the 157 members transferred from other Methodist churches?"

He answered: "One hundred fifty of them."

I shuddered. I felt that this pastor was depending upon his denominational strength to produce members in the years to come. He knew too well that he belonged to a denomination that numbered its national membership in the millions. The possibility of hundreds of Methodists moving into the growing community in the next 10 years was great.

Today that "successful" church has nearly 1,000 members. The tragedy is that it should have 3,000! It was an instant "success" because of its denominational pull.

But if you depend on transfers for the growth of your church membership, you are doomed to die! No church deserves to grow or live unless its purpose is to win unchurched people to Jesus Christ.

When I arrived in Garden Grove in 1955 with my wife as the only other member, I remembered that I belonged to a small denomination of only 200,000 in America. I calculated that in 10 years I could expect no more than 70 people from my denomination to move into this territory. Therefore, we would never grow unless we could successfully impress and win the 50 percent of the people living in the community who were totally unchurched. This lack of strong denominational backing proved to be the first and greatest blessing our church ever received!

Yes, success that is dependent upon denominational ties can be an obstacle!

Six: Fear of Debt

A fear of increasing indebtedness has kept one church from deciding to borrow the added money to enlarge its sanctuary and improve its parking problem. As a result, the church has not increased but has declined in size and consequently declined in income. If an institution faces a strong growth potential, it almost always pays to borrow the money to expand immediately! Unfortunately, the mortgage-burning ceremony becomes in churches what the gold watch and retirement papers become to the retired person, a symbol marking the end of productivity.

Our policy has been to borrow as much as we could, as fast as we could, to meet needs as quickly as we could. But be careful now and understand what I am saying.

There are some guidelines which are most important as you borrow money:

First, never borrow to the extent that it will whittle away your net worth. Your net worth must always be growing, so as to provide a sound financial base on which to operate.

Second, never borrow money to pay for interest on debt. Before you increase your corporate debt, broaden your financial base to demonstrate a regular cash flow that can at least pay for the added interest cost of the proposed increased debt.

In other words, if you needed another $200,000 to build classrooms or offices and the interest on that new debt would be 10 percent then you would have a campaign to increase your weekly income at least $400 to pay the added annual interest. The cash to reduce the principal could—in most instances—be expected to come from the increased growth resulting from the increased service offered by the expanded facilities built with the increased debt.

To borrow dollars to pay for interest is a proven path to bankruptcy.

Third, never borrow more than you can amortize over a 20-year period. In our budget we have a figure we call debt service. That figure extended over 20 years would totally pay off all our indebtedness.

The truth is, financial debt frequently is a spur to church growth. Members of the church know that their support is needed there, and people need to be needed. As a result, they do not resist maximum contributions. And where their treasure is, there will their hearts be also (see Matt. 6:21).

The files of another church reveal a 22-year-old institution that, for all practical purposes, is a dead church. It had good growth at the outset, continued to increase steadily until it was 10 years old, then leveled off. Growth came to a standstill at that time because the two church services were virtually filled and this meant that there was no longer surplus parking.

About this time, I was called in by the pastor to offer my advice on their developmental planning. I recommended that they contemplate borrowing $200,000 which, at that time, could have been secured at 6 percent interest over a 20-year period. The $200,000 was to be used to build a sanctuary to seat 700 people and to increase their parking by 250 cars.

The response of the church board was, "But we have a $50,000 debt now. We have to wait until we get that paid off, then we will think about borrowing more money." The result was that the church failed to keep up its dynamism. The community got the impression that the church was no longer growing—as, in fact, it was not. The church got the reputation of being static, not moving, not going anywhere, not doing anything. Consequently, growth tapered off.

Now, many years later, the debt is paid off, but the attendance has also declined. The dynamic personalities within the church that made it grow in the beginning moved away in discouragement and attached themselves to institutions that were more alive and aggressive.

Debt consciousness and the fear of debt can kill a church. In the case at hand, the borrowing of another $200,000 would have increased the budget by only $16,000 the first year, enough to cover the first year's interest payment. This would have amounted to a little more than $300 a week. There is no doubt that the enlarged sanctuary, with the additional parking, could easily have brought in $16,000 in the first year!

Seven: Lack of Conviction

At one time, not a few pastors and lay people began to question the reality of God and the authority of the holy Scriptures. The only institution that can grow is the institution that is totally convinced of its ministry and its message. No salesman can sell a product unless he is thoroughly sold on it himself first! No church will grow if it is not uncontrollably enthusiastic about its faith!

Eight: Distracted from Primary Mission

There is no doubt that the pastor of the church must be responsible in offering community leadership. He should be the conscience of the community. The church that exercises its evangelism without seeking to relieve social problems is a lopsided institution.

But church historians may well record that the church in the late 1950s and especially in the 1960s was overly involved in social and political activities to the utter neglect of its mission of seeking to bring the good news of Jesus Christ to unchurched people in the community. In every age and every historical phase, there have been fashions and fads that could easily distract a pastor or his people from their primary mission, which is to preach the good news to hungry hearts.

Arthur F. Burns, former chairman of the Federal Reserve Board, said at Los Angeles on December 7, 1970, while explaining the near disastrous inflation of the 1960s: "Many businessmen became so preoccupied . . . that they lost sight of the primary business objective of seeking larger profits through improved technology, marketing and management. *When talented corporate execu-*

tives devote their finest hours to arranging speculative maneuvers, the productivity of their businesses inevitably suffer, and so does the nation's productivity."

Wise words! During this same period, our finest churchmen were preoccupied with "glamorous," "fashionable" and "speculative merger and maneuvers"— distracted from their primary objective of winning the 100-million Americans who are not Christians!

"To merge two old, declining, denominations is NOT growth!" I declared when in the 1960s the Reformed Church in America was considering merger with the Southern Presbyterian Church. "Take two old, insecure people and let them marry. It may be a beautiful idea but don't expect the union to be fruitful with new children!"

Nine: The Controversial Pulpit

Controversy has been a major cause of membership decline in Protestanism. There is a proper time and place for the church to deal with controversial theological, political, social, biblical issues. But the pulpit is seldom the right time or the right place for the following reasons:

First, the fact that an issue is controversial means that sincere people disagree. Every person deserves to be treated respectfully even if you disagree with him. And you insult his dignity if, behind the shielded protection of a pulpit, you authoritatively challenge his position without, in fairness, giving him a chance to ask questions or share his viewpoint.

And if you ever insult the dignity of a person, that person will not be converted, he'll only be inflamed. At best he'll walk out and never return. At worst he'll become a bitter enemy.

Controversy should only be handled in a setting like a classroom where no person feels he's being indoctrinated without a chance to ask honest questions. In the disastrous '60s two words were "in words" for many churchmen. They were "confrontation" and "dialogue." Crazy! For confrontation always results in polarization and a mental climate where dialogue becomes impossible! Little wonder church membership plummeted!

Ten: Short-Sighted Leadership

Probably the foremost obstacle to church growth that comes to light as we study the hundreds of Self-Study Guides in our Institute for Successful Church Leadership is what might best be termed "short-sighted leadership."

Three-year and five-year pastorates are common, if not average. As a result, the average church has no 10-year plan, no 15-year plan, no 20-year plan. I shall be forever indebted to Dr. Raymond Lindquist, a former pastor of the First Presbyterian Church in Hollywood, who lectured at the seminary when I was a theological student. "Boys," he said, "never take a call to a church unless you can envision spending your life there."

When I came to Garden Grove, it was with the belief that this field would hold enough opportunity for my energies to be released fruitfully for years to come. As a result, I laid out a 40-year plan.

I was 28 when I began the church. My denominational constitution suggested 68 as a retirement age, leaving me 40 years to work in this field. What could I possibly do if I gave 40 years of my energies to one church?

When you have that amount of time, you can start to dream big. In the same manner, an artist who is told to imagine a painting that may fill a canvas 100 feet long by 20 feet high is going to envision a far bigger picture than an artist who is given a canvas only 8 inches by 12 inches in size!

Eleven: Impossibility Thinking

Undoubtedly the most widespread obstacle to success, both inside and outside the church, is what I choose to call "impossibility thinking." Jesus Christ said, "If you have faith as a grain of mustard seed, you will say to this mountain, 'Move hence to yonder place,' and it will move; and nothing will be impossible to you" (Matt. 17:20, *RSV*). You would suppose then that the Church Christ founded would be packed with possibility thinkers! While men of the business world and in the scientific community have been shooting for the moon, the Protestant Church has been inflicted with impossibility thinking.

In an earlier book, I define impossibility thinkers as "people who make swift, sweeping passes over a proposed idea, scanning it with a sharp, negative eye, looking only for the distasteful aspect. They look for reasons why something won't work instead of visualizing ways in which it could work. So they are inclined to say no to a proposal, never giving the idea a fair hearing.

"Impossibility thinkers are people who immediately and instinctively react to any positive suggestion with a sweeping assortment of reasons why it can't be done, or why it is a bad idea, or how someone else tried it and failed or, and this is usually their clinching argument, how much it will cost! They are people who suffer from a perilous mental malignancy I call the impossibility complex. They are problem imaginators, failure predictors, trouble visualizers, obstacle envisioners and exaggerated-cost estimators!

"Their attitude produces doubt, stimulates fear and generates a mental climate of pessimism and fatigue. They are worry creators, optimism deflators, confidence squelchers. The end result? Positive ideas buried, dreams smashed and projects torpedoed."[1]

The solution? Somehow, Protestanism must experience a revival of possibility thinking, the belief that we are co-workers with an Almighty God who can accomplish anything that would be a great thing for His cause in this world!

Note

1. Robert H. Schuller, *Move Ahead with Possibility Thinking* (New York: Doubleday & Company, 1967), pp. 14-15.

Chapter 12

HOW TO SELL YOUR IDEAS SUCCESSFULLY

You have determined under God to become an inspiring leader of your church. And looking toward the twenty-first century, you have established exciting goals for your church. You have also saturated your mind with the Christ Spirit of possibility thinking.

So how do you go about sharing and successfully selling your ideas to the people who alone can help you make those dreams come true? I can summarize my first 15 years in the Garden Grove Community Church pulpit as time spent primarily in setting goals, testing them before God and then selling them successfully to the people who really did it all.

Steps in Selling Successfully

What is successful selling? It is not manipulation; it is communication. *Successful selling is communicating to people a truth they weren't aware of before.* Now follow these steps:

One: Concentration on the problem

If you don't have a problem, the odds are you won't

move ahead. To try to sell the idea of a new sanctuary if a congregation already has a fine, serviceable facility will not be easy. But let the building burn down and the problem becomes obvious.

So test your idea. Does it really fill a vital need? Does it solve a serious problem? Does it heal a hurt?

Two: Dramatize the problem

Remember this: you will very likely fail in any enterprise that does not offer solutions to real and honest problems. Therefore, possibility thinking is correct when it says that every problem is an opportunity. The only reason we were able to develop the walk-in, drive-in church, internationally pacesetting as it was, was due to the fact that we had a terribly real problem!

After three years of operation, I found myself with a congregation worshiping at 9:30 on a Sunday morning in a beautiful chapel located on a two-acre grassy suburban lot in the heart of the Garden Grove community. At 11 o'clock every Sunday morning, I found myself the pastor of our drive-in congregation meeting in a drive-in theater three miles away on the freeway. We had a major problem.

For future planning we could not envision continuing this arrangement indefinitely. It became unthinkable to contemplate planning future operations along these lines. After all, there were children from the drive-in church families who were attempting to learn their Sunday School lessons around splintery picnic tables, with thumbtacks holding down their coloring papers from strong winds. Unexpected showers would send the little children scrambling, dripping and shivering into the shelter of the family car! So we dramatized these problems.

We dramatized the real honest, human problems: a woman without any legs who could only worship in the drive-in church seated in a little basket! A paraplegic with his wheel chair folded in the back seat. "These people have a right to a church of their own," we suggested. So you must similarly dramatize your problem until it is honestly emotionalized.

Three: Help your people take a long view

Enable your people to see the problem down the long road ahead through projected studies of the future. Show them that the problem will not disappear by ignoring it. Ask the question: Will the problem go away if we do nothing about it?

For instance, we pointed out to our people in Garden Grove that the drive-in theater where we worshiped had refused us a lease for our Sunday use of their facility. We met there on a week-to-week basis only. Any Sunday we might be told that we could no longer conduct church services there. Should that happen and our growing congregation suddenly be evicted, we would become spiritual refugees on the edge of the freeway. What an embarrassment to Jesus Christ's program this would be!

Four: Ask all to give God a chance to work

Yes, ask everyone to join in giving God a chance to work a miracle if this is what He wants. Taking the long look, it was easy to point out that the drive-in theater might not want to keep us on indefinitely as permanent residents. And, as it turned out, this supposition proved correct. For 10 years later, swap meets became a highly lucrative business at this very drive-in, as well as at other outdoor theaters. It was only a matter of time before we would have been moved out anyway.

Cost account the solution to the problem. Ask the question: Will the solution come cheaper if we wait 5 to 10 years? In most cases this will get action NOW! If the ready cash is not available NOW, ask for freedom to find a solution to the money problem.

It is most unlikely that a majority of people would resist a motion to "give God a chance to work a miracle." You may have to communicate to your people an awareness of how the money problem can be met. Here you simply exercise possibility thinking yourself.

Calculate how money can grow. You can begin a fund with $5. Calculate how easy it is to build a fund of $5 into $100. What are all the possible ways in which you could raise money to build a fund to $100 and what are all the possible ways to increase this $100 to $1,000? What if you added $1,000 a year for five years? What if you made it $5,000 a year for 10 years? What if you made it $10,000 a year for 20 years? What if you made it $15,000 a year for 30 years? What does it add up to?

You may have to show them how, if you increase your parking lot by 100 cars, you can increase your church families by 100 families a year, each contributing an average of $600 a year, which adds up to a gross annual added income of $60,000. Multiply this by 20 years and what do you come up with? Actually you should formulate and mimeograph these figures and distribute them to your key people.

Five: Offer creative solutions

Your next step now is to offer various creative solutions to this dramatic, emotional, factual problem. In our case, we called a congregational meeting, and I explained that continuing the routine of conducting two church services in two separate locations was unthinkable. I would not and could not contemplate being the pastor of two separate, growing churches. I had been called to organize *one* church.

I offered three solutions:

Solution One: Drop the drive-in ministry work and let the sick and the handicapped, the old and the infirm go home and listen on the radio the way they do all across America.

Solution Two: Separate the two institutions into two separate organizations, each with its own pastor. I would resign from both situations so both groups could start fresh without my personal leadership.

Solution Three: I offered to merge both churches into a single new creative development to be known as a "walk-in, drive-in" church.

I then proceeded to show all of the advantages of the third alternative. I pointed out how this could become a truly large church with a great program for people of all ages. If the churches separated, I told them that it was my opinion that the little church in Garden Grove would never be able to expand beyond its two acres and would always be a mediocre, medium-sized church in an ever-growing town. "It would be like shooting elephants with a .22 single-shot rifle," I warned.

I emphasized that if we merged, we could build something great, something powerful, something pacesetting, something exciting and something that could be helpful to thousands of people. At this juncture, I opened the floor for questions.

Not surprisingly, one of the first questions raised was: "Reverend Schuller, where do you expect to get the money to buy the land, not to mention all of the buildings, that you're talking about?"

To which I replied—as you must reply—"Our job is to be great thinkers for God. We must trust God to provide if He wants to have this facility. Our God is not a pauper.

"My Bible says that 'my God shall supply all your need

according to his riches' (Phil. 4:19). The Bible also says, 'If you have faith as a grain of mustard seed, you will say to this mountain, "Move . . . ," and it will move; and nothing will be impossible to you' (Matt. 17:20, *RSV*).

"The question is not: *'What will it cost?' The all important question is: 'Would it be a great thing for God?'* If so, I am sure that He will find a solution to the financial situation if we give Him time."

A few other questions were raised. At this point Dr. Wilfred Landrus, one of my leading laymen, rose and quietly read from a small slip of paper a resolution he had been scrawling with a ball-point pen. His resolution read: "I move, Mr. President, that this congregation go on record under God as favoring the merger of the two churches in a new development."

Immediately that positive motion became the leadership of the moment, proving again that the man who makes the positive motion is the leader. It was immediately seconded. Then there was time for discussion.

Parliamentary procedure was adhered to rigidly under my chairmanship. No one was permitted to speak more than twice for or against the proposal. The motion was then put to the house. It was passed by a vote of 54 to 48. The decision was made. The idea was virtually sold!

Six: Alert top lay leaders in advance

Make sure the top positive thinkers in your congregation are alerted in advance and are behind you all the way. How? By tapping the most trusted, competent, positive, enthusiastic lay leaders and privately advising them of what "God is leading you to lead with." Prayerfully draw them into a circle of mutual confidence and trust.

Ask them for their support. Tell them you need them. You do! Tell them God needs them. He does!

Be honest; don't be a manipulator. Tell them why you have called them into this inner circle. "I trust you. You are big persons. You are able to envision possibilities; you are able to imagine solutions to problems; you are able to move forward with a daring faith.

"You are the kind of men and women needed to fill the lay leadership vacuum in this church. God is counting on you. I am counting on you!"

Seven: Present your recommendation; Win a decision for commitment

Now present your recommendation to the official board or to the congregation and make the decision a definite commitment. First, be assured of the support of your key lay leaders. Then, guided by their wisdom, lay the idea before the board and one of the positive laymen will make a motion, while a second supports it. The idea is now about to become a decision!

Reread again the steps of how to sell your ideas successfully. Always begin with *Step 1:* Make sure your idea solves a real problem. Talk about the problem. Always follow this with *Step 2:* Dramatize the problem as extensively and emotionally as possible. Follow this immediately with *Step 3:* Take the long view of the situation.

Now move on to *Step 4:* Show your solution and ask people to join in giving God a chance to work His miracle. You are then ready, presumably, with key laymen deeply involved in advance for your strong leadership thrust.

In my personal experience, I have always found it very helpful and advantageous to give the initial promotional thrust to the entire congregation in the form of a sermon. My congregation expects me to be their leader. They are not offended if I give a sermon and show the problems that are facing our congregation today, how these problems are going to get worse and how there are several solutions, but here is the best one of all!

I advise them that this is what we're going to give God a chance to do! I tell them we're going to move ahead in faith and expect miracles to happen! A positive, inspiring and highly motivating sermon leads to action.

You'll have to judge the temper of your own situation and determine if this is the way you wish to handle it, or if you prefer to have your official decision-making board approve it first and then present it to the full congregation in the form of a sermon. With the purchase of the $1-million, 10-acre piece of property adjoining our original property, I took it first to the church board. Then, with their approval, I presented it in the form of a sermon to the congregation. It was the right way to handle it at that time.

The next steps are very simple. All you have to do is to start a fund if your idea is going to cost money. And then hire an architect if your idea calls for the construction of a building.

Steps in Handling Impossibility Thinkers

"But how do you handle the impossibility thinkers? What do you do with the obstacle people who insist on obstructing your plan, your project, your dream?" This is a question I am often asked by ministers who attend our institutes. In answer, I say, "Make sure, first of all, that Christ is the head of your church and in the master role over your personal and private life. It is my belief that sometimes God allows our dreams to be frustrated because we are not ready for success if it happens immediately."

Here is my testimony:

I had successfully "sold" the concept of a walk-in, drive-in church to the congregation. They voted by a slight majority to adopt the policy of working toward a merged church. Up to that point, I had succeeded.

However, the opposition was deep-seated. Its members refused to accept defeat. They were instrumental in bringing in the first staff addition to our church, a man who was not my personal choice. The opposition gravitated toward him and used him as their negative leader.

Nothing is more difficult than trying to maintain the momentum of success-producing enthusiasm when there is a serious split within a church. Well, I had this experience! Those were the dark, despairing months of my life.

When I could tolerate it no longer, I prayed a very deep prayer, "God, I can stand no more of this. I don't know who is for me and who is against me. I am asking you for your help. If you want this church that we envision to be built, then you will have to solve this problem. I can't."

The next thought that flowed into my mind was the Bible verse—and I heard it clearly emphasized: *"I will build my church"* (Matt. 16:18).

I leaped to my feet, and perhaps over-dramatically, threw a gesture to my empty office chair and said, "Then, Jesus Christ, do it! You be the head of this church. You take command. You solve the problems. And you handle the problem people. And if you don't mind, Lord, I'm going on vacation. I'm tired."

When I returned four weeks later, I discovered that the staff minister had been called to another field of work and had accepted the assignment. The opposition had lost its leadership. But the parting pastor challenged the congregation to "beware of a man who only preaches positive thinking and doesn't preach the full gospel of Jesus Christ." So the obstacle people continued to hang in there until they saw themselves truly defeated.

The truth is that God used that difficult experience to wrestle ultimate leadership from me! I think I really thought *I* was the *leader*. From that moment on, the center chair at my board meeting has been empty. *Christ* is the real Chairman of the Board.

How do you handle negative-thinking obstructionists? Begin by surrendering your innermost self—and your church—to the Lordship and leadership of Christ. Now follow these tips on handling impossibility thinking laymen.

One: Don't attract them to the church

You attract negative thinkers by preaching negative sermons. I think of one minister of a particular church that has been analyzed by our Institute. This minister's sermons are consistently negative. For about two years, he was anti-Catholic. Then, for several years, he shifted to anti-Communism. Next he became anti-ecumenical. Finally he became anti-glossolalia.

During every one of these phases, he attracted into his congregation people who were inflamed against certain issues. That's like putting carcasses in your backyard and then wondering why you attract vultures instead of hummingbirds. You need to hang out hummingbird feeders to attract hummingbirds.

Two: Don't feed them

If you do have impossibility thinkers in your church, don't feed them. Then they will wander off in their hunger. If you are not already aware of it, you will soon discover that most impossibility thinkers are neurotic negativists. A neurotic negativist needs to be fed a negative sermon constantly. Stop preaching negative sermons, and negative thinkers will soon become "hungry for the whole gospel."

What they really mean is "hungry for *bad* news"! If you don't provide it, they'll wander off to some pulpit-pounder down the street.

Three: Don't build a stage for them

If you have these negative people in your church—and every church does—don't build a stage for them; don't create an opportunity for them to sound off. *Robert's Rules of Order and Parliamentary Procedure* is so designed that the president of the corporation and the chairman of the board can keep impossibility thinkers from disrupting a meeting or taking the reins.

You simply do not appoint an impossibility thinker as the chairman of a committee. It's amazing how many ministers do this, thinking they will "win the man's favor and convert him." That's like suggesting that your daughter marry a crook in order to convert him.

You build a stage for impossibility thinkers every time you give everyone in the congregation the chance to express their opinions on a controversial issue. You build a platform for the impossibility thinker to sound off, to gain support for his negative position when you publicly ask for everybody's opinion on an upcoming decision. Furthermore, this is not "democracy." This is indecisive, uncertain, insecure leadership.

Four: Know when and how To confront obstacle people

When and *how* should obstructionists be confronted? And *who* should do the confronting? To find the answers to these questions, go to the one, two or three most loyal, most Christlike positive thinkers in your congregation and seek their advice.

Generally speaking—and it would be a rare exception

when this principle would not hold—the pastor should never confront the negative-thinking, obstructionist layman. Another layman should do the confronting and spare the pastor—not for the selfish reason that a pastor is unwilling to suffer the scars of battle, but for the sake of the church.

There are times when a confrontation must take place. This should be done by the strongest and most prominent, positive-thinking layman in the church. When it is done and how it should be handled is something that must be prayerfully thought through in every individual case. Perhaps the impossibility thinker may have to be frankly advised to "resign from the church board." If the decision has been made to move ahead on a major project or projects, he has no right to continue to be an obstructionist!

In many instances, the obstacle person can be replaced by a full-time or a part-time staff member who is hired to fill the slot that the impossibility thinker occupies. And, of course, your bylaws will specify that the senior pastor approve all additions to the staff and will have a hand in selecting them personally. In this way, a positive thinker can be placed in the position.

Five: Attract possibility thinkers

Work hard to attract possibility thinkers and, ultimately, the congregation will be led by possibility-thinking church members. A young minister at one of our Institute sessions returned to his eastern church with great enthusiasm. However, two weeks later, he was rudely treated by one of his church's key laymen.

When the minister complained about the matter to his wife, her reply was, "Dear, you made him into that kind of a person by the kind of sermons you've been preaching ever since you've been here. You've been preaching negative sermons, critical sermons and 'here's-what's-wrong' sermons. He is only giving back to you what you have been giving to him."

Now, this pastor is involved in developing in-depth, possibility-thinking attitudes throughout the church. It's a lengthy procedure, but given enough years, possibility thinkers will be attracted and they will win out.

Six: Put possibility thinkers in power positions

Church bylaws can help you entrench possibility thinkers in power positions. Remember that in your bylaws the minister is an ex-officio member of each committee. The minister also appoints the chairmen of the committees. The bylaws require that no new business will be handled or heard in the board meeting unless it comes as a positive recommendation from a standing or special committee. That means that committee meetings are the place to nip impossibility thoughts in the bud before they reach the church board.

Your bylaws will also specify that you have the freedom to build a staff, subject to the board's approval. You select both the staff and the key men on executive committees. The staff then becomes a committee of its own with the power to offer recommendations to the church board.

If some impossibility thinker speaks up at a board meeting with some negative idea, you as board chairman can handle his suggestion very skillfully and sweetly by "referring the matter" to whatever is the appropriate committee. Or you may decide to refer it to the staff for their study with instructions to report back at a later date. If you fail to specify a time for the report to be returned, the negative proposal can simply die in committee.

Meanwhile, you will make sure that your committees are staffed by powerful possibility thinkers.

Seven: Positive ideas are stronger
Than negative ones

Remember, not only are positive ideas stronger than negative ideas, positive ideas outlive negative ideas. Positive ideas thrive on enthusiasm. And enthusiastic people have more energy, live longer and generate more force than negative-thinking personalities.

Great ideas never die. People may quit on the idea but the idea seldom, if ever, quits by itself. So have faith, my friend!

Eight: Show love for impossibility thinkers

Yes, do keep showing nothing but love for the impossibility thinkers. If you allow hate thoughts, resentment thoughts or other negative thoughts or emotions to dominate you, these emotions will show up in your words or in your life. And you will lose ground as a result. "Whom the gods would destroy, they first make mad" is an old Greek proverb.

Keep cool. Remain Christlike. And the majority who have backed you so far will continue to love you. Your love for the impossibility thinkers may not convert them, but it will keep them from winning added support.

Whatever you do, continue to practice the power of possibility thinking! Keep believing in the promise of Christ who said, "If you have faith as a grain of mustard seed, you will say to this mountain, 'Move . . . ,' and it will move; and nothing will be impossible to you" (Matt. 17:20, *RSV*).

Now, forget about the obstructionists. Go on adding and winning new members to your church. Your new converts will soon outnumber, outvote and overpower the opposition.

Chapter 13

HOW TO MAKE AN INSPIRING IMPRESSION

It was 1955, and I had failed to find an empty hall to rent anywhere in all of Orange County. So I finally turned to a drive-in theater for a place to begin holding Sunday services. Then hearing of this turn of events, the ministers of the First Methodist Church, the First Baptist Church and other established denominational churches of Garden Grove extended their sincere sympathies to me.

Yes, my wonderful friends in the ministerial association genuinely felt sorry for me. Why? In that drive-in theater, I would have no roof over my head, no pews for people to sit in and no classrooms for Sunday School purposes. Moreover, we would be located outside the eastern city limits of Garden Grove.

What Have You Got Going for You?

The other churches all had the advantages of buildings, pews, organ and Sunday School classrooms. And, for the most part, they were located in downtown Garden Grove. Yet even as they were sympathizing with me, I replied,

An Easter morning service, 1955, at the drive-in theater.

"But don't feel sorry for me. After all, I have three things going for me in the drive-in theater that none of you have."

"And what are they?" the pastor of the Methodist Church asked.

"Number one," I answered, "I have superb accessibility. The Orange Drive-In Theatre is right on the Santa Ana Freeway, and that's the heaviest traveled road in the State of California. People can drive 20 miles in a few minutes and be at my church. Nobody has a better road leading up to their front door than I do! And you have to have a road leading up to your front door before you need a building.

"Number two, I have virtually unlimited parking space. I could invite the biggest crowd-getter in the world to speak in the Orange Drive-In Theatre and not have to worry about turning people away. We have parking for 1,700 cars!"

I pointed out that the existing churches in Garden Grove had virtually no parking lots whatever. Furthermore, the seating capacities of their churches were decidedly limited and they wouldn't be able to consider inviting "great crowd-getters" if they wanted to.

"Number three, I have a much larger market than you men do. You are in the heart of one town. I am on a main road which intersects three large cities—Anaheim, Garden Grove and Santa Ana!

"You are at the heart of a town; I am at the heart of a county. So, don't feel sorry for me. I have a vast market of unchurched people to reach. All I have to do now is make a big, beautiful, successful and inspiring impression on all of these unchurched people in the county and we'll build a great church for our Lord."

How Do You Make an Impression?

Some months after we had launched our church services in this drive-in theater, I wrote a letter to Dr. Norman Vincent Peale, the most sought-after speaker in America at that time. I invited him to be a guest speaker in our church some Sunday. *The Power of Positive Thinking* was Dr. Peale's most successful book, and it was on all the best-seller lists at that time.

Inviting Dr. Peale was my attempt to impress unchurched people in my community. I knew that the unchurched people in Orange County were not impressed by my name. I was a nobody. They would never cross the street to come to hear me. But they were reading Norman Vincent Peale.

Somehow I had to make a big, walloping impression on the whole county to let everyone know that (a) I was in business; (b) this was an inspiring business; (c) we were a successful business; (d) we were really going to town and they ought to get on the bandwagon. By inviting Dr.

Peale, I hoped to convey these inspiring impressions to unchurched people in Orange County, California.

I was delighted when Dr. Peale accepted my invitation. The morning of his appearance arrived, and there was bumper-to-bumper traffic up and down the freeway as cars flocked into the Orange Drive-In Theatre. When eleven o'clock arrived, the place was jammed with 1,700 cars, plus cars parked in the aisles. What an enormous array of vehicles! Because of Dr. Peale's presence, the unchurched of our community had also responded to our church's invitation. And they had responded in over-whelming numbers!

It was at this very moment in modern American church history that Dr. Peale was beginning to be the subject of attack by both the conservative and liberal elements of Protestantism. I was warned not to invite Dr. Peale to the church because "the fundamentalists of the area will think that you are not really fundamental." And the friend went on to say, "And the liberals will all make you out as being too conservative."

To all this, I replied, "I am not interested in impressing Christians of the conservative or liberal persuasion. I am here only to impress unchurched people. And Dr. Peale is widely read by unchurched persons.

"Furthermore, I am interested in building a church that can put 'strong wings on weary hearts.' I am also interested in attracting positive-thinking, enthusiastic people into the membership. I believe Dr. Peale is precisely the right man to invite! He will make the kind of impression I want to make on the unchurched community."

My observation proved to be accurate. For 12 months after that service, we took hundreds of members into the church who came originally to hear Dr. Peale speak "in person."

Who Are You Trying to Impress, Schuller?

Many years later, after we had our own walk-in, drive-in church built, I was walking across our magnificent grounds and ran into a wonderful old farmer from the Middle West who had stopped by to "see what this big deal was all about." With enthusiasm, I ushered him around the area. I took him into the pulpit of the sanctuary, pressed a button, and we watched the glass walls slide open. "This makes it possible for people in the drive-in church to see me at the same time people in the sanctuary have visual communication with me," I explained.

Then I flipped a switch and 12 fountains leaped into being out of a block-long pool of water. I took him through the gardens and up and down the Tower. When I finally wound up this personally-conducted tour, my visitor looked me full in the face and asked me the cutting question: "Just who are you trying to impress, Schuller?"

Up to that moment, no one had ever been that blunt with me. It was brutal, but it was the greatest thing that could have happened! It forced me to analyze our motives.

I gave him an honest answer. "We're trying to impress non-Christians and unchurched people. We are trying to make a big, beautiful impression upon the affluent non-religious American who is riding by on this busy freeway.

"It's obvious that we are not trying to impress the Christians! They would tend to be most critical of the expenditure of money we have made. They would tell us that we should give this money to missions.

"Nor are we trying to impress the social workers in the County Welfare Department. They would tell us that we ought to be content to remain in the Orange Drive-In Theatre and give the money to feed the poor. But suppose we *had* given this money to feed the poor? What would we have today? We would still have hungry, poor people and God would not have this tremendous base of operations which He is using to inspire people to become more successful, more affluent, more generous, more genuinely unselfish in their giving of themselves."

As a result of our experience with the old farmer, we formulated in the Self-Study Guides distributed to participants of our Institute for Successful Church Leadership this revolutionary question: "Who are *you* trying to impress?" After having studied many hundreds of these Self-Study Guides, we can report on the answers to this all-important question.

It is obvious that the average pastor in the average church is not making an all-out effort to impress unchurched people—or his church would have more unchurched people in its pews and in its program.

Some ministers are subconsciously trying to impress the minister who originally impressed them as young boys. "I have always held in my mind the image of my dear old pastor," one minister said to me, "and I wanted as a young boy to become a preacher who would preach the kind of a sermon that would draw praise from the pastor I admired." He continued, "As I analyze my sermons, I find that I am really subconsciously trying to impress that dear old pastor who, incidentally, died many years ago!"

Other ministers are trying to impress their theology professors. Subconsciously, they are still striving to get a top mark in their class on sermonizing! So their profound vocabulary of theological and biblical terms is designed to impress—not the unchurched persons—but the enlightened theologian.

Still other ministers and church leaders are trying to impress the "bishop" or the "top executive officers of the denomination." They very carefully take public positions and decide how to vote on controversial issues, based upon what kind of impression this would make on the leaders of their denomination. They are consciously or subconsciously thinking that they may be promoted to a bigger and better church if they make a good impression on their superiors.

The weakness of this kind of thinking should be transparently clear. In the first place, a man ceases to be effective when he dishonestly seeks only to impress his peers. This is not the way to build a church! Your denominational peers are not going to get converted, move out to your community, join your church and make it grow.

If you, pastor, can impress the unchurched people in your community, your church can grow faster until you will have, by the blessing of God, a better church than the denomination could ever turn over to you! And, meanwhile, you will have been honest to your own convictions and will not have become a tool of an ecclesiastical machine. Be your own person, under God!

Still other ministers are seeking to impress the Christians who move into their communities. Again, this becomes obvious by simply looking at the sermon titles in the average church page of the community newspaper. You'll find, for the most part, that they are designed to impress religious people.

When we started our church in Garden Grove, God gave me the common sense to understand that I should never expect to win the Presbyterians, Methodists, Episcopalians, Lutherans, Baptists, Seventh-Day Adventists, Congregationalists, the Open Bible people or members of the many other groups. After all, if they were already members of one of these denominations, they could be expected to join the local denominational church of their choice. Why should they switch? Why should they join our church? And if they did, what gain would that count for the Kingdom of Christ?

Our only hope of building up a vital and growing church was to impress and win unchurched people. To that end, everything was designed from the very beginning to make a big impression upon the kind of unchurched people who lived in our area. This is the only way any minister can make a church grow.

And the good news that I have for you is that your church—unless it is located in a tiny town in a rural section—is unquestionably surrounded by a vast majority of people who are not committed to any faith, to any religion, to any denomination! *That means that there is an enormous potential for your church growth.*

There is a great market for your product! All of these people—although they may not realize it—really want the gospel of Jesus Christ. So go to work and attract these people. Be an inspiring impression-maker!

How do you impress unchurched people?

Sincerity impresses!

Begin by trying to impress them with your sincere desire to help in solving their personal daily problems.

Ring door bells. Some minister asked me how to spell the word success and I replied, "W-O-R-K!" I rang more than 3,500 door bells the first 12 months I was in Garden Grove.

I made an all-out effort to impress people with my willingness to help them with their daily problems. I made an all-out effort to impress them with my sincere desire to be a helpful and friendly human being in their community. Obviously, this pays off! But be sincere. People can spot a phony a mile off.

Success impresses!

Then seek to make an impression of success.

The first service of worship we conducted in the drive-in theater was a service where we used *printed* morning programs. From the beginning, I have refused to use mimeographed Sunday bulletins. A mimeographed bulletin says, "We can't afford to print our Sunday bulletins and we save a lot of money by mimeographing them."

I was insistent upon creating a success image in the very beginning and, therefore, I allocated, from the slim resources at my disposal, $20 to have the morning church bulletins printed by a very fine printer. I still continue that policy. The quality of your church bulletins, the photographs used, the caliber of the music you select, the architecture of your buildings—all of these things create an impression, be it good or bad. So create a good image.

Beauty impresses!

When we were to build our beautiful walk-in, drive-in church a half-mile west of this drive-in theater alongside the same heavily traveled freeway, I determined to hire the finest architect I could possibly find. I was well aware of the fact that, in attempting to create something entirely new, a walk-in, drive-in church, the project would have to be executed in such excellent architectural taste that we would not be shot down by critics but would be praised for the quality of the design.

We selected Richard Neutra, who took my original drawings of the walk-in, drive-in sanctuary, the fountains, the pools and the tower and sketched them out in an award-winning concept. It was another attempt on our part to make a favorable impression on unchurched people. And it worked! Architectural magazines in several languages around the world published stories about the church, and pictures of it appeared internationally. As a result, unchurched people interested principally in architecture came to our property just to see the building, and many remained to hear our message, accept Christ and become vital members.

Multiplied millions who drive by our church are attracted to the sight of a huge cross on top of a 13-floor tower. The top of the cross reaches to a height of 252 feet above the ground. It is the tallest cross—90 feet—to stand on any cathedral tower anywhere in the world.

I have been deeply influenced by Richard Neutra. We worked closely together for 12 years planning and building our walk-in, drive-in church. Together, we agreed upon the principles that were to be carried out in our church architecture. "The secular and sacred must be integrated in architecture," we both agreed. Therefore, we deliberately designed clear glass windows so people seated in the pews can see "the world out there."

A religious experience that is experienced in the sanctuary does not seem totally divorced from daily life if, out of the corner of your eye, you can see a jetliner gliding through the sky at the moment that you experience Christ coming into your life. In the distance, you can see cars moving over a bridge on the busy highway at the very moment the pastor is praying. The evolution of your soul and spiritual life is more significant and beautiful when integrated with the secular world.

Meanwhile, unchurched people who come to the church are impressed. One can enter into many sanctuaries where all sorts of profound symbolism is woven into the architecture. This may have real meaning to the Christians. But if the sanctuary is designed first of all to impress unchurched people, remember that these meaningless symbols only confuse and distract the non-Christian.

There are those who argue this point with me. But I know of no one who disagrees with my position on this issue whose church is growing faster than ours! And I have observed that those who quarrel with this position on church architecture and insist on letting it be dark and gloomy, resplendent with all sorts of mysterious symbolism, are themselves pastors of churches that are not for the most part meeting with enormous success in winning and converting the unchurched person.

Again the question must be raised: "Who are you trying to impress?"

Mr. Neutra made an interesting point to me one day. "Why," he asked, "did churches ever get into the custom of building structures that obstruct from their view the outside, secular world?"

I offered the usual answer. "I suppose it comes from the concept of God being in the sanctuary or in and around the altar."

He enlightened me. "But Christians sought fellowship with Jesus on the mountaintop, in the out-of-doors. They had experiences with Christ under the open sky and in the sanctuary and on the beach. Then why did Christians develop the kind of church that they did?"

He proceeded to answer his own question. "In the early days, the Christians were forced underground. They worshiped for years in the catacombs. Here, in dark underground caverns, candles were required to give light. Consequently, little children, with their impressionable minds, were raised to have religious experiences in a setting where the world was shut out and only candles flickered. The altar was frequently a coffin or a box made to hold the bones of martyrs. These were the natural niches in the hallways of the below-ground catacombs.

"So, when these Christian children became adults and

finally emerged into the sunlight with freedom to build churches above the ground, they designed the structures that would recreate what, in their minds and experiences, was a religious mood. It had to be reminiscent of the catacomb setting. Consequently, the buildings were designed to be dark, with flickering candles on a gloomy altar at the end of the corridor."

Even today, building committee members planning a new church attempt to design a sanctuary that fits their religious childhood impression of what a church should appear to be. So, in planning a church, *they are unconsciously seeking to impress those who were raised in a church instead of trying to design a structure that would make an impression on unchurched, secular Americans.* One of the great tragedies is right here. Hundreds of thousands of churches are designed to stimulate, not the positive emotions of joy and hope that come with the fall of sunlight in the room; rather they are designed to stimulate the negative emotions of darkness, dreariness and gloom! I have sadly advised one church to sell its new structure because the emotional statement of the structure is so negative it is impossible to feel joyful in that building!

When Mr. Neutra suggested that he would like to set the stone *vertically* on our building, I immediately agreed. He explained, "Stone is always set horizontally or random, but the new international style, with its aluminum, steel and sheets of glass, has created magnificent vertical lines. It seems to me that we should continue the theme of verticality by setting stone in a vertical manner. After all," commented Mr. Neutra, "you don't wear a clubstripe tie with a pin-stripe suit."

And so our church became the first building ever designed anywhere in the world where stone was set vertically. As a result, this made a big impression on architects, builders, contractors and the masons themselves. Photographs appeared all over the place! People came to see the beautiful buildings, with their vertical stone, and some of them returned on Sunday mornings and joined the church!

Modernity impresses!

At this point, many churches suffer from terrible errors of design judgment. I ride past many old churches with their dated architecture. And I feel painfully sorry for the pastor who is trying to impress modern, unchurched people when the biggest impression he is making in the community is colored and influenced by an out-of-this-world architecture.

Such a church announces to one and all: "This church is old-fashioned, out-of-date, from bygone generations without any exciting plans for the future." Is that what your church architecture says? If so, you have a problem.

And this brings up a principle from which our Institute for Successful Church Leadership never wavers: the growth of the church is the only thing that matters. Money does not count. Winning people to Christ is all that matters. If a church structure stands in the way of growth, then remove, remodel or relocate the structure!

Honesty impresses!

In designing a church building, a church program, a church advertisement or a church organization, you must be an inspiring impression-maker. In all these areas people are impressed with honesty. There have been many mistakes in church architecture. For example, not a few unchurched people who come into a church are impressed negatively with the phony props that adorn the auditorium, the artificial lighting, the carefully contrived staging, the sentimental-solemn effect. These features are obviously designed to manipulate a person's emotions into an unreal religious mood.

Unchurched people see the phoniness of this. One of these people said to me after having been in such a sanctuary: "I felt like I was in a religious night club. I go to one night club that has an African motif. I go to another bar that has an Old English motif. I am thinking of another restaurant I sometimes patronize. It has a Hawaiian mood. Now, in all of these places I am emotionally conditioned to believe, for a fleeting moment, that I am in Africa, England or Hawaii.

"Then, when I went to that church with its dark walls and deeply stained windows and indirect lighting on an illuminated cross with flickering candles, I felt as though I were in still another world. It's contrived. I felt manipulated. It's a phony setup."

The same man who made that remark came to our church and was impressed by the honesty of the entire architectural arrangement.

Superb architecture seeks not to impress people with ornamental beauty. Rather, the structure hopefully becomes inconspicuous and nature becomes the center of attention. And so, one is impressed with the sky, the water, the flowers, the trees and the green grass. All of which means that the structure becomes a vehicle for effective communication.

Richard Neutra taught the doctrine of bio-realism. According to this doctrine, man was designed by God with a built-in tranquilizing system. Eyes look upon rounded hills, sweeping green pastures and tranquil pools of water, and man's nervous system responds by producing a feeling of deep relaxation. The church building, it follows, should be a vehicle for effective communication between God and man, and between man and his fellowman.

Effective communication is a process whereby a positive suggestion is placed in a suggestible mind and is at home. God designed the human organism in such a way that when we are deeply relaxed and very calm, we become receptive to an outward suggestion. And that is nothing more than a form of hypnosis! Medical doctors do not use the term "hypnosis." They describe this state as "deep relaxation."

So the doctrine of bio-realism would say that a church building should be the kind of a structure where people, upon entering, feel tranquil, calm and relaxed. They will therefore be in a mental mood where they will be receptive to outward suggestion, respond accordingly and make commitments. With this objective, the structure should not seek to excite, but to tranquilize. That is why Mr. Neutra deliberately avoided bright colors, which tend to excite, and held to more natural, organic colors which tend to tranquilize.

Who Are *You* Trying To Impress?

Your church will grow if you are trying to impress unchurched people. Be an inspiring impression-maker and watch your church go to town!

Impress the community

How can you impress the unchurched people in *your* community? That's for you to find out. If you make enough calls on homes, you will begin to catch a reading.

Find out where the unchurched people in your community neighborhood are hurting. Where do they experience difficulties? What are their daily problems? What are their needs?

Find the honest answers to these questions, then you will know how to impress them. You will then be able to design the program to meet their needs and their wants. And when you put this kind of a program into operation, you will be swamped with success!

Discover the mood of your neighborhood. Who are the heroes of your community? Who are the civic leaders, the writers, the actors and other prominent personages that the unchurched people in your community admire? Grab hold of the coattails of these heroes. Invite them to your church. Use them unashamedly! Your job is to impress the nonchurched people in your community.

I discovered one day that there were over 1,300 medical doctors living in Orange County, California. About that same time, I ran across a newspaper article which proclaimed, "Newly elected president of the American Medical Association is an unusual man. He happens to be a successful physician and at the same time is a very ardent churchman, teaching Sunday School every Sunday." I immediately wrote a letter to the doctor and invited him to be a guest speaker in our pulpit.

When he accepted, I sent a letter to all the members of the American Medical Association in Orange County, inviting them to hear the newly elected president of the medical association. They were impressed. Many of the doctors who had never come to our church to hear Dr. Schuller speak, or even to hear Dr. Norman Peale speak, did come to hear the new president of the AMA.

On another occasion, I discovered that there were over 3,000 life insurance salesmen in our area. "Who is the man that life insurance salesmen would come to listen to?" I asked myself. I came up with the answer, "W. Clement Stone." I managed to get an acceptance from Mr. Stone.

Then we mailed a letter to all of the life insurance salesmen, as well as a letter to all of the securities salesmen in the area. And they were impressed! Many of them came simply to hear a man whom they had heard about and admired.

Impress the unchurched

The secret of winning unchurched people into the church is really quite simple. Find out *what* would impress the unchurched people in your community and find out *who* would impress them. Find out what kind of *needs* exist in the private lives of the unchurched people in your community.

Discover the *cultural temper* of the unchurched people. Then forget what Christians may think. Forget what your denominational leaders might think. Go out and make a big, inspiring impression on these unchurched people! And they'll come in! And when they do, may they find the beautiful Jesus Christ living in your life and in the lives of the people in your church. When they find the beautiful love and joy of Christ, they will never want to let it go.

Success, for God's glory, is in your hands right now, if you follow through on this question: *"Who are you trying to impress?"*

Chapter 14

FUND RAISING
CAN BE FUN

It is the contention of the Institute for Successful Church Leadership that *no church has a money problem; churches only have idea problems!* Big, inspiring, human need-filling ideas are money-makers! Successful goals always produce their own financial support if they're widely and enthusiastically publicized! Only fear, small faith or timid thinking can cause failure.

So fund raising really becomes fun!

Now, don't ever use the lack of money as an excuse for not beginning! Remember—*it doesn't cost a dime to dream!* It doesn't cost a dime to stand in your inspiring pulpit on a Sunday morning and preach a sermon to your people on the subject: "How to Make Your Dreams Come True," and then honestly lay before them the inspiring dream that God has given to you for the church where you serve!

Now that you have a dream, and assuming that your great goal has passed the success-spotting principles, move ahead with great faith. In all of your money-raising activities, follow these principles:

Remember that you will never get money from people by scolding, generating guilt feelings, or perpetrating other negative insults.

I once heard a minister offer this horrible prayer when the offering was dedicated to the Lord in a church service: "Here, Lord, in spite of all we say and do, is what we really think of you." It was a dirty dig, a cheap insult. Clever? Yes! Sharp? Indeed! But also stupid! There are many people who were not able to give what they wanted to that morning. You never generate maximum response by a negative approach.

Remember that you can spoil the whole "money tree" if you give the impression that you are having financial problems!

Nobody likes to invest in a shaky business. Plead and beg and you will only reveal your weakness. And a weak institution does not inspire generous contributions.

There were times in the history of our church when we were really fighting for enough money to pay the next week's bills. Then, before the Sunday offering, instead of laying this weakness before the people and throwing *my problem* upon the tired shoulders of the persons who came to church to unload *their problems,* I made a statement to this effect: "You people are wonderful. You come here week after week and give so generously, even though we never appeal and plead for your financial help. You are simply thoughtful and generous folk.

"There have been times when we were desperate for financial help. We prayed to God. We trusted Him and always He was able to meet our needs through wonderful people like you! I just felt this morning that I wanted to tell you how grateful I am, and how I love you for what you are doing! May God bless you! Thank you again. Now, let us worship God with our tithes and morning offerings." That approach has always been successful.

Remember that you will spoil the money tree if you go after small pickings, such as suppers, sales and second offerings.

At the outset, Mrs. Schuller and I, as the only two members of the church, established the policy that we would never attempt to raise money through bazaars and similar affairs. We would rather, once a year, frankly, openly and honestly, lay before our people a beautiful surprise package filled with exciting ideas that they would want to buy! And we'd give them a chance to buy it! They would make their pledges of financial support and we would carry out our church year from this response. And a simple little financial appeal a week or a month or two months before the annual financial appeal would be enough, we knew, to stunt the whole tree!

To achieve maximum response, you must let everyone know that you are counting on them—and on them alone!

Make it clear that you are not going to receive financial support from the denomination in the form of a subsidy; you are not going to ask local businessmen to support your project; and you are not going to make appeals from the pulpit on Sunday morning! To do so would only create an image that you are not financially strong, and it would, at the same time, frighten off the unchurched person who is coming to church to seek strength and not to be weakened by listening to someone complain about his financial difficulties.

Again, remind yourself that the only way to generate maximum financial response is to throw out an exciting, inspiring, human need-filling, problem-solving project.

Give your people a tremendous dream and an enormous and inspiring challenge, and they will love to give! Help them to *visualize* and *emotionalize* the project!

Never be afraid to ask people to give money for a great cause.

It is important to have a sense of timing here. Obviously, timing will vary from situation to situation.

In our experience at the Crystal Cathedral, we have been reticent about asking for financial support more than once a year. There have been rare exceptions when we interrupted the year for a special financial campaign. When an important opportunity came along, we did not allow it to keep us from giving God a chance to work another miracle through the people.

However, as a matter of policy, *we generally restrict ourselves to a once-a-year appeal. Then we give it all we've got!* We open up with all the power at our disposal.

The point here is: don't be afraid to ask people to give money for a great cause. People love to spend their money. They can't wait to spend it on a new car, a new house, new clothes, anything that excites, stimulates or inspires their imagination or offers help and healing and hope to their family, marriage or private life!

A great project for the church is exactly what people want. They can't wait to give generously toward it! One illustration here might be helpful to you. The roughest job I ever had was trying to raise $1,800 for a dishwasher in the kitchen of our church. It was far easier to raise a million dollars for the Tower of Hope! Or a million dollars for a new 10 acres of property! Big, imaginative, problem-solving projects really turn people on!

Every year you must offer some new challenge in the form of a new program, a new project, a new building, a new addition to the staff or a new missionary project.

Every year you *must* add something *new!* If you fail to

do this, you are saying to the people: "We have stopped. We are moving backward. We can't move ahead. We have run out of great ideas!"

You are making this growth-retarding decision based on *your negative assumption* that God has no other possible sources of financial aid to meet your increased budget! If you cannot add something new, you are not growing. If you are not growing, you are not living on the edge of exciting faith! And you are not giving God a chance to perform His miracles!

Now, you must get organized to communicate this exciting challenge to the people in the most effective way.

In our church, we have always had an annual "every member" canvass. On four special occasions in the first 15-year history of the church, we employed professional fund-raisers to organize and communicate financial challenge to the people. Without exception, these proved to be exciting experiences. Some people did object. But we refused to surrender leadership to the hands of objection-minded people! Rather, they, for the most part, were caught up with new life, new enthusiasm, new excitement as the projects moved along.

In later years, the techniques of "organizing to communicate effectively and inspiringly" shifted from annual "every member" visitations to an annual church dinner. We did this in the fall, generally in November. The congregation was invited to be the guest of the church for dinner. We selected the finest restaurants in the finest hotels in the entire area. Beautiful decorations and inspiring entertainment made it an exciting fun night. There was music, there was laughter, there was great inspiration. It became a tradition as "the great night out for everyone."

At this dinner, the people were given an inspiring, challenging look at what surprises the budget for the new year held for Jesus Christ. In portraying our message, we used graphic slides projected in multi-media on a huge screen. The entire program of the church, from janitor to missionary, was emotionalized and dramatized through color graphics.

The congregation was then informed that the budget could be raised no matter how impossible the task looked.

The program then called for a quiet moment of dedication as everyone was invited to sign a pledge card, fill in the amount, drop it in the offering plate as it passed.

And so, in one fun-filled, inspiration-packed, forward-looking, mountain-moving night, the church took another giant step upward! *This was done every year!*

Our 15th year, 1970, marked our first departure from the traditional dinner. We simply did not have room for the anticipated crowd. However, we carried out the same program, in effect, renting the Convention Center in nearby Anaheim, and we had 6,800 in attendance. A producer and director were secured to write a fast-moving, one-hour music-and-humor-filled show. The show led up to my slot where, for 20 minutes, I unfolded with word pictures the tremendous challenge of the new year, with its greatly enlarged budget, and led the attendees to the signing of their pledges.

The point is, something that entails such a concentrated effort must be done annually!

Always, on the Sunday before your pledging party, emphasize tithing. Emphasize it throughout the season.

By that, I do not mean two or three "messages on money." On the Sunday before the annual dinner, I preach my "once-a-year message" on tithing. I warn the people before I begin by saying: "Isn't it wonderful to come to this church week after week, Sunday after Sunday, and never hear a word about money? There is only one Sunday a year when I talk about it. Of course it takes money to run a church. But we don't raise it through special appeals, extra offerings, pitiful or scolding announcements every week!

"Once a year, I share an exciting promise that God has given to us in His holy Scriptures! It's the most fantastic key to financial security I know of! Let me tell you about it." And I launch into my annual tithing talk. At the same time of year, members of the congregation are also receiving tracts on tithing through the mail.

Weekly offering envelopes are mailed to all of those who pledge. A follow-up letter is mailed to all who do not pledge at the annual "night out," and not a word is ever mentioned about financial needs again until the next year!

And so, for 52 weeks people can attend the church without being badgered for tickets to this supper or donations to that cause!

Our financial success seems to prove the assumptions of the Institute for Successful Church Leadership that people will give all you need if you focus on real solutions to real needs and present the story in a positive, inspiring and enthusiastic way! Remember, Jesus said, "Ask, and it shall be given you; seek, and ye shall find; knock, and it shall be opened unto you" (Luke 11:9).

Never let money problems stop you. They may delay you but don't let them defeat you. Remember—nobody has a money "problem." It's always a *symptom*, not a problem. The real problem is lack of dynamic, need-filling ideas, a lack of courage and nerve or a lack of faith!

Don't ever again use the lack of money as an excuse, unless your God is terribly poor. Mine isn't! We found that out as we raised several million additional dollars the first 20 years for capital financing. When we needed to raise money for land and buildings, for more land and more buildings I found out the biggest problem every time was not God's power but my feeble faith!

So remember: Financial problems are never the result of a lack of money; they are the result of a lack of faith and a lack of ideas. You have to believe it before you see it!

Chapter 15

THREE KEYS TO CERTAIN SUCCESS

nspiring preaching! Exciting, human-need-filling programs! Enthusiastic advertisements and publicity!
These are the three miracle-working keys that can unlock
the doorway into a fantastic future for your church!

Inspiring Preaching

I instruct ministers who attend our Institute for Successful Church Leadership to "send me copies of the three
most outstanding sermons you've ever preached." And if
there is any one statement that covers most of these sermons, it is simply that they are *sermons preached* by
preachers. Yet, if we are truly interested in impressing
unchurched people, we must realize that the secular society has a deep-seated negative impression of "preachers"
and "sermons."

So, many more years ago than I can remember, I
stopped referring to myself as a "preacher" and my morning messages as "sermons." Our morning bulletin simply
states, "Morning Message." As a layman in our church

once explained, "Schuller doesn't preach. He witnesses."

You see, the average unchurched person envisions the preacher as someone who offers only a red-faced verbal spanking from the pulpit, his sermon little more than a scolding, finger-pointing, wrist-slapping, pulpit-pounding rebuke. And quite probably, a study of the sermons preached in days past throughout the United States of America would justify this image of Protestant "preaching." In those days, unchurched people, perhaps facing a personal or family crisis, would enter a church on Sunday only to hear a judgmental, suspicion-producing sermon, advocating the single "Christian" position on some controversial subject. And had they entered the church across the street, they probably would have had another sermon preached with equally negative intensity advocating an opposing, but no less "Christian," position on the same subject.

In an earlier chapter we outlined our case for never using the pulpit for controversial issues. The truth is that no man is preaching the gospel when he stops giving people exciting and inspiring good news from the Sunday pulpit! People will rush to hear exciting good news!

Unless you have some good news every Sunday morning, pastor, you are not prepared to speak from the pulpit. I don't consider myself prepared to enter the pulpit on Sunday morning unless I can share some exciting experience I had with God over the past seven days or a work I saw God perform in a human life in a daily life situation!

That's keeping the gospel up-to-date. That's keeping good news as alive as today's newspaper. And this is what the world desperately needs!

When we began our church in the Orange Drive-In Theatre, I had accessibility, surplus parking and good news every Sunday! And my messages have continually stressed the upswing of life. While many Protestant pastors suffer from a neurotic anxiety over the tormenting question of "How can we be relevant to today's world?" I recall the words of a great preacher saying to his students many years ago: "Boys, preach to broken hearts and you will always be up-to-date!"

I have enormous confidence in the power of the spoken word when it conveys good news—its power to sway, to influence, to mold, to change lives! Recently, an unchurched family in southern California lost their four-year-old child in their backyard swimming pool. Carrying their grief, they went to a church hoping to find comfort and consolation, but they only got a social-political harangue. Then they found a church that was able to put "strong wings on their weary hearts." They stayed, they were saved and they are serving today!

The late Louis Cassells once wrote about what he aptly called the "Protestant Blahs." In a perceptive article, he analyzed the problems facing the modern church. He wrote: "A professional man of Bethesda, Maryland, told me he had quit going to church because 'it seemed kinda pointless to sit there Sunday after Sunday while the preacher bawls me out for attitudes I don't have.'"

Another letter, in the same article, is from a woman in Columbus, Ohio, who writes, "We are tired of being told from the pulpit that we have been coming to church all our lives for the wrong reasons—such as because we wanted to belong to a country club, or to build a fancy building, or to take shelter away from the world's troubles."

Then Cassells came to the theme of the article: "That brings me to what I consider to be the most important reason why people are drifting away from the Protestant fold. *They haven't found in church what they hoped to find—a confident faith in God.*"

In the same article, the author quotes the Methodist theologian, Dr. Albert C. Outler: "The middle class is reacting to the way we have assumed they were the golden goose and the whipping boys at the same time. They are fed up with the general disposition of the church to scold them rather than minister to them."

Finally the author concludes: "Many middle class churchgoing families don't necessarily disagree with— they may even heartily approve—the stand their pastor takes on Vietnam or race relations. What distresses them is the feeling that the pastor is so preoccupied with the plight of distant people who happen to be black and poor that he completely ignores the urgent personal problems of his own parishioners who happen to be white and a little better off economically. Genuine agony of mind and body and spirit can exist in a suburban rambler as well as in a cold-water flat."

Again Cassells: "Let me emphasize that I am not contending for one moment that ministers should be less concerned with the needs of the poor and oppressed. I am simply arguing that they *also* should display a little compassion and pastoral concern for human suffering which they can discover, if they will only take the trouble to look for it, in their own flocks."[1]

Some time ago, in a perceptive article, *Look* magazine had an interesting symposium contributed by a variety of thinkers in our country. It was an attempt to analyze the problems of our world at the beginning of a new decade. Near the close of the issue, they got to the root of it all when they said, "Joy is the missing ingredient in our culture—the healing force that can join individual impulse with a common good."

In the same article, Vincent Harding wrote: "In most of America, there is no sense of joy at all, that is, apart from age four down. A society that I am seeking is a society where joyousness is a part of the very fabric of life. I want a society in which people can touch each other without fear."[2]

Oddly enough, the one institution, namely the Christian church, that traditionally specializes in generating joy, building faith and spreading optimism, is the institution that seemingly has been affected and afflicted in the second half of the twentieth century with cynicism, bitterness and negativism. So the world goes hungry for the joy and the faith that the good news of Christ can offer.

Somehow, we must discover the enormous power there is in the real gospel of Christ. When a minister steps into a pulpit with genuine enthusiasm, exciting energy, positive statements of hope, people will flock to listen.

I recall attending the World Psychiatric Congress in 1967 in Madrid, Spain. At the closing session, there was a round-table discussion on the subject: "Human Values in Psychotherapy." The first lecturer, Dr. Rome, past president of the American Psychiatric Association, spoke for 30 minutes on the subject, "Faith." In effect, he said that it was the duty of the 4,000 psychiatrists from around the world to build faith in the hearts and lives of their clients, since the traditional faith-building institutions no longer seemed to be carrying out this vital function!

He was followed by a doctor from Germany who spoke for 30 minutes on "Hope." This speaker discussed the enormous healing power of hope: "Many of us have had patients who sat under our analysis for months without any sign of recovery until, one day, a spark appeared in their flat, dull eyes: it was the spark of the birth of hope! And healing began in that miracle moment!"

The third lecturer was from Lima, Peru. Believe it or not, he spoke on the subject, "Love." He said: "Nothing is more powerful in its healing potential than nonjudgmental love. Nonselective, nonjudgmental love is the greatest healing force in the world."

I went out of that assembly depressed, and in the next moment, overjoyed! Overjoyed that I had discovered the reason why our church was growing by leaps and bounds! We were meeting human need on the deepest level because our morning messages were consistently designed to build faith, generate hope and illustrate vital, noncritical love. But I was also depressed because I could see the Protestant church declining in America for the simple reason that most ministers seemed not to understand this very simple secret of successful preaching!

I had learned this lesson myself the morning I introduced Dr. Peale to that great drive-in audience. After the elaborate introduction I gave him, he stepped to the podium, looked across the more than 1,700 automobiles jammed with people and said, "What would Jesus Christ have to say to you if He could stand here and talk to you through me today?"

He then went on to preach a sermon so powerfully positive, uplifting and inspiring that I determined then to change my own style from "preaching" to "witnessing." Until that moment, I looked upon the job of a sermon to be fundamentally directed toward generating a sense of guilt in guilty hearts. What I had failed to realize was that unchurched people, who have no vital relationship with God, have a much deeper sense of guilt than we Christians realize. It is this sense of guilt that keeps them out of church, the same way an overweight man avoids stepping on a bathroom scale.

Now—here's how you can preach to pack your church with unchurched people.

1. Don't "preach sermons."

You can introduce people to the distinctive beliefs of your church after they enter your pastor's classes, but *don't try to sell them on your peculiar doctrines in a sermon on Sunday morning!* They are not ready for it yet.

Let your Sunday morning services aim at inspiration, entertainment and a basic commitment to Jesus Christ. Then get them into a small classroom setting where they will be more receptive to the deeper doctrines of your church.

Witness to the experience you had with your God this past week. If you've had no experience with Him, the chances are you were not calling on the sick or counseling with the troubled!

2. Don't be controversial in the pulpit.

Save that for a small group meeting where there can be respectful dialogue which alone leads to conversion of attitudes. In controversy you may relieve your frustration, and you will certainly earn enough opposition to boast that you are "being persecuted for righteousness' sake" (Matt. 5:10). But you will, in almost every instance, do your "cause" more harm than good!

3. Always be positive.

Make every sermon you preach positive. How can you tell if it's positive? Simply by asking yourself, "Is this stimulating positive emotions?"

Remember, too, that humor is a positive emotion. It is healthy. It is healing. It is unifying. It is harmony-creating.

There is a great deal of therapeutic and spiritual value in wholesome entertainment that comes in the form of warm and wonderful humor. So work at it. Make your sermons fun to listen to. Make them a positive witness!

Your hardest job will be resisting the constant temptation to "attack the enemies you see in the world." Remember, until you are able to verbalize your concern in the form of a positive, inspiring idea or dream, until then you are ill prepared to speak out!

4. Let every message stimulate the positive emotions of the listeners.

Positive emotions are: love, joy, peace, kindness, gentleness, goodness, faith, hope, humor, aspiration, trust, respect, self-confidence, enthusiasm, ambition, courage, optimism! Never play the negative emotions: fear, suspicion, anger, prejudice, sorrow, despair, self-hate, pessimism.

Make your list now. See how many positive emotions you can identify. Now make an equally long list of negative emotions and vow never to let your message or your pulpit announcements or the words of the anthems, hymns or prayers be allowed to send out and stimulate negative vibrations.

Follow this advice. Keep it up week after week, year after year, and you will literally transform the personality of your congregation! It will be fun to go to your church!

5. Keep your messages well illustrated.

Remember we deal with people who are too busy to think; they have time only to pick up on impressions. We deal with a graphic mentality, not a logic mentality. Communication that is effective draws a big picture, then adds a short sentence.

Billboard advertising is the best illustration of how to communicate from the platform that addresses people who are living and thinking at a fast pace. The most effective messages will have three or more sharply identified points that can be made in a sentence or two, then illustrated with honest down-to-earth, positive, emotion-generating stories. Then they are summarized with a powerful one-liner for emphasis.

6. Be sure to aim every message at some specific human problem.

Remember the theme of this book, the secret of successful churchmanship: find a hurt and heal it.

7. Don't be afraid of repeating yourself.

It's impossible for a minister to "preach the same sermon" again! You'll be a different person the second time around. Your listeners will be changed too! So I have a message every year on "How to Overcome Fear" and another on "How to Find Peace of Mind." The messages take on new meaning in each new phase of life!

8. Never "preach" on something you don't feel very strong about!

And people will marvel at your week-after-week enthusiasm and sincerity—two of the most important ingredients of successful speaking. So the place to start looking for sermon ideas is in your heart, not in your head! Use your heart first, and your head will follow!

9. Good sermons are like great architecture: "Make it strong but don't let it feel heavy." A second architectural principle also applies: "Form must always follow function. Never reverse the order!"

In other words, sermons are designed to help someone function! I've heard miserable messages that were form first—beautiful poetry and snobbish quotations full of ego boosting and name dropping. They served more to self-congratulate the speaker than to serve the hurts of the listener.

10. Expect positive results.

A minister once fell into depression because, he confessed, "I've preached for years and nothing seems to happen."

"Tell me," his sympathetic listening friend asked,

"when you go into your pulpit and while you share your thoughts do you *expect* anything to happen?" That question pointed up the pastor's problem!

If your message begins with your heart, aims at a real human problem, and *concludes with a call to decision,* then you can and will expect positive results. It is this positive expectation that will make your message sound like it comes from an excited young person standing on tiptoes! Plan your conclusion carefully and design it to call your listeners to a personal commitment and the dynamism of great expectations will inject real vitality throughout the whole service!

11. Always lead people to Jesus Christ!

It's really true—unchurched people are fascinated by this famous name. A missionary to Japan said to me, "It's strange—people here don't want to hear about Christianity, although they are really interested in Jesus Christ."

"Then don't preach Christianity," I advised. "Christianity is like all religions, full of shortcomings, sins and hypocrisy. But *do* preach Christ! Tell the world about Him!

"Live so close to Him that he is your dearest Friend. Invite Him to live in the front and back corners of every drawer in every room within your mind. And when you speak it will be Christ speaking, smiling, loving, laughing and uplifting the hearts of listeners.

"There is, after all, one unfilled need that exists in every human heart every Sunday. Every Christian and every non-Christian comes to church needing a fresh encounter with the inspiring, encouraging, new-hope-producing Spirit of the Eternal God. Bring Christ alive into their minds and hearts and you'll be a winner in the pulpit!"

12. Build people—never destroy them!

One of the most moving spiritual experiences of my life stemmed from the musical production, *Man of La Man-*

cha. For suddenly I saw the man of La Mancha as an allegory of the Christ. He is such a positive thinker! When he sees a prostitute, he lauds her as "My Lady."

She, wild-eyed, almost bare-breasted, open-mouthed, leers at him, saying in a voice filled with mocking disbelief: "Me a lady? I was born in a ditch by a mother who left me there, naked and cold and too hungry to cry. I never blamed her. I am sure she left, hoping that I would have the good sense to die."

The man of La Mancha continued to look at her, continues to believe the best of her, continues to appeal to her subconscious self-image as he announces grandly: "Your name is not Aldonza. I give you a new name. You are my lady. And I give you the name 'Dulcinea.'"

She later appears in hysterics on the stage, having been raped in the barn by rough travelers. The man of La Mancha again affirms his belief in her goodness.

But, wounded, crushed, filled with self-hate, she screams at him: "Don't call me a lady! God, won't you look at me! I am only a kitchen slut reeking with sweat! A strumpet men use and forget! I am only Aldonza. I am nothing at all!" And she runs off the stage.

As she makes her exit, he calls to her, "My lady!" And after a short pause, looking out into the shadows, he again calls, "My lady!" And off in the stillness, he calls out the new name he has given her: "Dulcinea!"

At the conclusion of the play, the man of La Mancha is dying of a broken heart. At this point, a strikingly beautiful Spanish lady approaches his bedside. "Who are you?" he asks with the feeble voice of a dying man. She has been kneeling at his side.

Now she arises, stands tall, and with queenly beauty announces: "My name? My name? My name is . . . Dulcinea!"

The work of redemption is complete! A self-hating, self-loathing, self-condemning person finally comes to believe that she can be beautiful and wholesome and lovely! You'll fill your church with unchurched people if you'll build them into the faith that through Christ they too can be beautiful.

Exciting Programs

Inspiring preaching must be backed up by exciting programs designed to impress unchurched people of every age. And the number one program of any church is the church school or Sunday School.

If you are sincerely interested in winning unchurched people, you should seriously consider scheduling your church school at the same time church is going on. We have discovered that unchurched people are interested in having their children in Sunday School even if they don't attend church services themselves. Early in our ministry, we found that some parents would drive their cars onto the church property, drop their children off and arrive later to pick their children up again.

So we scheduled adult church services at the same time that Sunday School was going on and discovered that almost all of these unchurched parents stayed for worship! It was more convenient than going home and coming back! And because our worship proved to be exciting, inspirational and entertaining, they not only stayed—they also enjoyed it. We found that our church school program did succeed in bringing the unchurched person into the pew on Sunday mornings.

Next we scheduled two morning services and two sessions of Sunday School, thereby getting twice the mileage out of all our physical facilities. By offering the full Sunday School program at each of those times, we obtain double utilization of all our educational facilities! A variety of combinations can thus be offered to people, meeting almost every conceivable requirement of many different lifestyles of people in the community.

Programming the church school obviously requires strong leadership on the supervisory level. The Protestant church has yet to learn the importance of hiring staff people in the role of supervisor. We can envision hiring a minister of education, but in the typical church this person is the only one hired to handle all of the administrative details of the church school, including the recruiting and training of teachers, supervision of the library, the allocation of class space, and so forth. As a result, one person simply will not have the time to give the close supervision over the teachers that this kind of activity demands.

We have made the discovery at the Crystal Cathedral that to hire a chief executive to head a department—without hiring the adequate supervisory help on the managerial level will prove to be inadequate and unsuccessful. Precisely for this reason, many staff situations fall apart. And the blame is too often placed mistakenly upon the minister of education or the senior pastor or the "failure of the people to respond and support him."

We can learn a great deal here from business, industry and the military organization. In the military, there may be a single general, but he needs colonels to inspire the majors with his orders, majors to inspire the captains, captains to inspire the lieutenants, lieutenants to inspire the sergeants, sergeants to inspire the corporals, and the corporals to inspire their small squads of privates. Notice that between the general and the squad there are several levels of full-time, professional supervisory officers.

We may look upon the head of a department as the idea-generating power plant! The several levels of employed staff persons unless you are fortunate enough to have extremely talented and dedicated volunteers are booster stations to "pick up" the power-generated idea from the head of the department and transmit it along down the line without allowing any of the power to be lost along the way. Very, very few church schools in America have been adequately staffed in this manner.

No wonder the Sunday Schools are falling apart! The army would fall apart, too, if it were as inadequately staffed as the church school. And the army has the power of unchallenged authority, with disciplinary powers to back up its authority!

Somehow, Protestant church planners must discover this principle: *Ideas lose their enthusiasm-power unless recharged by personnel operating on a supervisory or managerial level.* Consequently, in our highly effective church school, we have an enormous staff. They are outstanding people.

Under the direction of such a competent staff, church school and youth activity programs are planned for children and adults of all ages. We have classes for almost every type of person. We have a class for mentally retarded children. This fills a vital human need. After all, they can't be left in the regular nursery.

We also discovered very quickly that our community has a number of single adults. Consequently, we organized a "singles" group. It has been said that the Crystal Cathedral was the first church to have a full-time minister to singles. It wasn't until we had passed the 5,000 membership figure that we had enough single adults in the various age brackets to grade this program closely, which is vital to real success. We now have a group of singles 20 to 35, singles 35 to 60, another group 40 to 60 and still another group of single adults 50 and over. The key to a successful program is to sharpen it, focus it and grade it as closely as possible!

Program your church for institutional success. I marvel at Dr. Harold Fickett, former pastor of the successful First Baptist Church in Van Nuys, California. I often had him lecture at our Institute for Successful Church Leadership simply to explain the unbelievable variety of clubs and organizations then in operation at his church. I believe he even had a bowling league for the deaf. He applied a basic principle of successful retailing: he increased his inventory to meet a greater market!

Remember what we have already said elsewhere in this book: make a careful study of your larger city, county or community and you can begin to identify the kind of programs that will meet and fill human needs.

Enthusiastic Publicity

If you have inspiring preaching and exciting programming, then all you need is enthusiastic publicity and your church will break all growth records!

The first thing I did when I came to Garden Grove to launch a new church was to spend $15 for a small mimeograph machine large enough to take a postcard. Next I spent another $40 for a hand-operated addressograph machine. Then I began ringing door bells, picking up names and addresses of any unchurched persons in the neighborhood that I could lay my hands on. I began building the mailing list!

Yes, before I held even my first service in Garden Grove, I picked up all the names and addresses I could. And all were added to the mailing list. Remember: *a mailing list is all-important. It is your first line of publicity. It is the way to build a church.* Our most prized possession in the Crystal Cathedral today is our mailing list with its thousands of families.

The second thing I did was to prepare an advertisement for the newspaper: "Come as you are in the family car," the ad read. "Starting Sunday, March 27, 1955, an exciting new church will begin to operate in the Orange Drive-In Theatre!" The Sunday morning bulletins were printed, as were the registration cards, to give the impression of a successful, going organization.

Immediately after our first Sunday in the drive-in theater, I sent out a postcard to everybody on the mailing list with an enthusiastic, success-predicting announcement: "Nearly half a hundred cars drove quietly into the beautiful setting of the Orange Drive-in Theatre this past Sunday to launch what may well become one of the great churches in the world." And with that immodest, enthusiasm-generating announcement, the people on the mailing list were led to believe that this was going to be a winning thing and that they had better get on the bandwagon right away!

Through the years, the strategy has always been as follows:

1. The newspaper advertisement published every Saturday is geared to bring unchurched people into the church. The ads are generally built around helpful sounding messages.

2. People are urged to register their attendance. The object is to get them on the mailing list!

3. The mailing list is worked weekly to build church attendance the following Sunday. This simple procedure, followed year after year after year, is the one single, simple secret of effective publicity at Crystal Cathedral.

Not always do we place the ads on the church page. When Dr. Peale was to speak in our church, we advertised on the woman's page, knowing he had a following there; on the business page, including the West Coast edition of the *Wall Street Journal* and on the sports page. We assumed that if we wanted to impress unchurched people we would have to put the ads elsewhere than exclusively on the church page.

For the first six years of our church in Garden Grove, I made it a point to go to the office on Monday morning and begin the week in the following manner:

First, I would write the copy for the weekly card that was to go out to the entire mailing list—a message geared to generate enthusiasm for the coming Sunday. Next, I would dictate or draft a news release which was later mailed to area newspapers, an article describing events planned for the upcoming Sunday. I would then lay out the ads advertising the messages to be presented during Sunday's services.

Personally, I feel that it is enormously important for the senior minister to be in charge of the publicity program of the church. By being personally responsible for the publicity, I was forced to create, produce and generate sermons and programs that were newsworthy and had real publicity value! And when I really felt that we had to break into the headlines, it simply meant that I would have to make every effort to bring some famous personality to our "unlimited parking" church, be it Norman Vincent Peale or Chuck Colson.

A very important question in the Self-Study Guide prepared by those who attend our Institute for Successful Church Leadership is: "How much of your church income is budgeted for advertising?" The answers are astounding! We recommend a minimum of 5 percent of the church budget for publicity purposes. If the church is ailing or struggling, then it had better go considerably higher.

Our first service of worship in the drive-in theater was held on March 27, 1955. By December of that year, we had taken in a little over $8,000. But during that same period of time I had reinvested in newspaper and radio advertisements over $4,000! That's 50 percent of the income put back into publicity!

Let the following principles guide you as you plan enthusiasm-generating publicity that will pack your church!

Expect a very small return.

That means you must think in terms of reaching thousands of people with advertisements if you want to win 10 to 100. Most churches fail in publicity because they do too little and go into it too small.

Remember that good advertisements never cost—they always pay.

All you need to do is win one family and their tithe or their offering over a period of three or four years will more than pay for the entire cost. The last item to be cut from the budget should be this money-producing item. That's what advertising is!

Consider a radius of 10 miles from your church as the drawing power of your congregation.

Many ministers fail because they think that people won't drive more than two or three miles. Nothing is further from the truth.

Aim at saturating the area in the 10-mile radius.

Don't worry about competition with other churches. If people are interested in another church they won't come to yours anyway. Meanwhile, your advertisement will help create a general momentum in the community which will say: "Religion is really alive out here!" And the other churches will indirectly benefit more than they realize! Your advertisement will only challenge other church members to be more active in their own congregations.

Advertise when people are in a buying mood.

In other words, you don't try to sell air-conditioners in December, but in the heat of summer! So plan your heaviest advertising in the seasons of the year when the unchurched people might conceivably be interested in attending church. This means, of course, a saturation campaign the week before Easter. For years we have sent a brochure to every home within a 10-mile radius of the church heralding our Easter services.

I discovered that in our community, as in every community of America, there is a business called "direct mailing." This type of business has the addresses of all the residences in the city and county.

We discovered, in working with the firm, that there were 130,000 homes within a 10-miles radius of our church, so we budgeted $5,000 to send an Easter invitation to each of these homes.

We became so excited over inviting 130,000 families, that we scheduled three services on Easter instead of two! We estimated that perhaps $1,000 would come in extra offerings and we figured that if we won only 10 families from the 130,000 invitations, those 10 families would give an average of $5,000 a year, paying for the entire project in 12 months' time! Of course, it worked out much better than that! A friend of mine, Rev. Guy Davidson, founder and pastor of a fantastic, successful church in Tempe, Arizona, advertises very heavily in the summer months because, "That's when most of the homes change hands—new people are moving in between the end of one school year and the beginning of another."

Determine the mental attitude of your area and analyze what would impress the unchurched people in your community.

Then let your advertisements portray the kind of an image that could appeal to these *unchurched* people. I am often asked for samples of our advertisements. I always refuse. They were geared to impress a certain *type* of person at a specific *time* in history. Each pastor must research his community *today*.

In setting up any publicity material, do not try to impress Christians or religious people.

They are already involved with the church. Concentrate on the 50 percent who are uncommitted to any faith.

Select sermon titles that will appeal to the unchurched. Consider a series of sermons and advertise them over a six-week period. In the first ad, you can announce the six titles. Try to appeal to the unchurched people on the level of their thinking and self-interests.

A suggested sermon title might be: "How to Make Marriage Succeed in Today's World." The title sounds like an article from a secular magazine. It actually sounds quite nonreligious, but you can put plenty of the Bible and Christ into it.

The idea is to get them to come to church in the first place! And if they are not interested in religion, chances are that they won't be attracted to church by religious-sounding titles.

Make certain that all of your publicity creates an image of your church that says:

- This is a positive-thinking church.
- This is a church that really believes in the power of Christ to transform human life.
- This is a church that welcomes everyone no matter what his or her background.
- This is a church that believes in building people up, not in tearing people down.

Continue the job of advertisement and publicity until you

are reasonably sure that every household in a 10-mile radius knows and understands that:

- You are in business.
- You are offering distinctive services that nobody else is offering.
- You have something they need.

So publicity is never finished. There are always people moving in and out of the community. Furthermore, as the church moves along five years, then to 10 years, then to 15 years, new and bigger programs of community service, education, evangelism and counseling will be offered which will require wholesale communication.

Follow the above public relations and advertising principles and, provided you also have inspiring sermons and exciting human-need-filling programs, this enthusiasm-generating publicity is guaranteed to make your church boom!

Notes

1. *Christian Herald*, October, 1969.
2. *Look* magazine, January 7, 1970.

Chapter 16

A FORWARD LOOK AT LEADERSHIP

The year—1955. My calling? To start a new church. But without a nucleus of followers, how could I begin? After all, there were no members—no believers.

We began as a mission. My number one purpose was to impress the nonreligious people in the community. And today, 30 years later, I still hold that if your first priority is to impress the Bible-caring, born-again believers who are members of your community and who are called the fellowship of the church, then you cannot hold much hope for growth.

Be a Mission

The key to church growth is to be willing to be a mission! As we got started, I did an analysis of our community, and I found out that half the people didn't go to church in this community. I think this is still true today.

But 50 percent of the people who didn't go to church did want their children to go to Sunday School. Why? Because they went to Sunday School when they were kids! And they had heard J. Edgar Hoover say, "Kids that belonged to the Boy Scouts and went to Sunday School never get in trouble."

So, to the unchurched families of 30 years ago, the Sunday School was very appealing. It made a promise. It promised to help parents succeed in raising their children to be good persons. There were denominations that understood this attitude and carried this possibility to its ultimate goal. To win families, they reasoned, try to win the kids. To be an effective mission, then, have a dynamic Sunday School. Build your whole church around the Sunday School. Unchurched people will send their kids to Sunday School.

Well, I believed that too. And so, when we started 30 years ago, we deliberately planned to have morning worship timed concurrently with Sunday School. Part of the plan was that we would not bus kids to the place. If we did that, we still would not get their unchurched parents coming.

I decided I would try to go into topical and relational messages that would interest nonreligious adults while they waited for their children who were in Sunday School. So, by deliberate design, I moved away from expository sermons—these would please the believers who hunger for the Word, but they would also turn off many people who do not yet believe that the Bible is the Word of God! So I made a calculated decision to go into topical sermons that would be geared to meeting human problems of people in the here and now.

The idea was that if I had a series of messages on how to overcome your fears, your anxieties, your worries and the like, maybe the parents would bring their kids to Sunday School and then stay over to hear this helpful presentation instead of a sermon. The strategy worked pretty well. Here we are 30 years later, a strong church!

But where are we nationally 30 years later? Times have changed. The unchurched families in our community today are no longer turned on by Sunday School. The name is no longer the buzz word it was three decades ago.

Why not?

I remember 25 years ago when members of my church would say, "Boy, the kids on my block—they're not going to church. They're not even going to Sunday School."

And I used to say to them, "Well, for gosh sakes, pile them into your car and take them to Sunday School."

That didn't work. What's happened? All of those kids that grew up from the streets and didn't go to Sunday School 25 years ago are yuppies today. They're married and they've got kids of their own. But because they didn't go to Sunday School, Sunday School is no longer the magic word in mission that it was 25 years ago.

Create Leaders

So what do we do? I suggest that we make an historical shift in the use of Sunday morning time traditionally allocation to "Sunday School." In doing so, we must come up with a new, creative, educational and character-forming program that will appeal to the secular unchurched parents in our pluralistic, unbelieving communities.

If we are going to try to reach the unchurched people in our community, then we'd better not call the program "Sunday School." That could be a big blunder! And if we want to get the unchurched kids, we'd probably better not call it "Church School." My suggestion? That we call the Sunday morning Christian education time "Leadership Training." So our new church school building will be called a Leadership Training Center.

At a recent dinner honoring one of our elders who has been a member of this church for 28 years, I said, "We'll call our new educational structure a Leadership Training Center." And I explained all of the things that would happen there.

But he said, "Bob, we have to have a church school building for the children! And for the families!"

I heard myself respond, "What are we in business as a church for anyway? We are in the business of creating leaders!"

We have for years been teaching a biblical philosophy that we call "Possibility Thinking." We have also been writing books on self-esteem—the biblical psychology of persons. In addition, we conduct Institutes for Successful Church Leadership. As a mission we ask people to become Christians. But what is a Christian anyway? We ask people to accept the salvation that Jesus offers. What is this salvation anyway? How do we take all of these scattered, isolated ministries, teachings, concepts, ideologies, theologies, philosophies and integrate them?

Organize Around Leadership

Everything has got to be organized around something. World timekeeping, for instance, is organized around Greenwich Mean Time. My gardener wears two watches. I say to him, "Why do you wear two watches?"

He answers, "I wear *that* watch to check up on *this* watch."

I had to tell him about Greenwich Mean Time. I said, "But, Morrie, how can you be sure *that* watch is right?"

And then I'd tell him the story about the woman who worked for the telephone company. Every day at five minutes to noon, a stranger would call and say, "Can you tell me the correct time, please?"

And she'd reply, "It's five minutes before high noon."

He thanked her and hung up. He called her every day, month after month, year after year, and she wondered who he was. It bugged her that she didn't know his identity, but fraternization was not allowed. She couldn't ask, "Who are you?" so she had to tolerate him.

After 25 years, she was ready to retire, so she decided that on her last day on the job, if he called, she was going to break the rule and ask, "Who are you anyway?" Well, he called.

She answered, "Five minutes to noon. But wait a minute. You've been calling every day for years. Now I want to ask you a question. Who are you anyway?"

"Oh," he said, "I'm the guy that blows the whistle in the town factory, and everybody in town sets their clocks by our whistle at high noon!"

"Oh my gosh," she answered, shocked. "I've been setting *my* clock by *your* whistle!"

So everything has to be organized around something. And time is organized around Greenwich Mean Time. Music is organized around Middle C. Mathematics is organized around the tables. In the development of streets and curbs, a city organizes everything around sea level.

When we were developing this property on which the Crystal Cathedral stands, we first had to pave the street and put in the curbs. So the cement trucks came and poured the forms for the curbs. The cement set, the forms were removed and the curbs looked beautiful! They should have, for they were expensive.

Then the city inspector came along. He looked and he looked and he looked, and pretty soon he came to me and said, "Schuller, the curbs have to come out."

"What do you mean?" I answered.

He repeated. "The curbs have to come out."

I gasped. "You can't be serious! They cost us a lot of money!"

"I'm sorry, but the elevation is wrong," he explained.

I said, "I don't care how high or low they are. We paid big money for them. We can't afford to tear them out."

I was adamant. So was he. I was stubborn. So was he.

"But the elevation is wrong," he said again.

"That's your tough luck," I declared. "Your inspector checked the forms before the cement was poured. He OK'd them! You're too late!"

He looked right at me. "I may be too late, but you're wrong. They're coming out!"

"No, they're not," I continued to insist. "Your inspector approved them."

"That was his mistake."

I argued for time. "Wait a minute."

His final look indicated the discussion was over. "Look, Schuller, let me tell you something. If you leave those curbs where they are, the water will not flow down the street. It will stay here and flow into the parking lot. And on a heavy day, you're going to have water in the buildings. Get this through your head, Schuller. You're not arguing with me, you're *arguing with sea level!*"

I gave in. Sea level won the argument! And yes, the jackhammers came and broke up the cement. They dumped the pieces on trucks and hauled them away. They put in new forms, and this time we checked three times before we poured the cement.

Everything is organized around something. We are proposing to organize our Christian Education program around "Leadership!" Even our children's classes will be called "Leadership Training Classes." We believe such an emphasis can appeal to religious and nonreligious people alike.

What Is Leadership?

Leadership, what is it? Where is it needed? When is it needed? What's required to become a leader? And how does this relate to the growth of the church? Bear in mind, this gets very exciting if you want to develop a mission and appeal to the kids, the young adults and the older persons who have no interest in religion. If you, in other words, want to be an effective mission, this leadership concept could be the strategy for the future.

What then is leadership? Is it being president of the United States? Being a chief executive officer? Being president or chairman of the committee? Or being the class teacher? No, not necessarily. That is a shallow definition of leadership. Leadership, what is it? *It is an awareness that at any given point and time, I'm probably facing a variety of possibilities.* Leadership, then, is the *consciousness that several options are open to me.* And I have the freedom to choose.

So, leadership is seeing possibilities and sizing up the options. It is considering the choices that are open to me. Leadership, then, is the activity of a mature person. And that maturity is not measured by the calendar; it can happen at the age of five or six.

Leadership is willing to face the awareness that I can—and probably must—make personal decisions, and making a decision is choosing the possibility, selecting an option! What it all amounts to is: Leadership is the determination that I am going to be an individual, not just a drop in the bucket. Not just a part of a collection, but a person! Not just a puppet, but a person. This determination means that leadership is the development of the kind of a character that intuitively rejects intimidation. Coercion, whether it is religious, psychological, cultural or social, can become a form of oppression. Leadership, then, is the development of the quality of a human being that has the courage to go it alone, if need be.

So, leadership is the building up of an internal support system: an emotional support system, a psychological support system, a spiritual support system, all for the purpose of motivating a person to try it all by himself, if need be. So motivated, he'll say, "I'll walk on water, I'm willing to fail if I have to. But I'm going to attempt the impossible, if that's the best option."

Now that's leadership!

Where Is Leadership Needed?

With that definition of leadership, we come to the second question: Where is it needed, this quality of personhood called leadership? In the White House? Yes. In the halls of Congress? Of course. But go back further than that.

Our definition of leadership means this level of awareness or consciousness is very important to a first-grade child. For that first-grader is going to be on the playground, and already on the playground a boy or girl is going to be exposed to a variety of human behavioral patterns that are the incarnation and expression of a conflicting and confusing collection of human values. One little kid grabs a toy and says, "It's mine," and then proceeds to beat the other kid over the head with it.

Now, if our curriculum on Sunday morning—what today is called "Sunday School"—is right on, then we will develop first-graders who are learning how to evaluate and respond, how to react and choose. Why? Because reactions and responses are multiple—very seldom are they solitary.

Almost always when you get into the area of responses and reactions, there are several options. The child on the playground can:

a. Get mad and haul off and kick the aggressor,

b. He can sulk and pout,

c. He can just slink away, or

d. He can go along and compromise.

Providing for character development is training for leadership. And it begins to happen, not at the high-school level, not at the adult level; it happens on the playground in the first grade. *So leadership is needed in the first grade.*

Kindergarten and first-grade kids need leadership training. I don't need to tell you how young people need it. The junior-high level young people are particularly responsive to peer pressure. The need in high school is self-evident.

Surely the singles need this kind of character development so they can stand strong. The Crystal Cathedral congregation was, I am told, the first church in the history of Christianity to have a full-time minister to singles. That ministry began just about 30 years ago. Why? Because we saw single adults who were being swept along by an intimidating society around them until it was hard for them to stand against the social and sexual pressures.

Do the singles need leadership? Do the high-school kids need it? How do you stand up against the possibility of rejection? How do you tolerate the prospect of ridicule? How do you live when you're "out" and not "in"? Where do you go from out?

Adults need leadership training to continue to chart their career program, to handle the problems and stresses in their marriages. How am I going to respond and react? Do I split? Make up? Do I accommodate?

We need leadership skills when we set goals for the development of a family unit. And older people need leadership abilities to maintain control over their changing circumstances:

"The kids are out of the nest now. What do we do with the house?"

"What do we do with our money? We've got to get our estate lined up."

"Our health isn't so good anymore. What's the best way to handle this?"

"We've got to make some changes now, Honey. I'm retiring."

Anytime you face the possibility of a change, you become a leader. That's because leadership is making responsible choices. And because leadership is making responsible choices, the qualities and strategies of leadership are desperately needed by everyone today in responding to the different pressures of age, of society, of secularism and of culture. *Responding,* mind you, not merely reacting. Responding means considering the choices and options open to us within the value system to which we are committed.

Now pause a moment and ask, "Is the church doing the job?" Are we really geared up in our curriculum, in our sermon content and in our theology, so that we are, in fact, *creating leaders?* I'm not sure. In fact, it seems to me that there are developments, historically, within mainline Protestantism, which is where I am, that almost militate against the development of leadership.

The thinking is done, let's say, at denominational headquarters. Distant specialists prepare materials. They establish programs. They dictate policy. Directives are sent down to the churches and all are expected to carry out the orders. A pastor or a church that resists is seen as noncooperative.

If I take the position in a pulpit that, as a preacher, I know all the answers, then I will deliver a *sermon. And I am going to tell you!* But am I then creating leaders? Or am I merely setting up my parishioners to be puppets?

Don't misunderstand me, I'm not quarreling with all this; I'm just examining the situation. Take a look at it with me. For when you stop and analyze it, a lot of what has been done in Sunday School literature and through denominational strategy as well as by pronouncements of preachers actually produces followers—not leaders. So if you want to get a high mark as a pastor in a denomination or as a church member within a congregation, become a good follower.

If that's the way we are structured in our curricula, in our theology and in our ecclesiology—to produce followers—then it's no wonder that our church members, when they get out in the world on Monday morning, follow the crowd. We have taught them to be followers! Bending to the pressure of the pulpit, our people follow the same behavioral pattern they have followed all week, bending to the pressures of society.

Who Needs to Be a Leader?

So who needs to be a leader? Everyone! Women need this quality, too. They don't want to be doormats any more than men do. Right here in this matter of leadership is where the terrible nature of male chauvinism appears. We men haven't recognized the right of women to be leaders themselves, to have their own opinions and choices, to select their own options.

Yet isn't the real driving force behind women's liberation efforts the desire of every woman to be an *individual*, to have her own identity? It is, and rightly so. For to be one's own person is a healthy desire. That's why a strong self-image is the hallmark of good health.

Leadership? Women need it. Men need it. Christians surely need it, particularly as we attempt to be positive in a pagan world. This positive, inspiring leadership is needed any time and any place that calls for integrity. That's the key word: *integrity!* For what is integrity? *It is making a personal decision that I know, for me at least, is the right thing to do.*

Yes, any time, any place that calls for integrity, we need leadership. In my mind, "integrity" is a better word than "morality." If we have integrity, we will have morality. And the ultimate immorality is to abandon, forfeit or abdicate our decision-making responsibilities to others out of fear of exercising leadership. To surrender leadership is to lose integrity as a person—and *that* is the ultimate immorality.

When Is Leadership Needed?

When, then, is leadership needed? It is needed in the good times, so I can dream dreams, spot opportunities, set my goals and, hopefully, make my mark in changing the world. Yes, leadership is needed in good times, of course. But it is also needed in the rough times; times when life collapses, your wife leaves you, your husband dies, cancer hits. In the toughest of tough times, you need leadership more than ever.

But how can I cope rather than be controlled, so that I can live above circumstances, not under them? Probably nothing plagues our society with greater depression today than a subconscious sense of being victimized. People feel they are the victims of forces beyond their control. And the feeling of powerlessness remains the same, even when individuals identify differently the particular force they believe is arrayed against them. Some see this force as an international thing; maybe the hydrogen bomb will fall. Some see it in terms of economic, political, racial, ethnic, cultural or religious oppression. Others see it as the plague of poverty or the spread of disease, whether it's cancer or something new like AIDS.

What's needed? Leadership ability is needed. I hope I've been trained by my church to be a leader with the quality of character that recognizes immediately, intuitively, instinctively, impulsively the need to look for all the possibilities, to expose all the options, to consider all the alternatives from which I can choose my action. Unless I've been trained to be such a person, I will in the face of difficulty be easily defeated. I'll toss in the towel, throw my hands up, walk away—and quit!

Why are so many young people committing suicide? Because they haven't been taught to be leaders. They know they are not in control, so they get depressed and discouraged. They can't cope, so they say, "There's not a thing I can do about it. I don't want to get into that world."

So when are leadership qualifications needed? Every moment that I face a choice or confront change. Any time more than a single option is open to my acting or reacting process. In other words, any time I can or should make a decision. This means I can never escape my responsibility to be a leader without abdicating my integrity as a person.

What Is Needed to Become a Leader?

What is needed to become a leader? What are the psychological or spiritual qualities that produce the character of a leader, whether a person is a first grader, a junior higher, a high schooler, single, married, male, female, red, yellow, black or white, whether one lives in a free society like America or in an oppressed society?

Self-confidence

First of all, you need self-confidence, an "I can" spirit. I call that spirit "possibility thinking." We get it from Jesus Christ who taught, "If you have faith as a grain of mustard seed, you can say to your mountain, 'Move,' and it will move, and nothing will be impossible to you" (see Matt. 17:20). If you want to understand what I have been trying to do with my life, my books, my sermons, the "Hour of Power" and the Institute for Successful Church Leadership, you can grab hold of the words "possibility thinking." They say what I am trying to say: "It's possible!"

So, if I were to organize my thinking around two words, they would be "It's possible!" That's what a leader does; he organizes his reactions, his responses, his decision-making process around those words. And he will say, "It's possible *if* I can devote five years to the project. It's possible *when* I have done my homework and I have collected the money, and I have hired the right people. It's possible *after* I have made a commitment and a decision, and I'm never going to turn my back on it. I'll spend my whole life to pull it off if need be."

It's possible if, it's possible when, it's possible after, it's possible *with*, yes, with the right people, with the right piece of property, with the right kind of a concept, with the right financial backing. I say nobody has a money problem; nobody has an energy problem; it's always an idea problem.

It's possible if, it's possible when, it's possible after, it's possible with, yes, it's possible, but do I want to pay the price? It's possible, but is it the right thing to do?

So what is needed to be a leader? "It's possible!" thinking is needed. The leader believes, "I can. I may be one, I may be alone, but if I speak up, somebody will hear me. And if I'm right, somebody may believe me. And if that is the case, I will make progress. If I just speak up, I can amount to something, no matter who I am, no matter where I am!"

Self-esteem

Yes, to be a leader, possibility thinking is needed. But that is not all. In 1967 when I wrote my first book, *Move Ahead with Possibility Thinking,* I thought I had all the answers. Boy, was I wrong. People wrote to me and said, "I've read the book, but it doesn't work for me. Why not?" "Well, Dr. Schuller, I'm too old . . . " Or, "I'm too this . . . " Or, "I'm too that . . . . "

So I came to an awareness that something was deeper than possibility thinking, and that is self-esteem. We came up then with this insight: "The *I am* always determines the *I can.*"

In other words, if you have a negative self-image, you probably cannot be an authentic possibility thinker. Now then, this is where salvation through Jesus Christ becomes such an explosive, liberating, life-transforming, personality-altering experience.

Somebody said to me the other day, "What is your favorite Bible verse?"

I said, "Guess."

They said, "If you are faced with a mountain, and have faith as a grain of mustard seed, you can say to your mountain, 'Move,' and it will move, and nothing will be impossible."

I said, "No, that was the first text I preached on, but that's not my favorite Bible verse."

And they kept guessing, but they never did guess the right one. My favorite Bible verse is Ephesians 2:8: "For by grace are ye saved through faith; and that not of yourselves: it is the gift of God."

Why? Well, what happens when we are saved? We are, before we are saved, conscious of our imperfections. We are aware that we are missing the mark! Internally, privately, secretly, intimately, behind all the bluster, we are ashamed of our mistakes, failures, errors and imperfections. Then, in salvation, we encounter the Ideal One, the Lamb of God without spot or blemish. And He treats us as though we are as good as He is! We know He knows the *worst* about us, yet He treats us as if we ourselves were sons of God! By grace are we saved through faith.

So salvation is a gift of God! Then what happens when we are saved? We receive the precious experience of grace—an *awareness of my value as a human being!* Now I am somebody! I have been grafted into a branch! I can bear fruit! Suddenly I have value! I have worth! I may be thin or fat, young or old, rich or poor, black or white, but I have value!

If I am an intimate, chosen, selected friend of Jesus Christ, forgiven and loved, it means that nobody else can put me down! When He became my best friend, He established my personal worth once and for all.

Possibility thinking is needed to be a leader. But before you can be a possibility thinker, you need a sense of self-worth, self-esteem, value as a person, and that's what happens, that's what is so revolutionary in the salvation process. For I don't think that self-esteem, in the final analysis, can be taught. It has to be caught. It has to be experienced.

So a positive self-esteem is needed to be a leader. A strong self-image! "I am" a redeemed child of God, by grace! This is exciting! So if you didn't catch it before, catch it now. For here is one of the most beautiful and exciting contradictions that truth has ever exposed to human thought: *When I am saved I experience true humility and, at the same time, I experience a beautiful pride!*

Yes, I am a child of God! I am proud of who I am! At the same time, I'm humble because I know that I am what I am by the grace of God! Now that's what you call an incredible, peerless human experience.

So, what's needed for leadership? The "I can" spirit— that's possibility thinking! And the "I am" spirit—that's self-esteem! How do we get it? By grace, through Jesus Christ.

Community

What else is needed for leadership to be sustained, strengthened and supported? Of course, we need a fellowship of positive people. That's why we need churches within the community. The church or *ekklesia*—the "called-out ones"—is the place where the chosen, those who are called out, believers in Christ can mutually support and affirm one another. That is the purpose of the church. And that's why everything that happens in the church should be for the encouragement of the positive mental attitude that's happening in possibility-thinking, self-esteeming people—in believers.

So not only do we need churches within the community, we need community within the church. And that means small groups within the church, groups small enough for me to share my problems. "Can you pray for me? Can you help me? I need some support here."

And what is strong encouragement but the reinforcement of my self-confidence that, in Christ, I can cope with life? I can control my reactions. I can succeed as a person. I can still be an effective leader. I do not need to surrender leadership to forces or fears or negative fantasies or even to unpleasant facts.

When Does Leadership Training Begin?

We will have renewal in the church when we build leadership. But it must start in infancy, at the childhood level. Eric Erikson, the distinguished child psychologist, says that in the first stage of child development, a child learns to trust. That happens from birth to the age of two, and that is why Erikson urges breast-feeding the baby, if possible. Why? What happens? Trust is formed, and trust is foundational to the development of what will later appear in the forms of possibility thinking and self-esteem.

Then leadership training in the church really starts when the baby is left in your church nursery! It continues at the preschool level. The self-image and the self-esteem of a person is definitely shaped more forcibly in the kindergarten and in the first-grade classroom than in any other grade level, a fact that is well documented. So it's a foregone conclusion that what happens to a child in the kindergarten and the first-grade level will determine the child's sense of self-esteem. Obviously, that self-esteem has to be developed strongly through the elementary years of education and then be strongly reinforced at the junior high and high school levels as well as at the adult levels.

In all the church's departments we must keep our focus on the primary goal of developing the human being's quality of character that will turn him or her into a leader! So, in our church, we're really not interested in making sure that we only teach the Bible until people know the Scriptures from cover to cover. We are primarily interested in developing Christian character, in developing Christians who will be leaders in their own lives and in society! It's not enough just to be able to recite Bible verses and repeat them. I'm all for that—my greatest treasure is my collection of memorized Bible verses! But at the same time we must develop *character.*

How Can We Develop Leadership Qualities?

How can we develop leadership qualities? How does this happen? It comes through what I call the triple *E.* Creating leadership through the big triple *E* is creating leadership through *experience, exposure* and *education*—all three.

Experience

I've alluded to the personal salvation experience and what it does, providing that experience was born in the healthy environment of self-esteem and not in the neurotic mental climate of slimy shame. As an evangelist, and I consider myself an evangelist, it's possible to manipulate and exploit the negative self-worth of people to make them feel how bad they are, how dirty they are and how unclean they are. That's an easy thing to do!

Any simpleton can get in the pulpit and make people feel low. That's easy! Because they're struggling with negative guilt at the time, we can exploit that guilt and make them feel how worthless and totally depraved they are! Then we motivate them to accept Jesus, so their names will be written in heaven's book and they won't go to hell. Now they are saved.

Well, I think that's a cheap shot. I believe in heaven, and I believe in hell, and I believe in salvation, but I think there is a right way, a healthy way, and there's a sick way of trying to go about converting people. The positive way was the strategy Jesus used: "Come and see" (see John 1:37-42, *RSV*). He also said, "Come to me, all who labor and are heavy laden" (see Matt. 11:28-30, *RSV*) and "You are the salt of the earth . . . you are the light of the world" (see Matt. 5:13-14, *RSV*). And we have His invitation, "Follow me, and I will make you fishers of men" (Matt. 4:19, *RSV*).

Exposure and Education

In addition to a positive salvation experience, we develop leadership awareness through exposure and through education. We come to the study of the sacred Scripture, the Word of God, the Holy Bible as a textbook on leadership. It starts that way, doesn't it? God created the whole world, and He put Adam and Eve in it, and He said, "OK, you're in charge" (see Gen. 1:26). So, Adam and Eve were supposed to be leaders! That meant they would have the freedom and the responsibility to make decisions, good ones or bad ones.

I see the development of a whole Sunday School curriculum based on the principles of leadership! Adam and Eve! Noah! Moses! Biblical prophets! Disciples! Jesus! The Church! Let the Church discover that it is the only institution on earth invested with this high and holy calling: to save people from sin, the sin of abdicating control of their lives to negative forces, and to turn them into strong, honest, open, thinking leaders as shining lights in a dark world! Suddenly all the Scriptures become very exciting, very alive and very positive!

When I was a boy, I heard a preacher speak on the text: "Come out from among them, and be ye separate, saith the Lord" (2 Cor. 6:17). I heard it as a very negative message and a call to separatistic, holier-than-thou, pharisaical behavior. But now I hear this text as a call to leadership! "Come out from among them" can mean "Don't just be a part of the collective crowd! Step out of the pack! Be a leader!"

Do we need leaders? If not, then what's the purpose of the Church? To get people's names in heaven so they don't go to hell? To come together on Sunday mornings and get a spiritual high? Yes, of course! But, if it stops there, what a pity! We haven't yet developed persons! We haven't yet developed characters! We haven't yet created integrity! We haven't yet produced leaders! And just because a person doesn't lie, kill and cheat doesn't mean he has integrity. He doesn't have integrity until he dares to stand up, think for himself, dream a dream, set a goal, take a chance and go for it!

So suddenly, Sunday School classes become Leadership Training Centers! Then all the truth of God—whether it's from the sacred Word of God, the Holy Bible, or whether it's distilled in good positive theology or fine psychological principles, all truth comes together and is integrated for the purpose of transforming human lives. Puppets become persons!

Then we may have the preachers, churches, parishioners who can produce programs that can attract both Christians and non-Christians alike! We will have a uniqe product and service to offer that even the world will be attracted to! Our church will have real possibilities for a fantastic future.

Chapter 17

HOW YOU CAN DREAM GREAT DREAMS

First of all, determine to succeed. Resolve now to believe in success. Christ was not a failure. He was a success, for He planned to live and die to be the sacrificial Saviour. Everything worked out exactly as He *planned* it. And in His parting words to His disciples, He urged them to *plan big plans* with the challenge, *go* "unto the uttermost part of the earth" (Acts 1:8).

How do possibility thinkers dream their dreams? Here's how—just follow these three steps as you plan, pray and prepare to become a great leader to build a great church for Jesus Christ:

One: Get in Touch with God's Spirit

He has a dream for your life and your church. He will reveal His dream by causing you to desire what He wants. Prayerfully ask God to fill your life full with His Holy Spirit. To do this search your soul. Remove any secret or public sin. Let nothing remain that could block the flow of God's Holy Spirit.

Now pray the prayer of surrender, "God I'm willing to

do and be whatever you want me to be. I'm yours to command." Then ask the Holy Spirit to fill your mind with God's dream for your life.

Big beautiful dreams will come. If they are impossible then be sure they have come from God! If they're small and safe and entail no risk, the chances are they are of your own creation.

Let the big ideas come. Just because they're impossible doesn't mean God can't make them happen. Listen to this dream, "For it is God who is at work within you, giving you the will and the power to achieve his purpose" (Phil. 2:13, *Phillips*). Now . . .

Two: Get in Touch with God's People

Show them your dream. God wants to use others, so they'll make it happen for you. It's His way of making sure that you'll remain humble after He starts showering success on your life!

My testimony is with the apostle Paul, "I can do all things through Christ" (Phil. 4:13). But I must also add, "I can't do anything without God's people."

Yes, God's people make the dreams come true! God has His people waiting in the wings to come out on stage at the right time, with the exact talent you'll need! There's someone out there with the skill or the will to remove the obstacles that will temporarily block your way!

Three: Get in Touch with God's Calendar

Out of my first several years' walk with God in building His church in Garden Grove I now share a lesson in prayer as I've learned it. I've talked in this book about faith, organizing, financing, planning. But believe me—before, during and after every move there was deep, constant prayer. And I testify that God always answers true prayer.

When the request is not right God says no. I prayed for 10 acres to build our church in downtown Garden Grove. God said *no.* Three years later He showed us our present site—20 acres at the freeway hub of Orange County!

When you are not right God says, "Grow." It took me two dark years of depression, facing opposition in the church before I got the message. I had not really surrendered the church to Him. I had the idea that the Lord and Schuller were partners. The time came when He said, "The partnership is through! You work for me!"

When the time is not right God says, "Slow." God's calendar is always right. Remember, God's delays are not God's denials. When you think you've failed you haven't. You just have to wait longer—work harder!

"Nothing is impossible," the Army Corps of Engineers used to say, "It just takes longer! Inch by inch anything's a cinch!" Faith is spelled P-A-T-I-E-N-C-E!

And when everything is right God says, "Go!" And doors will open. Dreams will come true. All because you decided to *bloom where you are planted.*

So, friend, dream your dreams and make them great! I have every confidence that you are about to turn a corner in your ministry, a turning with lasting, lifetime results. It is a turning that will take you from discouragement and near defeat to optimism and unexpected victories, from one level of success to another—to ever higher levels of accomplishment that you ever dreamed of before you started real possibility thinking!

Why am I so sure? Because the principles of success are all here. You've already read them. Now believe them and apply them. They will work, if you work them!

And if this is done, your twentieth-century church in America will see a fantastic future unfold before it as it moves into the twenty-first century. And what will the future of the next century hold for all the small churches in America?

1. Some small churches will begin to grow, will plan to relocate and will become tremendous centers of dynamic inspiration by the twenty-first century.

2. Other small churches will merge with other local small churches to do something big and beautiful for Christ in their city.

3. Other small, boxed-in churches will fold up and die! Some should!

4. Others will be sold to the city and community for branch libraries, child-care centers and other uses, while the nucleus moves out to a new and larger center!

5. Some reader of this book will build the greatest and most unique church in America. With seven-days a week activity! It will be a sensation for Christ!

Rise up, O [Church] of God,
Have done with lesser things,
Give heart and soul and mind and strength
To serve the King of kings. [1]

Note

1. Adapted from "Rise Up, O Men of God" by William P. Merrill. Public domain.

Much of the content of this book is based on lectures
given by Dr. Robert H. Schuller at his Institute for
Successful Church Leadership.
To receive information on these seminars, write to:

Dr. Herman J. Ridder
R.H.S. Institute
12141 Lewis Street
Garden Grove, California 92640

To receive copies of morning messages delivered by
Dr. Schuller, write to:
Dr. Robert Schuller
Hour of Power
Garden Grove, California 92640